Winging It

Improv's Power & Peril in the Time of Trump

RANDY FERTEL

SPRING PUBLICATIONS
THOMPSON, CONN.

PRAISE FOR Winging It

At the farmers market, I'm responding to color, and smell, and I'm following my intuition. In my kitchen when I'm imagining where things will lead, I'm improvising. In his artful and authoritative new book *Winging It,* Randy Fertel explores how improvisation shapes and enlivens our wider world. Yield to your impulses, act spontaneously, and get this book—it's a revelation..
  —Alice Waters, Founder of Chez Panisse and the Edible Schoolyard

Winging It soars. Author Randy Fertel is a whipsmart, plate-spinning savant, an audacious flying circus wingman. Every performer faces unknown risks, but Fertel takes it to a whole new level, and it's a very exciting ride.
  —Michelle Shocked, singer/songwriter

In *Winging It,* Randy Fertel presents a wide ranging and masterful study of the art of improvisation that will delight scholars and lay readers alike. The work's true fascination lies in its adept analysis of the political implications of the quicksilver art form. It is a work to be savored slowly and thoughtfully, especially in anticipation of the upcoming elections.
  —Jessica B. Harris, author of *High on the Hog: How African American Cuisine Transformed America*

Winging It dances with the reader atop a mountain of scholarship, original thinking, and profound applicability. Written in the spirit and style of improvisation, this book charms the reader into a fresh perspective on our discombobulated world, touching on social media, popular culture, literary classics, neuroscience, AI, and politics. It's smart, fun, insightful, and relevant to life today and the incomprehensibles we live within. Don't walk, *improvise* your way to the bookstore to grab this irresistible tour de force from Randy Fertel.
  —Eric Booth, author of *Making Change* and *The Everyday Work of Art*

A masterwork—voracious in scope…and about as hopeful as can be in these troubling times.
    —Bruce Boyd Raeburn, Curator Emeritus, Hogan Archive of
        New Orleans Music and New Orleans Jazz, Tulane University

In *Winging It,* Randy Fertel returns to his life-long fascination with improvisation, following its threads from antiquity to the magic and madness of our unsettling present. Fertel will scare you and free you, as he peers deeply into the light and the dark spaces where improvisation ennobles or vexes our lives and culture. Radio is my home and I love the starring role he ascribes to listening, both in the construction of this rollicking and seductive book and within improv itself.
    —Davia Nelson, The Kitchen Sisters, Radio/Podcast Producer

In the new century, we're all winging it now. Randy Fertel gives us an impressive and artful view of cultural patterns that are roiling our world in so many ways. His knowledge is encyclopedic and his feeling for the complexities and double binds we face is deep and humane.
    —Stephen Nachmanovitch, author of *Free Play* and *The Art of Is*

Randy Fertel is a master at unveiling theatrical illusion. In this brilliant book, he shines a piercing light into the shadows of the so-called improv style in politics. *Winging It* reveals the concealed instincts and the fierce emotional currents that keep a rapacious predator aloft.
    —Murray Stein, author of *Jung's Map of the Soul*

Winging It is a remarkable feat of scholarship, analysis and imagination, an eclectic blend of insights from many realms of thought and study that equips the reader to make sense of such disparate phenomena as "artificial" (and pseudo-) intelligence, Benoît Mandelbrot's fractal geometry, Oscar Wilde's "*meticulously* prepared art" of spontaneity, and the perverse fascination of Donald "the Dark Trickster" Trump. Fertel's healing faith in intuition rings from every page.
    —Tom Mueller, author of *How to Make a Killing: Blood, Death and
        Dollars in American Medicine*

Winging It goes everywhere to make clear the universal nature of Fertel's premise, always with authority to back it, that our physical nature shares with our minds what makes us human.
    —Gerry Dryansky, Senior European Correspondent for
        Condé Nast Traveler

Published by Spring Publications
Thompson, Conn.
www.springpublications.com

© 2024 by Spring Publications and Randy Fertel
All rights reserved

First edition 2024 (1.4)

Cover art:
Hieronymus Bosch
The Garden of Earthly Delights: Hell (detail)
1490–1500
Oil on oak panel
Museo del Prado, Madrid

Library of Congress Control Number: 2023947923
ISBN: 978-0-88214-158-9

CONTENTS

PRELUDE
The Mainstream's Revenge:
Second City Flips Improv's Script
9

INTRODUCTION
What Do Improvisations Share?
11

CHAPTER ONE
Improvisation's Dark Side:
Hookup Sex, COVID-19, and Donald J. Trump
18

CHAPTER TWO
Spontaneous or Scripted?
The Goldilocks Challenge
33

CHAPTER THREE
Eureka!
Improv, Invention, and Paradigm Shifts
47

CHAPTER FOUR
The Rhetoric of Spontaneity:
Serious Man vs. Rhetorical Man
64

CHAPTER FIVE
*"I'm Going to Slop You Up":
The Rules of Rule-Breaking*
71

CHAPTER SIX
*What the Neuroscience of Psychedelics
Tells Us about Improvisation*
88

CHAPTER SEVEN
*Improv's Bravura Performer:
Charisma's Starring Role*
104

CHAPTER EIGHT
The Dark Side of Intuition and Instinct
119

CHAPTER NINE
*Hamilton as Signifying Trickster:
America's Experiment in Exceptionalism*
137

CHAPTER TEN
The Rhetoric of Spontaneity in Your Facebook Feed
164

CONCLUSION
Re-Embracing Trickster Through Collective Intelligence
193

NOTES
217

ACKNOWLEDGMENTS
244

for
Ron Ridenhour
Truth-teller

PRELUDE

The Mainstream's Revenge: Second City Flips Improv's Script

An improv troupe, eight men and women, arrayed on a bare stage, stand or sit on bentwood chairs. The men wear coats and ties, the women cocktail dresses. Each snaps their fingers, claps, or taps a syncopated rhythm. One man plays a chair seat like a bongo. Each has his or her own timing, but what the ensemble plays is not chaos but polyrhythm. Loose from the start, the beat becomes wilder and more energetic. They are having great fun.

A man enters stage left. He out-hipsters these hipsters with his goatee and dark sunglasses, a cigarette dangling from his lips, his lapels upturned. Furtively, he looks left and right. He carries a doctor's bag. Opening it, he takes out a metronome, decisively puts it on a table, and starts it ticking. Tick-tock. Tick-tock. He rushes out.

The chic ensemble frowns, trying to maintain their syncopated polyrhythm, but the metronome defeats them. They've lost the beat. The scene collapses. Blackout.

INTRODUCTION

What Do Improvisations Share?

> Spontaneity is a meticulously prepared art.
> —Oscar Wilde

Nightly on hundreds of dedicated stages with bare sets and in hundreds of classrooms at Second City and similar comedy club venues, professional and amateur improvisers demonstrate the power of "being at the ready." They all follow the prime directive of improvisation, the simple rule of agreement, often expressed as *Yes, and...*

Keith Johnstone, founder of Britain's and then Canada's improv movements, offers this example of the rule of agreement at work:

> Say that the first player to kill an idea loses; for example:
> — "You seem out of breath. Been running?"
> — "It's my asthma..."*

This asthma attack breaks the thread because it doesn't pick up the idea of running. To find a reason for breathing hard that keeps the story going requires free association: *Yes, I was running from that ogre.* The more surprising or outrageous the free association, the better. Then the first player will pick up the thread: *Whoa, that ogre's got quite an underbite doesn't he?* Each free association is a challenge to the rational metronome that dominates our lives.

Here's a famous example of *Yes, and...* in a jazz setting. Jazz keyboardist Herbie Hancock recounts that in the mid-1960s he played a blatantly wrong chord during a Miles Davis Quintet gig. Hancock's bad chord, meant to be a simple hand-off to Miles, hung out there, Hancock said, like a piece of "rotten fruit."

"Miles pauses for a fraction of a second," Hancock wrote, "and then he plays some notes that somehow, miraculously, make my chord sound

---

* References are not numbered but can be found in the Notes section at the back of the book, arranged by chapters and listed by key phrases.

right. In that moment I believe my mouth actually fell open. What kind of alchemy was this?"

What kind of alchemy? It was the *"Yes, and..."* kind of alchemy engendered by the rule of agreement, the kind where the improviser makes an offer and her partner, attending with all her senses, picks it up and makes a counteroffer. Such call and response is alchemical. It transforms culture.

We take it on faith that effective narrative demands conflict. John and Mary wed, *but...*, and you're in a Tennessee Williams play. The rule of agreement begs to differ that conflict is the only way forward. John and Mary wed, *and...* constellates a community.

Jazz improvisation transformed global popular culture in the first half of the twentieth century. If jazz has since then lost its ascendency in the cultural marketplace, improv's dominance in film and TV helps explain the rush to improv clubs and classrooms. Actors who got their start at Chicago's founding improv theater, Second City, or similar troupes from coast to coast, soon peopled the *Saturday Night Live* stage—John Belushi, Gilda Radner, Bill Murray, Mike Myers, Jim Carrey, among many. Comedy improv led to some of the highest grossing films of the 1980s and beyond: Harold Ramis's *Caddyshack*, Ivan Reitman's *Ghostbusters*, Christopher Guest's *This is Spinal Tap* and *Best in Show*, the Farrelly brothers' *Dumb and Dumber*, or any of Judd Apatow's minor masterpieces, including *The 40-Year-Old Virgin*.

Hamlet these may not be. But such movies grabbed box office, giving audiences something they wanted, and not just laughs. We all long to live in the moment. At times we all long, like Belushi, samurai sword in hand, to slash back against our normal, everyday, metronome-bound rational lives. Belushi's death hit us hard. Then John Candy's and Chris Farley's. But because of them the spirit that once animated sixteenth-century *Commedia dell'Arte*'s street theater now commands center stage. Masters of improv become culture heroes. Everyone wants a piece of what improv offers. Everyone wants their voice, mistaken or not, to be heard.

Improv has been an element in high culture since Antiquity. In the Renaissance, to show their smarts courtiers cultivated *sprezzatura*, what Baldassare Castiglione defines as "a certain nonchalance, so as to conceal all art and make whatever one does or says appear to be without effort and almost without any thought about it" (*The Book of the Courtier*, 1528). John Milton describes his epic poem *Paradise Lost,* though dense and finely worked, as "my unpremeditated verse." Laurence Sterne tells us that his eighteenth-century novel *Tristram Shandy*—"This rhapsodical work"— proceeds "out of all rule." In the Romantic lyric, the spontaneous dams break: poetry is not artifice but "the spontaneous overflow of powerful feeling recollected in tranquility."

Minstrelsy, then country blues, then gospel, then jazz and their heirs—rhythm and blues, rock and roll, funk, punk, and hip hop—all these carried improvisation into popular culture, shaping how we play, how we dance, and how we think. Today, just after ChatGPT's release, a new book appeared with the title, *Impromptu: Amplifying Our Humanity through AI.* Everyone wants to share in improvisation's mysterious power, in what Oscar Wilde, that master of paradox, called spontaneity's "meticulously prepared art."

Improvisation's alchemy is now sought in board rooms, churches, and academic classrooms. Hollywood actor Alan Alda used improv games in crafting his Center for Communicating Science at Stony Brook University. Teaching improv, The Center seeks to free scientists of jargon and technical details, because "before people can understand complex information, they need to trust and feel connected to its source." Improv's promise of unmediated experience has played a surprising role in the history of modern science, as this book will demonstrate.

The global Applied Improvisation Network has thousands of members. The International Institute for Critical Studies in Improvisation (IICSI) covers Canada coast to coast, with research sites from Newfoundland to British Columbia. IICSI scholars publish prolifically on the role of improvisation in ethics, community organizing, theatre, jazz, and many other disciplines. The two-volume *Oxford Handbook of Critical Improvisation Studies* (2016) is a doorstopper as is the *Routledge Handbook of Philosophy and Improvisation in the Arts* (2022) for which I was one of 48 contributors.

The *Oxford Handbook* gave a name to what I've been doing all along: critical improvisation studies. I'm glad to embrace the term and to find colleagues tilling the same field. But while many agree about a few general principles—like the rule of agreement (*Yes, and...*) and the role of call and response—few ask what is for me the central question: What is shared among the many rows of the field we're all tilling? How do these different artistic, academic, and scientific disciplines constitute a field? What connects the dots?

We need a unified field theory of improvisation. That is the project I pursue: how improvisation constitutes a discourse with perennial formal patterns, constraints, and themes. George Lewis, a distinguished alum of the radical jazz improv group, The Association for the Advancement of Creative Musicians (AACM), and a professor of musicology at Columbia, says in his *Oxford Handbook* preface that no definition of improvisation guided the essays' selection. A wise move, no doubt, for a compendium of many voices. But surely, given its growing dominance in world culture, improvisation needs defining.

Stumbling on Improv

I first stumbled on an example of literary improvisation in a graduate seminar. Our day's topic was Shakespeare's contemporary, Thomas Nashe. We'd read his pamphlet, *Pierce Pennylesse, His Supplication to the Devil* (1592), wildly popular in its day, which complained in a witty, digressive, "extemporal" satire how hard it was for a writer to make a living. His eponymous name, Pierce, is pronounced "purse." His is pennyless. The pamphlet's cleverness underscored the injustice. *If I am so smart,* Nashe wondered, *why am I so poor?*

The seminar leader got the ball rolling with a throwaway line. *He doubted we'd ever read anything like this before.* Everyone nodded, prepared to move on to the discussion. But that nonchalant remark stopped me short and sealed my fate. Nashe's purse was empty, but my mind teemed with some of my favorite authors. Doors opened. Behind them I saw Erasmus's *Praise of Folly,* Sterne's *Tristram Shandy,* Byron's *Don Juan,* and Stendhal's *The Red and the Black* and numerous others, all promising some measure of spontaneity.

I was a budding Romanticist at the time so many of the spontaneity-professing Romantics—Blake, Wordsworth, Coleridge, Keats, and the gang—were among the writers that sprung to mind. The Surrealists weren't far behind. The jazz of my native city, New Orleans, too, was in that number. Art that claims spontaneous composition seemed, according to this flash of insight, to bear a strong family resemblance. I wondered whether there was a tradition linked by that trope—*You've never seen anything like this before*—something fashioned extempore without traditional models. The Greeks separated human endeavor into nine categories overseen by nine muses who determined each discourse's rule-bound decorum. Was there a *sub-rosa* tradition of improvisation dating even to Antiquity that flaunted rules and disdained the right way to do things?

Forty years after that seminar, I published a book on improv, *A Taste for Chaos: The Art of Literary Improvisation.* It argued that the central texts of the Western tradition—The Canon—began on the margins as improvisations using spontaneity's persuasive power to push back against the dominant rationalist culture.

Three months after publication, Donald J. Trump came down the golden escalator. His ungoverned speeches, his way of "governing," and his entire presidency (and beyond) reeked of improv in darker garb. Improvisation was too important to remain in the ivory tower. I launched an annual conference on "Improv Across the Disciplines" at the New Orleans Jazz Museum and started thinking about a book for a general audience.

Einstein's Sacred Gift and Faithful Servant

Post-Enlightenment culture instructs us to talk and think and act based on logic and the rationalist, scientific method. Things have causes, evidence must be brought, procedure must be followed, and logic rules the day. If that is so, why should free association have such a role in our culture? For Dada founder, Tristan Tzara, "Thought is made in the mouth." For Beat poet, Allen Ginsburg, "First thought, best thought." From jazz, rock and roll, and hip-hop to Second City and *Saturday Night Live,* improv's indecorous roughness pushes back against the white-lab-coat rigor of the scientific method. Donald Trump didn't invent alternative facts. Improvisers have long embraced subjectivity's role in meaning-making.

The battle between objective reason and subjective free association can be explained by new findings in neuroscience. The brain behaves as two separate and different minds, each enacting a different way of attending to the world, top-down or bottom-up. Neuroscientists confirm what has often been attributed to Einstein—"The intuitive mind is a sacred gift...and the rational mind [is] a faithful servant. We have created a society that honors the servant and has forgotten the gift."

Neuroscientists call Einstein's intuitive mind Hot Cognition and the rational mind Cold Cognition. Anatomy identifies the hitch

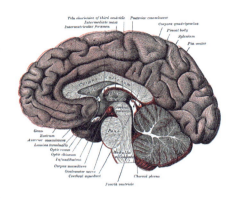

The corpus callosum

between the intuitive and rational minds: the corpus callosum, a C-shaped nerve fiber bundle, found beneath the cerebral cortex and stretching across the brain's midline. Different kinds of attention communicate within that bundle of nerve fibers. But it's the reasoning brain—Cold Cognition—that controls the communication. That's where Hot Cognition—Einstein's sacred gift, intuition—gets demoted to a subservient role.

Neuroscientists' two minds helps explain what is happening when we improvise. Cold Cognition applies reason and logic to our perceptions. It draws on memories to determine our behavior in the next moment based on similarities to the past and likely outcomes. Cold Cognition is voluntary, meaning that it is consciously called into action. Hot Cognition—automatic and autonomously outside our control—is focused on the details of the present moment and determines our behavior *right now* by noting the anomalies, positive or negative. When that car comes speeding toward us, Hot Cognition takes control of our autonomic system and dodges away.

Deeply inscribed by bio-evolution in our thinking and behavior, Hot Cognition drives creativity and innovation which Cold Cognition formalizes into rules and guardrails which Hot Cognition eventually again breaks through. Cold Cognition formulates paradigms that shape how we know the world. Responding to anomalies, Hot Cognition inspires paradigm shifts.

Neuroscience is in its infancy and Hot and Cold Cognition—the terms I'll use here—go by many names. Once, it was believed these functions were located hemispherically: Right and Left Brain. Now the hemispheric idea is challenged: the functions can be differentiated but are not localized. The two kinds of attention generally correlate to Princeton economist and psychologist Daniel Kahneman's Fast Thinking/System 1 and Slow Thinking/System 2. Both are susceptible to ingrained cognitive biases in our decision-making which Kahneman won the Nobel Prize for describing.

In the chapters that follow, we follow improvisation as the engine of creativity and cultural innovation, roles which ancient myths have recorded and which the Marvel Cinematic Universe (MCU) continues to explore. We'll explore improvisation's roots in bio-evolution and its triumphant role in the coronavirus vaccine. We'll find improvisation's promise of unmediated experience in hookup sex, psychedelic trips, Fred Astaire's tap dancing, Frans Hals's brushstrokes, and in the emergence of global popular culture infusing jazz, rock and roll, rhythm and blues, tap-dance, and hip-hop.

In our civic life, Cold Cognition creates hierarchies of power and value. *This,* it says, *is within bounds; that, not.* It separates the voiced from the voiceless. Hot Cognition urges that all experience, including embodied experience, not just what happens in our Cold Cognition, deserves attention. For Hot Cognition every voice *should* be heard, informing the American experiment in democracy, from the Founding Fathers to Lin-Manuel Miranda's *Hamilton*. And there—in our democracy—appears the central paradox of improvisation, that it is both light and dark, creative and destructive, a power and a peril. Improv is the engine of both democracy and demagogy.

All improvisation—light and dark—is a response to the traumas that have riddled the modern era. Creative improvisation is an effort to write a new life narrative. Diabolical improvisation promises a new narrative but sows only chaos and more trauma.

CHAPTER ONE

Improvisation's Dark Side: Hookup Sex, COVID-19, and Donald J. Trump

Improvisation in general primes us to anticipate positive innovation and life-affirming art. Comic improv primes us to expect laughs. But improvisation has a dark side. Spontaneity is no proof of authenticity or authority. How often have your intuitions or instincts steered you wrong? As Daniel Kahneman told Sam Harris in his podcast, "So it turns out you can have intuitions for bad reasons. All it takes is a thought that comes to your mind automatically and with high confidence, and you'll think that it's an intuition, and you'll trust it. But the correlation between confidence and accuracy is not high." Intuition is a function of Kahneman's Fast Thinking/System 1: Hot Cognition. High confidence—charisma—makes it possible. Charisma, as we'll see, is part of the improviser's DNA.

Many improvisations in literary history warn us against spontaneity's dark side. The Romantic period embraced the imagination's spontaneous overflow of powerful feelings, and yet Samuel Taylor Coleridge in *Kubla Khan,* an unfinished poem written in a dream, urges us:

> Beware! Beware!
> His flashing eyes, his floating hair!
> Weave a circle round him thrice,
> And close your eyes with holy dread,
> For he on honey-dew hath fed,
> And drunk the milk of Paradise.

Before the first New Orleans Improv Conference in 2018, my email blast promoting a political panel on "The Dark Side of Improv: Politics" earned a scathing reply from a preeminent scholar at Rutgers's Institute of Jazz Studies. With Louis Armstrong's "It's a Wonderful World" perhaps ringing in his ears, he wrote back curtly: "Why give improvisation a bad name? It's not a synonym for lies or bullshit!"

I understand his concern. Improv is a robust form but, try as it might, it does not share the values of the dominant culture. One can feel protective. Yet American democracy itself then was suffering through the presidency of a master improviser and charismatic bullshitter. A media savant, Trump faked his way through one of the most consequential presidencies in American history with off-the-cuff tweets and policies developed on the fly. Like improvisers since Antiquity, he used the impression of his improvising— the persuasive power of spontaneity—as proof of his naturalness, authenticity, and authority. His improvising gave him the authority to break norms (and laws). His transformation of American politics was, well, *huge*.

Great listening is one of improvisers' secret powers, and, alas for the republic, Trump was attuned to the MAGA crowds and adjusted his speeches and policies based on applause and retweets. It is well documented that the Mexican Wall policy resulted from the jolt of audience enthusiasm that exploded when he mentioned the possibility of a wall. "Amazingly, for something so central to the current U.S. president," Stuart Anderson remarks, "the wall came about as a 'mnemonic device' thought up by a pair of political consultants to remind Donald Trump to talk about illegal immigration." Suddenly his candidacy and presidency were all about Building the Wall.

Meanwhile, the left didn't hear the fear and anger its pro-globalization policies largely merited.

That improv has a dark side does not negate its historic contributions to culture. As Carl Jung knew, everything solid casts a shadow. Improv is the engine of creativity and cultural innovation. Innovation always begins with disruption, a pushback against the dominant culture. Some innovators, while promising renewal, settle for destruction. The claim of spontaneous composition has power. In that power peril also lurks.

Hookup Sex as Improv

Reading Tulane sociologist Lisa Wade on the sexual hookup culture on American campuses today, I can't *not* hear *improvisation*. This form of casual sex, is, according to Wade, "spontaneous, but scripted; order out of disorder; an unruly routine. It is, in short, a feat of social engineering." Each of those tensions is characteristic of improvisation. While purporting to be without purpose, just a whim or lark, improv covertly takes aim at feats of social engineering.

Not that hooking up is something new under the sun. Nor does Wade's concern stem from a surging epidemic of hookups. According to data compiled by the Online College Social Life Survey (OCSLS), college students average only two sexual encounters per year. The critical difference, argues Wade, lies in the hookup imperative: students feel they are *supposed* to have *meaningless* sex. Embodied intimacy without emotional intimacy.

Wade's research derives, in part, from student journals "about sex and romance on campus." What she learns is that hooking up usually begins by "getting shit-faced" prior to college parties. At the parties, women dance rhythmically, pressing their backsides against the men—butts to balls, I've heard it called. One student described the dancing as "clothed sex with a stranger."

Once the students are intoxicated, "crowdsourcing" initiates the hookup. Turned away from their impromptu dance partners, women look to their friends to signal whether the young man is "hot." The quest is not for a relationship but to enhance one's social status. "The goal is fast, random, no-strings-attached sex," wrote one student. Above all, it must be meaningless. Choose badly—someone not hot enough or not on a varsity sports team—and you can always blame the alcohol. Fall in love and you're out of the game.

Who benefits from this orderly disorder is disputed. Sociologists Kathleen Bogle (*Hooking Up: Sex, Dating, and Relationships on Campus,* 2008) and Michael Kimmel (*Guyland,* 2008) agree that hooking up is "guys' sex." Only guys benefit. But journalists Hanna Rosen in the *Atlantic* and Kate Taylor in the *New York Times* have argued "that casual sex allows women to put their careers and education before men."

Granted, many of Wade's students attend a famous party school in New Orleans, a famous party town. But hookup culture has engulfed campuses of all kinds, public and private, religious and secular, with or without major athletic programs or Greek life. For Wade, while some individuals—men, women, and those across the gender continuum—may thrive in hookup culture, she sounds an overall alarm about its nature, "coercive and omnipresent," resulting in students feeling "depressed, anxious, and overwhelmed."

It has the appeal of pushing back against Mom and Dad's sexual revolution while going it one better. After all, emotional commitment led statistically to divorce. Let's try not just lots of casual sex; let's make sure its meaningless too. *Yes, and...*

Improvisation can change individual lives and the larger culture. It brought us many of the positive innovations we thrive on, from the scientific revolution to rock and roll. But the new paradigm is not always positive. Generations to come may not date or seek lasting relationships because social pressures at college, just like those Renaissance courtiers, committed them to "a certain nonchalance" and to avoid serious relationships. To understand improvisation's culture-changing power, we must understand both its creative spirit and its destructive power.

An Improvised Pandemic and Improvising its Cure

Improvisation promises novelty—something you've never seen before. But novelty can equally be a curse, as the *novel* coronavirus has all too thoroughly demonstrated. Like improvisation, COVID-19 is a hybrid form we'd never seen before. The pandemic and the heroics behind the vaccine are two more reasons we should look closely at improvisation, both its dark and positive aspects.

The novel coronavirus, like other viruses, is pure RNA. It can replicate but, unlike DNA-based life forms, can't regenerate. Like other viruses, it has no neural system. Yet, pursuing replication, it can kill you.

Like many scientific breakthroughs—the heliocentric universe, X-rays, penicillin—the coronavirus vaccine came about not purposefully but through serendipity. Dr. Katalin Karikó, a biochemist, first had the insight that led to the Pfizer/BioNTech and Moderna vaccines. From her intuition emerged hypotheses and experiments that demonstrated the use of mRNA to suppress what makes RNA-based creatures like COVID infectious.

A Hungarian immigrant, Karikó was the daughter of a village butcher.

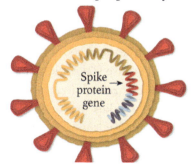

The coronavirus with its characteristic spikes

As a child, she had watched her father carve pigs into primal cuts—leg, shoulder, short loin, rib loin—by slicing at the joints, called articulations, where bones meet and are held together by ligaments. In her lab, Karikó noticed that the single-strand molecule mRNA ("m" stands for messenger), worked at the articulations of double-strand DNA proteins, the ribosomes. Ribosomes, the site of protein synthesis in the cell, link amino acids together in the order specified by the mRNA molecules. Her early experiments suggested that mRNA could direct any cell to make any protein, at will. But there were hurdles. Early efforts worked in petri dishes but not in live mice. The mRNA molecules appeared to the immune system as an invasion of pathogens, triggering an inflammatory immune reaction that killed the mice.

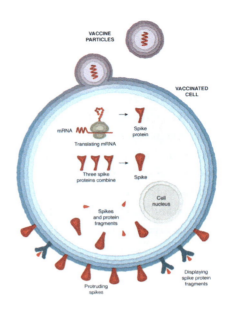

In 1998, Karikó met Drew Weissman, a University of Pennsylvania professor of immunology. "I had always wanted to try mRNA," says Weissman about his quest for new vaccines, "and here was somebody at the copy machine telling me that she was an RNA scientist." When later interviewed by the *New York Times* about her ability to "make anything with RNA," Karikó commented, "I felt like a god."

However, by the time she met Weissman, Karikó was adrift without a lab or funding, a god with no seat on Olympus. Karikó had been denied tenure because she could not secure funding from agencies that typically reward research confirming what is known rather than discoveries on the frontier. It takes bravado—characteristic of improvisers—to go beyond conventional wisdom. Impressed by that bravado, Weissman introduced her to Anthony Fauci, director of the National Institute of Allergy and Infectious Diseases. Through this chance connection to Weissman and Fauci, Karikó found a way where there had been no way.

ONE: *Improvisation's Dark Side*

In 2005, Karikó's next breakthrough came by paying attention to the anomalies. While the early version of the mRNA molecule caused the customary immune reaction, the control placebo, containing transfer or tRNA, didn't trigger that response. Karikó added tRNA to her mRNA molecule. The immune response stopped. Using tRNA as a passkey, the mRNA worked its magic on the ribosomes. The mice lived.

Karikó's vaccine prepares the body to handle viral anomalies. How? The mRNA in the vaccine teaches your cells to make copies of the coronavirus's characteristic "corona" or "crown" spike protein. This tricks our bodies into creating antibodies in advance of the invading coronavirus. Once vaccinated, the immune system works, Walter Isaacson explains, "by remembering essentially a mug shot of any virus that attacks it and then creating a weapon system that targets that virus whenever it attacks."

Karikó saw her experiments' failures as opportunities. Each was a Eureka! moment. Looked at as a *Yes, and...*, each was a *hermaion,* a happy accident, named for Hermes, the god of chance. By the mid 2010s, they had several viral vaccines in animal trials. Pfizer and Moderna licensed their mRNA patents.

When in December 2019 news of the virus emerged from Wuhan, China, Karikó and Weissman's associates at Pfizer and Moderna were at the ready. On January 10, 2020, Chinese scientists posted the virus's genome sequence. Moderna, with a speed that Hermes might have envied, had a COVID vaccine prototype within days. Happy accident indeed.

Dr. David Langer, a neurosurgeon and Karikó associate, told the *New York Times* that, working with her, "he realized that one key to real scientific understanding is to design experiments that always tell you something, even if it is something you don't want to hear. The crucial data often come from the control [the placebo], he learned—the part of the experiment that involves a dummy substance for comparison." In improvisation there are no mistakes. "Rotten fruit" can inspire genius.

Karikó's genius was her willingness to accept each failure and keep trying. As Karikó commented in her gruff European accent "The bench is there, the science is good. All you need is daily fidelity to your desk." Cold Cognition provided the structures and protocols of basic science, refined by thousands of hours in the lab—a meticulously prepared art. But the Eureka moments often come from emergent anomalies recognized by Hot Cognition. Thriving on anomalies, Karikó played both parts in the Herbie Hancock/Miles Davis handoff, alchemizing her own rotten fruit into gold.

The Commonwealth Fund estimates that Karikó's work on the vaccine saved 3.2 million lives and avoided nearly 120 million more COVID-19 infections. The vaccination program saved the United States more than $1 trillion in healthcare costs. Karikó and Weissman now are exploring mRNA's application to other medical conditions, including HIV, cancer, and sickle-cell anemia. Their pioneering mRNA technology is reshaping the landscape of vaccine development and the future of gene therapies. Attending to anomalies has resulted in a paradigm shift that goes by the name synthetic biology.

Today, Karikó is an adjunct professor at the University of Pennsylvania and Senior Vice President at BioNTech Pharmaceuticals. Karikó and Weissman have garnered many awards, including the $3 million Breakthrough Prize in Life Sciences. (As an academic post-doc, Karikó had never made more than $60,000 a year). The British evolutionary geneticist Richard Dawkins, as well as the Canadian stem cell biologist Derrick Rossi, Moderna's co-founder, called for Weissman and Karikó to receive the Nobel Prize. In October 2023, they were awarded the Nobel Prize in Physiology or Medicine. They had mounted Olympus. Their discovery "fundamentally changed our understanding of how mRNA interacts with our immune system," the Nobel panel said, adding that the work "contributed to the unprecedented rate of vaccine development during one of the greatest threats to human health in modern times."

Will the AI technology called CRISPR that Karikó employs bring utopia or apocalypse? We don't know. What we do know is that it follows the pattern that improvisation has long deployed: promising innovation through disruption.

Holy Moly: The Improviser-in-Chief

COVID and Karikó's vaccine against it work like the mythic plant moly in Homer's *Odyssey*. The sorceress Circe uses moly to enchant men, turning them into swine. But in the right hands and in the right dose, moly serves as a vaccine against Circe's magic. Sent by Zeus, Hermes provides his great grandson Odysseus with moly which protects him. Surprised,

ONE: *Improvisation's Dark Side*

Circe responds:
> No other man
> has drunk it and withstood the magic charm.
> But you are different. Your mind is not
> enchanted. You must be Odysseus,
> the man who can adapt to anything.

No wonder Karikó felt like a god: with a touch of charisma she turns the virus into vaccine.

In the *Homeric Hymn to Hermes* (c. sixth century BCE), baby Hermes is a mere demigod, the son of Zeus and the nymph Maia. He is determined to win the last remaining seat on Mount Olympus, home of the gods. On the day of his birth, he steals and carves his brother Apollo's heretofore immortal cattle—at the joints or articulations—into sacrificial lots. By these novel disconnections, Hermes connects the gods and humankind and earns his status as messenger of the gods. Apollo is furious at the sacrilege. How does Hermes respond? He farts in the sun god's face, an act that so violates the deity's dignity that, despite himself, Apollo laughs. Laughter clears the path from conflict to harmony.

Lord of Liars and Prince of Thieves, like Tricksters across the globe, Hermes doesn't know shame. His freedom from shame is handy for another reason. He is a figure of unrestrained appetites. Like his Trickster brethren in other cultures, he is always horny and always hungry. Shame doesn't keep him from passing through locked doors.

Mythical stories, of course, produce legions of archetypes. Are they merely chance survivals, fragments of the long-lost thought processes of ancient Mediterranean peoples, or are they signals, transmitted across the abyss of time, that can connect us to deep meanings, enduring truths? Can such figures exist universally, as the depth psychologist Carl Jung argued when he made them the cornerstone of his concept of the collective unconscious? Can they sustain the universalizing systems of mythographic and literary analysis that Jung's follower Joseph Campbell sought to erect in *The Hero with a Thousand Faces* and *The Masks of God*? In short, what are we dealing with here: universal truths, fuzzy-headed nonsense, or something else altogether, something genetically imprinted?

I had the good fortune to pose that last question to James Hillman, a post-Jungian who founded the discipline of archetypal psychology. Hillman's psychology is polytheistic. He argues that the gods aren't dead but inhabit us, living in our unconscious and sometimes rising to seize and direct our everyday lives. Very much a Trickster himself, hearing my question, Hillman laughed. "Randy," he said, "it's simple. We all have the same body. For 30,000 years and more, it's always been this body. Archetypes are perennial expressions of the body and its parts."

Archetypes aren't a genetic inheritance. They emerge from the embodied experience we all inevitably share *because* of our genetic inheritance. Neuroscience now confirms the central role of embodied emotions in our cognitive lives. Those feelings arise from our bodies and inspire not only images and stories but archetypes, complexes of images, metaphors, and narratives that we come to associate with the mythic gods in various pantheons. You don't have to read Joseph Campbell to appreciate *Star Wars*.

Such archetypes form because the body evokes strong emotions. The body leans toward or away from some object. Complicated emotions arise. You're hungry but that's your neighbor's mammoth haunch; you're horny but that's your neighbor's mate. Trickster and his playful stories are one way to experience our ambivalences in an unthreatening way. He expresses our longings but we see how silly they can be. He reminds us that, though we have elevated thoughts, still we fart. Seeming to mirror our blunders introduces an element of farce. Of course, we desire the Aphrodite or Ares next door, but we needn't be enmeshed by our longing. In the spirit of Hermes, myths provide us with a compensatory way to laugh off our troublesome desires without denying them.

What you do not bring to consciousness, Jung intoned, you act out as fate. Seeing the gods as metaphors for our embodied emotions helps bring them to consciousness. Feeling ourselves reflected in mythic narratives helps us avoid the nets they describe. Archetypes are often contradictory and always complicated, the Trickster archetype perhaps most of all because he patrols the boundary between Hot and Cold Cognition—the abiding drama of our mental lives. Mythic stories help us accommodate to our hunger's shame; we are insatiable; we must kill to feed ourselves. They help us embrace and our hunger's glory: satisfying hunger delights us, nurtures those we love, and turns matter into mind and spirit. Our tendency to covet our neighbor's spouse is just one of the reasons that our genitals, the source of so much joy and pleasure, also bring us so much trouble.

I am continually amazed at the deep understanding of human experience embedded in the details of myth. While we mostly remember the myths in broad strokes, the gods (or the devil, as different versions of the saying go), are in the details. It is in the details recorded by poets and mythographers that we find myths' profound understanding of human nature. When we attend to the details, archetypal myths explain things in a deep way, etiologically, back to their origins. Want to know how civilization began? Listen to the myths told time immemorial around the campfire. As Neil Gaiman, one of today's finest mythographers, writes, "You know myths and legends still have power; they get buried and forgotten, but they're like land mines."

Where does innovation, something new under the sun, come from? What is the nature of creativity? In answer to these questions the Greeks had a lot to say, not just about their experience but about ours. Now those truths are told on silver or flat screens. We resist archaic myths and yet we binge the latest Marvel Cinematic Universe (MCU) films and series, which are replete with mythological references and heroes' journeys. The first of the MCU series, *Iron Man* (2008) was largely improvised by director Jon Favreau, who developed the script on an almost daily basis, and by the eponymous lead played by ever playful Robert Downey, Jr. "They had no script, man," the film's villain Jeff Bridges groused. At the center of the MCU, the world's highest grossing film franchise, with total worldwide box office revenue of 22.56 billion U.S. dollars, is the ongoing battle between Reason—Ultron, Thanos, Iron Man—and Unreason: Loki, Doctor Strange, Black Widow, Wanda, and Vision, all Tricksters.

Trickster is a universal figure. To MCU's many Tricksters we can add Native American and African figures—Coyote and Crow, Br'er Rabbit and the spider Anansi. What Tricksters share is cunning beyond mere rationality, the quality of crafty or creative intelligence that obsessed the Greeks. They called it *metis,* named for Zeus' first wife Metis, an oceanic, shape-shifting Titan.

Winging It

In the Greek Olympiad only five figures have this craft of *metic* intelligence: the Titans Metis and Prometheus, and the gods Hephaestus, Athena, and Hermes. All five represent innovation of the most profound sort, because each is associated with the birth of culture and civilization. Prometheus stole fire and gave it to humankind. Athena designed the horse's bit and plowshare that Hephaestus forged; Hermes invented fire and the rituals of sacrifice. To this list of *metic* beings we can add one human: the ever-wily, polytropic (ever-turning), ever-cunning Odysseus, great-grandson of Hermes. Without Odysseus, there would have been no fall of Troy, no birth of pan-Hellenic culture, no Western culture as we know it. *Metic* intelligence and the mythic stories that embody it encompass both our longing for innovation and for agency, of freedom from the metronome, and the trouble such longing gets us into. Though these culture-heroes disrupt the existing order, they are essentially creators. They may bring chaos, but they do so in a way that catalyzes the emergence of a new, richer, more capacious order. They are all improvisers, responding to the moment, creating something new under the sun. Their myths are land mines, some of the creative, some of the destructive sort.

We have then a working definition of improvisation's meticulously prepared art: spontaneous, but scripted; order out of disorder; a routine unruliness; a feat of social engineering. And we have put our finger on its ruling spirit: the disruptive, *metic* intelligence of Trickster.

Trickster Trump

It's safe to assume that Donald Trump has not read Joseph Campbell. But who among us is more motivated by *id*—where archetypes live?

A mere demigod from outlying Queens, Trump always longed to play with the big boys who dominated Olympian Manhattan. He was a lord of liars and patron of thieves, "the country's most accomplished trickster." Like Hermes, he is a man of unquenchable appetites. Unlike Hermes, not so friendly.

Matt Wuerker © 2019 | POLITICO

ONE: *Improvisation's Dark Side*

A man of appetites, Trump claimed, "My gut tells me more sometimes than anybody else's brain can ever tell me." Trump's gut told him that democracy's articulations—easiest to sever—were embedded in civil society's norms. He enchanted his base with his Twitter feed and the free-associative riffs at his rallies. It quickly became clear that his ramblings were shtick, oft-repeated. But there was power in the impression of spontaneity he achieved. His improvised discourse blared the message, *Trust me, only I can do it.*

Matt Wuerker © 2019 | POLITICO

Asked by Wolf Blitzer if he was responding intuitively when he threatened to withdraw support from NATO, Trump's answer was clear: "Off the cuff…I'm an intuitive person," he explained, "I didn't read books on NATO." As presidential historian Jon Meachum commented, "unabashedly improvisational, Trump revels in his lack of conventional political or policy experience." "I'm a very instinctual person," Trump trumpets, "but my instinct turns out to be right." Except when his instinct led him to dismiss the threat of COVID as no worse than the flu or to promote bleach injections to cure a deadly virus—proofs of Kahneman's distrust of confidence.

Tasked with assessing Donald Trump's health policy record, the Lancet Commission reported that forty percent of the more than 400,000 COVID deaths during his term could have been averted.

Many doubt Trump's intellectual capacity to improvise. Robin Williams he isn't. But what matters is the *appearance* of impromptu behavior. That, he is good at. It is the appearance of spontaneity that has power and peril. Unschooled, Trump presents himself as the "natural man," authentic, free of politicking's artifice, trustworthy. Trump's embrace of folly-as-persuader harks back to the Renaissance when the former monk and priest Erasmus claimed that his mock oration *Praise of Folly* "is unpremeditated but all the truer for that." Embracing speed and carelessness, Erasmus was aiming at the Scholastics, or Schoolmen, followers of Aristotle and Aquinas, remembered mostly for long debates about how many angels can dance on the head of a pin. British philosopher Alfred North Whitehead called their reign, "the rationalistic orgy of the Middle Ages." We call them the Dark Ages, but they were lit up by Cold Cognition. One of the Schoolmen was Duns Scotus from whom we get the word *dunce*. In Erasmus's ironic hands, embracing folly was a way to challenge the Schoolmen's more dangerous, hyperrational follies. Had they remained dominant in western culture, the scientific method would never have emerged.

In the bizarre world led by Trump the Improviser, being a dunce makes you head of the class. According to his worldview, we can *Make America Great Again* by rejecting the best and brightest, the elites. Instead, we should follow Trump's *gut*. As Salena Zito argued, "The press takes him literally but not seriously. His supporters take him seriously, but not literally." The MAGAs know Trump is selling shtick but believe what he means is, *just as I am now breaking the norms of civic discourse, I'll break political norms to bring your jobs back home.* They may know that Trump's promise to save the coal industry is empty, but they trust his promise to care for those whom Hillary Clinton dismissed as deplorables. Each Tweet, according to the *Atlantic,* was "a fragment of presidential id" that fed on, and fed, his base's anger.

Progressives know that Trump cares only for the one percent, evidenced by his tax cuts for the super wealthy. But oft repeated, his lies and "alternative facts" worked *bigly.* The *Washington Post* counted more than 30,000 lies in his four years in office. "Alternative facts" is right out of improvisation's playbook where subjectivity plays a critical role in experience. To his followers, Trump is authentic because, like them, he isn't a member of the rationalist elites.

It's counterintuitive that the embrace of folly has the power to persuade. It's absurd that a reality show host and serial liar with a spray tan can strike anyone as authentic. And yet in Trump's hands, smart is stupid and stupid smart, the way back to an imagined American paradise before the Civil and Voting Rights Acts.

Trump's claim of spontaneity and its resonance with his base has pulled us into an alternate universe where the values and norms of democracy and civic life—reason, expertise, evidence—are seen as the problem, not the solution. He promised to drain the swamp. Instead, when choosing cabinet members, he rejected field experts in favor of political henchmen who acknowledged they knew nothing about the departments they led.

Above all, he was authentic because he was a master of the rhetoric of spontaneity and its cultivated roughness. What really mattered was the *appearance* of impromptu behavior. As they say in Hollywood, "if you can fake sincerity, you can make it in this town." Trump's appearance of improvising is the magic trick that gives him, against all reason, "the ability to exude sincerity as far as a Llama can spit"—to borrow a trope from the great A.J. Liebling. Trump is spontaneous and scripted and routinely unruly. That appearance of spontaneity begets both power and peril. Understanding Trump's manipulative spontaneity can arm the electorate against the next onslaught and help it recover from the trauma he brought upon the American psyche.

Trump and Trauma

The word *trauma* comes from the Greek, meaning wound. Traumatic events, argues Judith Herman in *Trauma and Recovery,* are "extraordinary, not because they occur rarely, but rather because they overwhelm the ordinary human adaptations to life." We all carry within us a life narrative, one that makes sense of our lives. If truth is war's first casualty, meaning—the truths we hold dear—is trauma's first victim. Trauma breaks the life narrative. It wounds whatever meaning we have subjectively constructed for our lives. Destroying personal meaning, trauma also breaks the narrative that holds the community together.

Most traumas involve the abuse of power. Rape, emotional abuse, immoral wars, *quid pro quos* to steal elections—all are abuses of power that inspire helplessness and terror and end our sense that justice reigns. The lens of trauma is one way to understand the abuse of power we experienced under Trump. Democracy has always been susceptible to trauma induced by demagogues whose first role is disruption: Andrew Jackson, Huey Long, Father Charles E. Coughlin, Joseph McCarthy. America always had white supremacists, guardians of The Lost Cause. Trump gave them permission to come out of their woodpile.

Trump's "alternative facts" and "fake news" were a direct assault on truth. To assault truth, personal or communal, is traumatizing. Congressman Jamie Raskin writes in his memoir *Unthinkable: Trauma, Truth, and the Trials of American Democracy* that, "Before the attempted coup of January 6 destroyed our fundamental expectations about the peaceful transfer of power in America, the norms of our constitutional democracy had already been overrun by years of political propaganda, social media disinformation, racist violence, conspiracy theorizing, and authoritarian demagoguery."

Though traumatic events range from extreme violence to more subtle forms of abuse, the basic disorders that result follow a common pathway. The salient characteristics include *hyperarousal,* or the persistent expectation of danger; *intrusion,* often as flashbacks of the traumatic moment; and *constriction,* experienced as the numbing response of surrender.

Recovery from trauma knits the life narrative back together. Restoring a sense of safety is the first step. Then we can bear witness to the harm. Telling the story and being heard equips us to take back control of our lives, returns our sense of agency. Control begins with a new understanding of the pre-trauma narrative. The trauma was *unthinkable*—Congressman Jamie Raskin's word from his memoir's title—due to our national myth of American exceptionalism, that decorous metronome that promises that democracy is as trustworthy as clockwork. Improvisation's syncopations—*here's the beat, no it's here*—pushes back against the American sense of entitlement. All the while, the traumatizer gaslights the victims: *there were good people on both sides.* The improviser pushes back: *no, this was not normal.*

Truth-tellers knit the story back together, including the dark threads. They model the hard work ahead as we rebuild the facts, norms, and the healthy balance of power envisioned by the framers.

The tribal polarization of America, which Trump has done so much to exploit, is one of most crucial problems we face. Dealing honestly with the trauma of Trump is the first step toward healing the divide. Telling our truth—and listening to the truth of both tribes—is an important step on the road to recovery. If dark improvisation has deeply wounded civil society, the way forward is not to stop improvising but to really listen, learning from the best improvisers—comics, scientists, musicians, dancers, and the Founding Fathers—our best listeners.

CHAPTER TWO

Spontaneous or Scripted? The Goldilocks Challenge

If the voice and spirit of improvisation is Trickster, the Lord of Liars, we should not be surprised to find a few lies, white or otherwise, in her discourse. Effortless? Composed in the moment of presentation? Just for fun? Maybe, maybe not.

It's hard to doubt those comedic improvisers who come out on a bare stage and suddenly improvise a sketch based on an audience prompt. But remember, we seek the essential connection among the many disparate discourses our culture loosely labels "improvised." What do comic improvisers have to do with Jack Kerouac's *On the Road,* written on a 130-foot scroll without punctuation over the course of three caffeine-fueled weeks? Kerouac called his spontaneous poetics "kickwriting." But many challenge the very idea of "literary" improvisation. Taking a look at an early draft of *A Taste for Chaos,* my chairman in Liberal Studies at The New School for Social Research dismissed it outright: *A book can't be improvised.* Books, one reasons, are composed over time, not in the moment. Is Kerouac's three weeks somehow short enough to make the cut? Using what measure are we to split such hairs? Should we put Goldilocks—she of the three bears—in charge of deciding if a discourse is improvised too little, too much, or just right?

Goldilocks' familiar questions lead to a dead end for critical improvisation studies. We adopt the spirit of Goldilocks when we feel compelled to decide if an improvisation was composed in the present *in just the right measure*—and dismiss those that don't measure up. Left to her devices, Goldilocks stops our critical adventure cold.

When we split hairs about how spontaneous an improvised text must be, what we miss is the rhetorical effect of how an artist defines her art. Emerson preferred "imperfect theories and sentences, which contain glimpses of truth" over "digested systems"—an improviser's vote for flexibility over rigidity. Dismissing poets with "a marked style," Walt Whitman thinks "the greatest poet…swears to his art, I will not be meddlesome, I will not have in my writing any elegance, or effect, or originality to hang in the way between me and the rest, like [a] curtain." Promising not to meddle, Whitman affirms his authenticity, that he will not let Cold Cognition's second thoughts interfere with his Hot, unmediated experience.

And yet *Leaves of Grass* went through six editions in his lifetime: 1855, 1856, 1860–61, 1867, 1871, 1881–82. Whitman also heavily annotated his personal copy of the 1860 edition in what is known as the "Blue Book." That makes six editions he meddled with. When Kerouac breathlessly presented *On the Road* to Robert Giroux, the famed editor told him the scroll needed an editor's blue pencil. Kerouac insisted it was dictated "by the Holy Ghost" and hit the street, if not the road. Kerouac doesn't mention which member of the Trinity helped him finally edit the scroll for six years. And, in fact, the scroll was his fourth draft. Was only the scroll improvised, Miss Goldilocks? Or only the first, pre-scroll draft? And yet with its aura of spontaneity *On the Road* helped inspire the disruptions of the 1960s. A few years later, James Brown helped to inspire the Black Pride movement, claiming that his improvised performances were sacrosanct: "when it comes from me, it's the real thing. It's God."

Isn't all writing and creativity a spontaneous act to some degree? Isn't all writing and creativity a premeditated act to some degree? Yet some art presents itself as impromptu and some as carefully crafted. What if we took them at their word, but rhetorically, not what they say but what they mean? What do those opposing gestures—spontaneity vs. premeditation—convey?

Do improvisers believe their own bravado or is it the voice of Hot Cognition having to push overly hard against the dominance of Cold Cognition to get a hearing? Maybe to be an improviser requires a modicum of cognitive dissonance, the left hand ignoring the right hand's role, and vice versa. Wilde's paradox gets it just right: "Spontaneity is a meticulously prepared art." So did Tristan Tzara: "thought is produced in the mouth." Both are true but their contradiction goes ignored. Improvisation is a hard-won skill. In the second century of the Christian era, rhetorician Quintilian called improvisation "the greatest fruit of our studies, the richest harvest of our long labours." Once mastered, its results occur in the moment.

Seeking perfection through mastery requires linear, step-by-step, structured human faculties. Setting the appearance of imperfection as a goal—to lack polish and orderliness—casts a vote for a new order where every voice must be heard, even those who have yet to attain mastery and enter the guild. Like Groucho Marx, no improviser would belong to a guild that would have her as a member.

Sourcing Improv

Stephen Colbert's commitment to improv's playfulness was rooted in tragedy. Colbert lost his father and two brothers in an airplane crash. Ten years old at the time, Colbert grieved by embracing nihilism: if these lives that meant so much to him didn't matter to the universe, then surely nothing mattered. Colbert's darkness was so extreme that a theater professor at Northwestern once urged him to seek counseling because he was "physically afraid that you were going to punch me today in class."

But, one night Colbert, now a theater and philosophy major, was taken to see his first comic improv. Colbert was struck by how in improv there were no mistakes, no need to fear "free fall." Realizing "the present social norm is [not] some sort of eternal truth," Colbert had found an avenue back to flourishing. The road forward lay not by denying but by embracing his damage. For Colbert, improv historian Sam Wasson remarks, "damage...was talent, the precursor of personality. 'Damaged people are very interesting,' [Colbert] said. 'The way they behave to cover up their damage is usually very entertaining.'" On Comedy Central's *The Colbert Report* he would play a caricature of a televised political pundit, in Colbert's words, a "well-intentioned, poorly informed, high-status idiot" who spends much of his time covering up his damage with hollow political rhetoric.

A corollary of embracing damage was embracing failure. In legitimate theater, mistakes—free fall—bring nothing but terror. There's no way forward when you drop a line or miss a cue. (It happened to me once in eighth grade before the entire school; the thought of it still makes me flinch.) In improv, mistakes are just an unexpected *Yes, and...* that results in an unexpected and liberating way forward: Hancock's "rotten fruit." In improv, nothing is more welcome than unpredictable surprises. Again

Wasson: "Colbert understood there can be no real unhappiness, 'because if there can be this much joy at a moment of this much agony and failure, there's something very healthy about that...You gotta learn to love when you're failing,' Colbert explained. 'The embracing of that, the discomfort of failing in front of an audience, leads you to penetrate through the fear that blinds you.'"

Another corollary of embracing damage and failure is embracing the indecorous. Colbert would take the stage in his underwear, sing too loudly in an elevator, pay for a bus ride in pennies. "I like to do things that are publicly embarrassing," he said, "to feel the embarrassment touch me and sink into me and then be gone." Wasson explains:

> Colbert's ensemble—indeed his entire generation—had a particular fascination with the excruciatingly uncomfortable. Into the 1990s, as "indie" and alternative sensibilities fought their way free of '80s corporate culture, frolicking in perversely "bad taste" became as much a political gesture as a cultural one. While comedy innovation always turns on violation—Mike Nichols, Elaine May, and others were "sick;" the Lampoon descendants rejoiced in blow jobs, acid, and Belushi—Second City's third great generation took theirs as an antidote to political correctness. Evil was good. Good was evil. Marginalized subcultures would now marginalize the mainstream.

And that is how improv comedy in its own small (and large) way changed the paradigm we live in. The Improviser-in-Chief would have his own way of marginalizing the mainstream.

Francis Coppola's Opportunism

In the late 1990s, the New Orleans Film Society hosted a dinner, a fundraiser for fans to honor Francis Coppola. The legendary director kept a place in the French Quarter, a renovated townhouse that had once been an Italian grocery. I was allowed to replace the restaurant's private dining room's wall art with photographs I had recently taken in Viet Nam. It was my homage to Coppola's *Apocalypse Now!* that for years I had taught in my college course, *Literature, Film, and the Experience of Viet Nam.*

I couldn't have been better paid for my trouble. Coppola gave a short speech about his career. People often asked him, he recounted, why he didn't just make films? "Why do I do all these other projects, my pasta factory in

Brooklyn and my ecolodges in Belize, on and on, the many projects that have nothing to do with film?"

"Well," he explained, "the answer is simply that what makes me the director I am, is what makes me do those other things. When an opportunity presents itself, like rescuing a pasta factory which had 19th-century rollers with burrs that make pasta that hold your marinara sauce, I seize the opportunity. It's no different from when my wife Eleanor came to me while we were filming *Apocalypse Now!* in the Philippines to tell me that the local tribal people serving as extras in the film were about to ritually slaughter a water buffalo." He threw a crew together. The vivid scene earned Coppola a stern rebuke from the American Humane Association. It was nevertheless a perfect symbol for the film's core idea that Kurtz's death was a ritual sacrifice. It was Coppola's call for America to be purged of its misdeeds during its misadventures in Southeast Asia.

Coppola didn't call it opportunism that day but strictly speaking, shorn of the word's dark connotations, that's what it was. It's the op*port*unism that Trickster is master of: finding a way through locked *portals* or gateways. It is the opportunism of the oppressed and marginalized: finding a way out of no way. Opportunism drives improvisers to assess a situation, feel something, and respond creatively.

Crass opportunism waits purposefully for the main chance, for the right moment to seize the day. It differs from opportunism of this creative sort. For the improviser every moment approached with the right attention is the right moment. The improviser confidently rushes through the gateway, finding a way through that was not there but, because of her subjective eye, suddenly appears out of nowhere.

Such joyful careening is what improvisers are best at. It's what we love to watch. It's a talent we'd love to deploy to get us through the straitjacket of our days. Crass opportunism is purposeful and dour; creative opportunism is playful and joyful. Miles with a smile alchemizes gold from Hancock's "rotten fruit." *Apocalypse Now!* creates a community ritually absolved of its toxic masculinity. Each opens our minds to appreciate the value of the valueless. Each assembles a community of those so attuned, who can follow their free associative leaps. Improvisation—the art of the unforeseen—leads the way.

Coppola's opportunism is shaped by his vision and his dreams. His biographer Peter Cowie reports his "dreams of improving the world: 'make a better telephone, develop a more efficient toaster, improve the style of baseball uniforms, build a beautiful little restaurant, run a revolutionary design school such as Germany's pre-war Bauhaus.'" He did build the restaurant, Wim's, named after Wim Wenders. He also revolutionized film distribution. Opening in hundreds of theaters across the country rather than just prestige venues in major cities, *The Godfather* was the first blockbuster, setting the pattern that *Jaws* and *Star Wars* and all those summer MCU films later followed.

Dionysus, Radical Trickster

Trump's opportunism makes everyday, crass opportunists—like Aaron Burr in Lin-Manuel Miranda's *Hamilton*, for example—look like milquetoast. Wielding the tropes of improvisation like a master, Trump promised, as improvisers often do, to create a better world by returning us to a more "natural" world, one governed (or ungoverned) by the foundational values of white supremacy that liberal woke culture increasingly denies. January 6, masquerading as a spontaneous improvisation, as chaos, was carefully planned by Trump and his henchmen, by Michael Flynn and Rudy Giuliani, by the Proud Boys and Oath Keepers. In a key image from that awful day, these last groups deployed a technique, called a "stack formation," learned in Viet Nam or in the Gulf Wars to march purposely forward, hand on the shoulder ahead, brothers and sisters leading and supporting one another. Unseen but there symbolically at the head marched Trump. There was nothing chaotic about it, except the result. If Del Close, the mad genius of comedic improv, urged his disciples to "Treat your audience like artists and poets...so they might have a chance to become them," Trump aimed for the lowest common denominator: fear and anger. As did his partner in crime, Social Media.

But Trump's improvising is not just some fluke. No, it is the inherent dark side of the improv that we love. Even his appeal to the lowest common denominator echoes improv's appeal—with an ironic wink—to the natural and instinctual in us: to Einstein's sacred gift. To study improv critically is to see with clear eyes how fine is the line between democracy and demagoguery. Charismatic voices full of bravado lead both. Both promise to make every voice count. Both challenge accepted norms. Both promise innovation that will enrich culture.

Hermes, Lord of Liars, is the engine behind the improv we know and love. Dionysus, Hermes's more extreme Trickster cousin, energizes Trump. Dionysus is a nature god, the oldest extant symbol in western culture, symbolized by the grape cultivation and wine fabrication he innovated. Dionysian intoxication represents transformation and rebirth, a challenge to hyperrationality. He is an outsider, known as "the god who comes." His coming is always an epiphany, always presenting himself in his charismatic state. He is "Bromios," the loud-roarer. But, promising innovation fueled by intoxication, all he brings is chaos. Hermes responds to Apollo's anger with an innocuous fart. In Euripides's *The Bacchae* he incites regicide, his own little January 6.

In the play, Dionysus promises to bring a new order to Thebes. But, even when his divinity is acknowledged, *The Bacchae* ends in anarchy. No Fortinbras, the Norwegian prince who replaces Hamlet, waits in the wings to reestablish order. The cover of Paul Woodruff's translation brilliantly turns Elvis Presley's official army photo into a criminal mugshot to link Dionysus's anarchy to the end of civilization the 1950s mainstream feared from the advent of rock and roll. In a sense, let's admit it now, they were right. The age of Aquarius was dawning, largely driven by improvisation.

Dionysian chaos is the kind an aspiring tyrant can profit from. "As a focus for communal celebration," British classicist Richard Seaford writes, "Dionysus is in the Athenian democracy imagined as subversive of autocracy, but for this very reason may...be appropriated by the autocrat." Autocrats in history rode in triumph as the "New Dionysus" to mobilize their base. Marc Anthony rode into Ephesus and Athens draped in grape leaves and carrying Dionysus's staff, the thyrsus, and promising to renew the republic. What he sought was its end. He, or Dionysus, inspired two more autocrats, Caligula and Nero, to parade as the New Dionysus. Perhaps tweeting is the new fiddling, except that Nero's fiddling was feckless, without purpose. Trump's tweets marshal his base. Trump expresses something utterly new yet foreshadowed in Antiquity, an American president demanding total loyalty bent like Marc Antony on destroying the republic.

Buying Trump's lies, the red-capped MAGA-heads show every indication of intoxication. For their progressive opponents, there is the rub. Who while intoxicated is open to rational discourse? How can this 40% of America be reached?

His followers may be intoxicated but Trump himself, who never touches alcohol, seems to suffer from what AA calls "dry drunk syndrome" (DDS) where one has achieved sobriety but hasn't recovered from the underlying traumas. The symptoms of DDS fit Trump to a tee:

- Wanting to be the center of attention
- Feeling like you're always the victim
- Having trouble communicating with other people
- Mood swings that range from depression to extreme happiness
- Anger and resentment towards family and friends who intervene
- Believing that sobriety is boring
- Not acknowledging the problems your substance abuse caused
- Believing you always know what's best
- Refusing to accept constructive criticism

Improv is always touched by our dark side, by what Jung calls the Shadow, that part of us we'd like to deny. Hermes, guide of souls to the underworld, is always subject to this darkness. We mustn't ignore it. But just as the devil in all of us does not negate our better angels, so Trump's dark improv does not negate the improv that has enriched rationality and culture. Neuroscience clarifies the pulse and throb of embodied emotion that drives improv's pushback against reason and normative culture. Heroic doses of psychedelics, as we'll see, open the ego's reducing valve and put us in touch, finally, with the unmediated experience that improv has long promised. Artists and scientists have demonstrated improv's allure. The embattled dance between Reason's discourse and improvisation has shaped the march of civilization.

Coppola's *The Godfather*:
The Battle between Hot and Cold Cognition

Effortless hard work—pardon my oxymoron—improvisation is also marked by the paradox of synchronicity. Synchronicity, acausal connection—doors with no way through that suddenly offer their keyholes—is another challenge to rational discourse. *The Godfather*'s birth was marked by a triple syn-

TWO: *Spontaneous or Scripted?*

chronicity. One morning in San Francisco, Coppola's eye is caught by a small ad in the *New York Times*. The puppeteer logo on the novel's cover attracted him "because it implied power, the story was going to be about power." Two more coincidences followed the same morning. Al Ruddy in town making *Little Fauss and Big Halsey* dropped in to say hello. During "this purely social visit," Coppola was called to the phone: Marlon Brando was calling to turn down the role Coppola had written for him in *The Conversation*. In *The Godfather Notebook,* Coppola calls attention to the coincidences: Paramount would soon assign Al Ruddy to produce *The Godfather,* and Marlon Brando would play Vito Corleone.

Coppola started the book but soon put it aside, turned off by the "odd" sub-plot "about Lucy Mancini and the surgeon who was hired to alter her private anatomy." But Paramount came calling and Coppola's "young protégé" at American Zoetrope, George Lucas, insisted: "You have to accept this job; we have no money and the sheriff is coming to chain up the front door." Coppola had founded his production company American Zoetrope in San Francisco's North Beach in an effort to disrupt and be free of the Hollywood studio system. As improvisers always do, Coppola targeted rigidified system first and last.

So Coppola reads the novel through and realizes that apart from Lucy's anatomical problems it was also an anatomy lesson about American capitalism: "a metaphor for American capitalism in the tale of a great king with three sons: the oldest was given his passion and aggressiveness, the second his sweet nature and childlike qualities, and the third his intelligence, cunning and coldness." Vito Corleone's middle child is a non-player. What matters is the opposition between his oldest and youngest male heirs, between Santino and Michael. He wants to save his youngest from inheriting his dark world, but Sonny's hotheadedness gets him killed in a rain of bullets. The *Godfather* trilogy is about Michael's cold embrace of his father's dark world. *The Godfather* is about who will pull the strings, the sacred gift or the unfaithful servant, Hermes or Apollo. The name of Michael's Sicilian wife, Apollonia, suggests where his loyalties lie. It will be a battle between Sonny's Hot and Michael's Cold Cognition, and about the cost of Michael's Pyrrhic victory, symbolic of American capitalism's postwar Pyrrhic victory.

Winging It

Accepting the project, using his college background in theater arts, Coppola begins to fashion his prompt book, cutting out the pages of the novel, making notes and underlining in multiple colors. Coppola's *The Godfather Notebook* describes in detail his effort to create a "master control," the three-ring binder, the reinforced sheets, the leather satchel he bought to transport and protect it. "It would be the repository of every idea I could think of about my future project." A cover sheet before each scene of the screenplay contained, according to Coppola, "the key criteria: (1) synopsis, (2) the times, (3) imagery and tone, (4) the core, (5) pitfalls." The core was derived from director Elia Kazan's idea that every scene in a play "comes down to 'a core idea.'" Coppola writes,

> It was appealing to me that if you nailed the clarity of that core in each scene, the audience would get that, and that would form the spine of the experience for them. I endeavored to distill the essence of each scene into a sentence, expressing in a few words what the point of the scene was.

Profoundly analytic and made "out of profound fear," Coppola's *Godfather Notebook* is an act of Cold Cognition, a prediction machine meant to cover and control every eventuality when Coppola yells, *roll film*. "The notebook," Coppola writes, "was a kind of multilayered road map for me to direct the film... I didn't need a script because I could have made the movie just from this notebook."

There was good reason for Coppola's fear. Not only was his career on the line, it was in the hands of a bunch of relative newbies. Coppola had won best screenplay for *Patton,* but in the director's chair he had only four unsuccessful, low-budget films to his credit. Producer Al Ruddy had co-created TV sitcom *Hogan's Heroes* but had produced only two minor films. Robert Evans, who would executive produce for Paramount, had produced two hits, *Rosemary's Baby* and *Love Story,* but, to his dismay, was still known as the ladies wear salesman (where he'd gotten his start).

With analytic Cold Cognition Coppola creates the *Godfather Notebook,* and then production starts. Hot Cognition kicks in.

Coppola almost loses control of the film because of an improvisation in the very first scene they shoot. In Vito's dark office, the undertaker Amerigo

TWO: *Spontaneous or Scripted?*

Bonasera with his resonant name (America, Goodnight), comes to say, "I believe in America." But his daughter has been molested by two well-connected American teenagers, and he has come to ask for the rough justice the American judicial system had not delivered. Beautifully shot in chiaroscuro by Gordon Willis, the sound was marred by the decision to put a cat in Marlon Brando's lap during the scene. How the cat got on the soundstage is unclear. Some say it was Coppola's last-minute idea; some say that ever-playful Brando had befriended the alley cat. The cat's purring so obscured Brando's lines, already infamous for his mumble, that the Paramount executives, equally upset by the uncorrected color of Willis's chiaroscuro, were ready to toss Coppola from the production. Coppola fast-talked his way back in. Willis corrected the color. Brando overdubbed the lines. Problem solved.

The purring cat with its hooded claws is another opportunistic synchronicity and perhaps worth the trouble it caused. "We're not murderers in spite of what this undertaker says," Vito tells Tom Hagen, smelling the rose in his buttonhole. Film critic Peter Cowie captures the symbolism: like the cat's hooded claws, "The words, so mundane and unexceptional, mask the vicious street violence of the Mafia."

With Vito dead, *The Godfather* ends with Michael standing as godfather to his nephew, Connie's son. During the baptism his henchmen murder the heads of the five families. As the priest casts out evil, the baptism is exquisitely intercut in a montage of the five murders. Michael has assumed his role as the Prince of Darkness, Hermes's dark role as Guide of Souls to Hades. In the confrontations with his brother-in-law Carlo, his sister, and his wife Kay that end the first film, Michael takes on Hermes's mantle of Lord of Liars.

Thieves and murderers and yet we root for them. We root for Michael and his henchmen in part because the five Mafia dons are more venal, and in part because Coppola's exquisite film treatment seems to say that the Corleones are a more accomplished version of us. We, too, long for justice, for loyalty, and for the mastery, free of the metronome's constraints, to get the job done.

Improv always enacts this battle between hard-won preparation and skill and the newbie's confrontation with the moment that comes. We are all newbies before the present moment. As the Nobel laureate Wisława Szymborska reminds us, our lives are inevitably improvised:

> Nothing can ever happen twice.
> In consequence, the sorry fact is
> that we arrive here improvised
> and leave without the chance to practice.

The central battle of improvisation is enacted both in Coppola's filmmaking methods—at once coldly analytic and improvised—and in the film's subject matter: Sonny's Hot and Michael's Cold Cognition.

Improvising a Road to Graceland

When I was a student in Paris, a brilliant fellow student from Barnard who shared my budding literary aspirations surprised me one day with an offhand remark about Simon and Garfunkel. "Their songs are overwritten," she offered. It was the early 1970s. I was clueless what that meant—overwritten?—and stunned one could find fault with Paul Simon's exquisite lyricism. Apparently, my friend was not alone. A couple years before, Arthur Schmidt in *Rolling Stone* had written that *Bookends* "exudes a sense of process, and it is slick."

Granted, Simon's lyrics were highly *composed,* hardly the creation of the moment. *There's a problem with that?* I wondered. Perhaps it marked the dawning of my interest in the special power of the spontaneous.

Paul Simon's creative method is largely the subject of Malcolm Gladwell's audio book *Miracle and Wonder: Conversations with Paul Simon*. If much of Simon's songbook is highly "composed," one exception is the title song of his album *Graceland*.

The album was inspired by Simon's listening to a borrowed cassette of the Soweto township jive (or *mbaqanga*) band The Boyoyo Boys. Their instrumental "Gumboots" would become the fourth song on *Graceland*. *Mbaqanga* means cornmeal porridge, which suggests their humble origins and aspirations.

This was long before "world music" was a thing. Besides, South Africa was a pariah state. The UN had imposed a boycott in 1980. But Simon was charmed and intrigued by "Gumboots." Despite the UN boycott, he arranged to travel to Johannesburg to work with some township artists, "with the idea," in Simon's words, "that the two musical cultures could intermingle in a way that would be interesting."

As Gladwell points out, the title song "was a departure for Simon because he didn't come to the studio with lyrics or melodies already written. This time all he had was a feeling." Simon planned to "just follow his ear," to pursue the feeling that he'd heard on the Boyoyo Boys cassette. It reminded him of the joy he heard in 1950s rock and roll. He went to South Africa to see what would emerge when the two confronted one another, rock and roll, heir to African rhythms, and "originary" African rhythms.

What emerged, however, was Simon's realization that the Boyoyo Boys sounded like early rock and roll in part because township musicians had long been imitating American music. The "originary" was derivative. (As Derrida has it: *toujours déjà*). Confronting this paradox, Gladwell offers a sweeping explanation of how this came about:

> Rhythms come to North America from Africa hundreds of years ago with the slave trade, get transformed in their new environment into R&B and gospel and do-wop and a hundred other things and then get refracted back to Africa: a musical jet stream encircling the earth round and round and [Simon] gets caught up in that stream as a kid and plunges in again as an adult years later and he can tell, I've been here before… That's where *Graceland* began, with the memory of a feeling.

The musical jet stream gives the lie to improvisation's claim that "you've never seen anything like this before." It takes the teeth out of objections to "world music." It defuses the charge of appropriation that haunts *Graceland*. Improvisation is not something new under the sun. Always a hybrid form tinkered from preexistent parts, it's just something *newer*. Never completely impromptu, spontaneous composition draws on the instinctive brain which is the seat of our personal and ancestral memories.

The first world-music album made by an American—*Graceland*—wasn't the only thing spontaneously to emerge in the recording studio. Simon explains the synchronicity to Gladwell:

> When I was composing the lyrics, I kept singing "Graceland, I'm going to Graceland, Graceland" and then whenever I sing it, I'd say of course

> I'm going to change that. This can't be a song about Elvis Presley, and I mean it's a South African band you know. And finally I just didn't stop singing that, "Graceland, I'm going to Graceland." Finally, I said, I guess I have to go to Graceland and find out what's going on here. I have to go there to find out why I can't drop this lyric. So I wrote the story about the journey that's in search of grace.

The song took months to write. If not completely impromptu, its emergent narrative perfectly captures the musical jet stream Simon was discovering. Playing with these "roots" musicians, he journeys to the roots both of rock and roll and of township music—roots that are themselves derivative appropriations—in search of what improvisation always seeks: a grace beyond the reach of art (and rationality).

Effortless? Composed in the moment of presentation? Maybe. Maybe not. But to insist on totally impromptu is to miss the rhetorical power of *seeming* impromptu. Perhaps an improvisation's effortless, impromptu nature is a lie. The salient truth the lie points to is that creative innovations they cannot fully be planned. However premeditated, what is new to some degree emerges in a way surprising to the artist.

CHAPTER THREE

Eureka!
Improv, Invention, and Paradigm Shifts

In their startling Selective Attention Test (1999), psychologists Simons and Chabris ask subjects to watch a video and to count how many times the team wearing white passes the basketball. As the two teams pass the balls, the experiment's true test begins: will viewers see a gorilla suit-clad person who walks onto the court? The gorilla even tries to steal the show, pausing center court to beat her chest. Few viewers attend to the gorilla because the challenge to discriminate between teams and count passes activates Cold Cognition and de-activates the ability to see an event so anomalous.

Daniel Simons | YouTube

Over 60% of viewers don't see the gorilla and afterwards insist it couldn't have happened. When Cold Cognition is in charge counting the passes, Hot Cognition chomps at the bit to get a hearing—to no avail. Not just the Information Age but our mental life itself is a roiling attention economy. Cold and Hot Cognition fight for attention in our overstimulated brains. When they don't work together "inattentional blindness" occurs.

Unwilling to shut off Hot Cognition, improvisers see, and get us to see, the anomalous: the strutting gorilla.

Shifting Paradigms

To understand improvisation's power and allure, we must understand the problem it seeks to solve. Improvisation may not truly be a different way of composing. But it always embodies a different way of knowing. It always seeks knowledge beyond reason's limits.

Improv would have us see more of the world and to use more of our brain, not just Cold Cognition. Ed Yong's recent work on the sensory life of animals is a helpful analogy to our selective attention. Bats can hear ultrasound that we can't. Like every animal we too are "enclosed within our own sensory bubble, perceiving but a tiny sliver of an immense world." Cold and Hot Cognition each have their sensory bubble. When Cold Cognition is in charge, we don't attend to anomalies. Improv seeks to widen our mental bubble.

If hearing ultrasound is bats' superpower, intuition—Einstein's "sacred gift"—is ours. For the godmother of comedic improv, Viola Spolin, intuition is the extra-rational faculty *par excellence*. Fearful that "intuitive" become "a catch-all word which we throw around or use for old concepts," Spolin urges that instead we "use it to denote that area of knowledge which [is] deeper than the 'survival dress' of mannerisms, prejudices, intellectualisms, and borrowings most of us wear to live out our daily lives" (e.g., the metronome). Spolin urges us to use intuition to break through "the walls of our cage, prejudices, frames of reference, and predetermined right and wrong...In this way there will be no fear that a system becomes a system."

Looking with intuition's "inward eye," we avoid knowing the world only through the metronome of fixed and deadened systems. The rigidity of systems—the precinct of Cold Cognition—is improvisation's perennial target. On the level of language, when an experience rigidifies into cliché, the innovator finds the new language to bring the experience back to life.

Improvisation is the discourse of paradigm shifts. Defined by Thomas Kuhn in his influential *The Structure of Scientific Revolutions* (1962), "paradigm shift" describes how science progresses not by a linear accumulation of new knowledge but rather by transforming the nature of the dominant scientific field. Paradigm shifts reflect change at a metalevel, not just *what* we know but *how* we know it—a change in the conceptual map.

THREE: *Eureka!—Improv, Invention, and Paradigm Shifts*

Experimentation solves puzzles about nature but also sometimes yields anomalies, results that don't fit the paradigm—new puzzles the reigning paradigm can't address, or even perceive. When anomalies present themselves, the paradigm explains them away as the scientists' or the experiments' mistakes, mere noise that can be ignored. Karikó's strength, recall, was that she didn't ignore failed results. When enough anomalies accumulate, the old paradigm reaches a crisis. The anomalies can no longer be ignored. A new paradigm emerges that incorporates earlier valid results and now explains the anomalies. A larger, richer vision of nature finds a new consensus. Galileo's and Copernicus's heliocentric view of the solar system replaces the geocentric. The new paradigm, first resisted but finally adopted, shifts our view not only of the solar system but also of nature and humanity, their value and meaning. Karikó's mRNA represents the leading edge of a paradigm shift in medical science.

One challenge Kuhn's theory faced among historians of science was the view that paradigms really shift only when the old generation dies out. Once they're gone, the rising generation can see through different lenses. Improvisation, however, not only makes the case for a new paradigm but demonstrates it in the moment. Following an improviser's metaphoric leaps activates our instincts and intuitions and makes improvisers of us all. Improvisation is an effort to shift the paradigm kinetically in real time, creating a community ready for the paradigm shift.

Improvisation thrives on anomalies, alchemically transforms noise into gold. Where Reason and Science seek the statistical norm, improvisation inhabits a present that is unique—by definition like no other in history, an anomaly. (Others will read that last sentence, but *your* reading it in the last moment was a unique event in history.) Improvisation challenges as too narrow the rationality that produced but can't explain anomalies. Making anomalies—like ogres with underbites—the "point of concentration," as Spolin terms each improvisation's focus, improv urges the need for a new, richer rationality informed by faculties that rationality has marginalized.

Winging It

Yes, and... is Epistemological?!?

At Satchmo Fest at the New Orleans Jazz Museum, I once gave a talk on Joyce's *Ulysses* as improv. I argued that Joyce's High Modernist improv was like Armstrong's. Both tinker their art together from many sources, high and low. Both teach us how to embrace more of the world. Joyce shows us the joy and humanity of embracing those thrown away like Leopold Bloom and Molly his wife, named for Odysseus's moly. Armstrong sees "the bright blessed day" and "the dark sacred night," both wonderful.

Afterwards, on the way out, a good friend and great New Orleans clarinetist Evan Christopher stopped me at the door. *You think that's what I'm thinking about when I play?* he asked with scorn.

For once at the ready, without a moment's hesitation I replied, *I didn't say, it's what you're thinking but what you're doing.* Embodied Hot Cognition is hot jazz's calling card.

What I didn't say then but what I think now is that what Evan does when he channels Sidney Bechet is to participate in a discourse with roots deeper than we usually imagine. Like Bechet and like Joyce, his mastery of jazz discourse expresses our longing for "a place where they all used to be happy once," as Bechet writes of jazz's roots in his memoir *Treat It Gentle*. Building community, his call and response gives voice to both our individuality and our *shared humanity,* as improv has always done.

The joy of knowing more than reason and social norms allow is baked into improv's *Yes, and...,* its rule of agreement, its call and response, its signifying. Enough *Yes, and...* and you've shifted the paradigm. Science makes distinctions, and as Wordsworth noted, "murders to dissect." Improv connects dots, weaves patterns, makes metaphoric leaps from which meaning and community emerge. Seizing more and more of life, improv, like evolution, tinkers. Neuroendocrinologist Robert Sapolsky calls attention, for example, to a brain region called the insula which tens of millions of years ego evolved to register the smell or taste of rancid food and automatically trigger spitting out the food or barfing, saving us from all kinds of intestinal woes. But when tens of thousands of years ago "humans invented constructs like morality and disgust at moral norm violations," Sapolsky explains,

> that's way too little time to have evolved a new brain region to "do" moral disgust. Instead, moral disgust was added to the insula's port-

THREE: *Eureka!—Improv, Invention, and Paradigm Shifts*

folio; as it's said, rather than inventing, evolution tinkers, improvising (elegantly or otherwise) with what's on hand. Our insula neurons don't distinguish between disgusting smells and disgusting behaviors, explaining metaphors about moral disgust leaving a bad taste in your mouth.

Tinkering rather than inventing, evolution, like improv, works by call and response: *hey, that's a nice neuron or brain region or gene, let's use it over here.* Joyce tinkers the *Odyssey* together with Dublin, Telemachus's quest to find his father with Stephen Dedalus's, and the result, *Ulysses*, transforms the English novel. Repeating evolution's dynamic processes lends improv some measure of its power. Improv-as-tinkerer returns us to life's beginnings—evolution—and pushes us toward the next paradigm: revolution. *yes I said yes I will Yes,* rejoices Joyce's Molly, named after the Hermes's cure-all herb, moly.

Fractals and the Challenge to Objectivity

One truth that improvisation discloses is the hollowness of science's cult of objectivity. Improv's truths always embody a subjective element. One of the founders of Chaos Science and the "father of fractals," Benoît Mandelbrot challenged the normative science of his day by calling attention to a problem in the notion of measurement, a key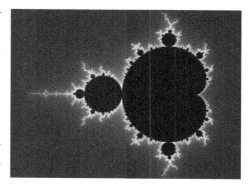

Mandelbrot Set

to scientific objectivity. In a landmark paper in *Science* (1967) he asked the simple, but disruptive question, "How Long Is the Coast of Britain?" The problem he points to is that the length is contingent on the unit of measurement you subjectively choose. Using 200 kilometers yields one number: 2400 km. Using 50 kilometers enables you to measure the bays and inlets that are part and parcel of the coast but which the larger measure ignores as noise. The smaller measure counterintuitively yields a larger number: 3400 km. And so on, down to millimeters or microns. The imperfections in the island's circumference give truer weight to your measurement: they have meaning. To insist on any given measure as transcendently normative is to put your thumb on the scale. The truer weight may not have more value, more utility, but Mandelbrot didn't seek utility. He sought disruption. He sought to challenge science's dependence on the utility of objective measurement. By looking at the coastline's statistical "imperfections," his "coastline paradox," as it was called, revealed the limits of our rational measures, their dependence despite themselves on subjective contingency. Science's vaunted objectivity took a tumble.

A whole new science emerged—a whole new way of knowing—when Mandelbrot switched from challenging measure to contemplating nonlinear equations (e.g., $ax^2 + by^2 = c$, where a, b, c are constants and x and y are variables). Most mathematicians took little interest in nonlinear equations which, as far as they were concerned, were mere noise. Studying them had no purpose. Such equations enabled Mandelbrot—with the aid of computer graphics—to describe turbulence, a "noise" phenomenon long resistant to mathematical description. They enabled him to find the scaled regularity of irregular and fragmented patterns, from mountainsides to cloud formations to the stock market's fluctuations. In a catalogue typical of improvisation, he declared that he found "a world of pure plastic beauty unsuspected till now" in natural forms that scientists dismissed as *"grainy, hydralike, in between, pimply, pocky, ramified, seaweedy, strange, tangled, tortuous, wiggly, wispy, wrinkled,* and the like."

Chaos science (and later Complexity science which it inspired) enlarged the way we know the world, the world we know, and our appreciation of its beauty. Calling attention to the contingency of perception, Mandelbrot took responsibility for how we shape what we see. We see the world according to the method of perception we have subjectively chosen. Where through science we perceive an objective world, through improvisation we perceive subjectively—perception that acknowledges the objective world while insisting that the phenomenologically experienced world also exists and needs attention.

With a playful element that shuns utility, Mandelbrot's fractal geometry nevertheless led to many scientific breakthroughs. It had wide practical applications in predicting various biological processes and morphology, in predicting stock market and weather fluctuations, in developing computer

THREE: *Eureka!—Improv, Invention, and Paradigm Shifts*

graphics (used making those CGI blockbusters that fill our summer screens). Challenging systematic order, improvisation begets a new, richer order.

Mandelbrot's openness to the non-linear, self-organizing aspects of nature is reflected in his characterization of the book that launched the science of Chaos. Open to new knowledge, Mandelbrot is also formally an improviser. His "openness" is formally and stylistically echoed by eschewing, as he says in his preface, the form of a systematic "textbook [or] treatise in mathematics" and his characterizing *The Fractal Geometry of Nature* instead as "a scientific Essay because it is written from a personal point of view and without attempting completeness. Also, like many Essays, it tends to digressions and interruptions." Essay—*something merely subjective, free associative, and, by definition tentative* (to essay or assay is "to try")—has been a common improviser's trope since Montaigne, that "accidental philosopher" and Bacon, the founder of the scientific method. Mandelbrot challenges mainstream science by seeking "to study those forms that Euclid leaves aside as being 'formless,' to investigate the morphology of the 'amorphous.'" Form and content are one.

In his encyclopedic tendency, his digressions, and his swerve from the traditional form, Mandelbrot echoes Bacon's *Essays* and Locke's *Essay on Human Understanding* that helped to build the foundation of science by challenging the hyperrationalism of medieval scholasticism—the Schoolmen. Mandelbrot's eccentric and playful first-person voice, so scandalous to mainstream scientists who did their best to marginalize him, unwittingly looks toward the Trickster persona of improvisation and helps implicitly to debunk the scientific positivism that has no room for the unreasonableness of life's complexity. *Fractals,* the best-selling book on higher mathematics in history, was followed by user-friendly software and full-color coffee-table books. Scientists belittle this popularization and yet it is inevitable: chaos science is a science of the world and for the people. Like improvisation. Yes, improv is a science: it seeks to define, to model, and to enable a larger way of knowing.

Mandelbrot's embrace of imperfection is true in that other familiar, world-popular improvisational form: jazz. In comedic improv, there is turbulence but no mistakes.

Inventing Fire

Did systematic reason or logic help our ancestors invent fire? Of course, we had the use of fire before it was "invented." Inspired by the delightful Romantic essayist Charles Lamb's "A Dissertation Upon [the First] Roast Pig," I imagine one of our ancestors saw the African savannah ablaze from a lightning strike and liked the taste of the roast pork found in the ashes. Next time she carefully nursed some of that fire home and kept the flames going. But inevitably that home fire went out. It's hard to have to wait for the next lightning strike when your mammoth haunch needs cooking. Among its many civilizing advantages, cooking made staples of otherwise inedible wheat, rice, and potatoes, all reasons for our "advance" from hunter-gatherers to settled farmers, and hence the birth of cities (from, *civitas*). From the hoarding of agricultural goods, hierarchies emerge that enthrone Reason and writing (to tally the hoards, lending power to its owners). The "invention"—the rational control—of fire is fundamental to civilization. But was its invention a rational process?

Eventually someone stumbled on starting fire by striking flint and iron ore over tinder. But how? There was no one to teach her. This foundation to civilization came out of nowhere, perhaps by free association or analogical thinking. David Perkins, founding member of Harvard's Project Zero, which studies the nature of creativity, calls it "breakthrough thinking" as opposed to "sequential thinking." To think by free association or by analogies is to find patterns by means of resemblances. To think, *this is like that,* is not entirely rational. *Metaphor* means to carry or throw across, to link what is not the same. *This* is *not* in fact *that. But what if for the moment...*

Analogy-making, the breakthrough leap of metaphors, runs deep in our humanness. For Douglas Hofstadter, a leader in the field of human creativity, "analogy is the fuel and fire of thinking" not just for art but also for science: "without concepts there can be no thought, and without analogies there can be no concepts." As British psychiatrist and neuroscientist Iain McGilchrist points out, "if we wanted examples, we have them at the highest levels: Darwin in biology, Freud in psychology, and Bohr in physics spring to mind." Eighteenth century philosopher David Hume weighed in early: "all our reasonings concerning matters of fact are founded on a species of analogy." Even Cold Cognition's predictive function works by analo-

THREE: *Eureka!—Improv, Invention, and Paradigm Shifts*

gies: *this is like that, therefore let's do this.* Rationality gives its systematic logic high marks while dismissing the key role of unsystematic, intuition-based metaphor and analogy.

That something can run "deep" in our nature is a metaphor you probably don't need cognitive linguists to help you understand. Cognitive linguists unite linguistics, psychology, and neuroscience to understand how we deploy figures of speech in engaging the world and in making meaning. "Running deep" fits our conceptual map of human nature which uses embodied metaphors associated with up and down, high and low.

Because we have the bodies we do—and have done for 30,000 years, James Hillman reminds us—certain metaphors are universal. "Up" is happy (my spirits *rose*); "down" is sad (I *fell into* a depression). You might respond that while analogies may have a role in primitive thinking, they didn't create high-level thinking like, for example, Boolean (binary) logic upon which our computers are based. One imagines that such logic (1s and 0s representing on and off switches) was born out of a totally structured, systematic mind: David Perkins's "sequential thinking;" neuroscience's Cold Cognition.

And yet, analogical thinking had a critical role in *applying* Boolean logic to computers and in founding the Information Age. Claude Shannon, an MIT graduate student in electrical engineering, once took a required philosophy course where he learned about George Boole, the nineteenth-century English logician, who assigned a value of 1 to true statements and 0 to false statements to show that logic problems could be solved like math equations. Boolean logic found no practical application until Shannon did a summer internship at AT&T's Bell Labs. Once there, Shannon made a sudden leap, a free association, when he saw he could apply Boolean logic to telephone call-routing to encode and transmit information electronically. No one had ever connected the two fields. That leap, as the historian of creativity Walter Isaacson put it, "became the basic concept underlying all digital computers." *Scientific American* named Shannon's paper ("The Mathematical Theory of Communication") "the Magna Carta of the Information Age." By his leap, analogical thinking lit the fire beneath post-industrialism. The Information Age and, we can add, the Attention Economy—the struggle for our scarce attention—was born.

Winging It

Like Einstein's advances in physics, Shannon's Eureka moment was first driven by intuition. Then he worked out the math. Einstein didn't speak until he was five; he thought in images—which shaped his "thought experiments," all imagistic and metaphorical in nature. To picture special relativity, he employed moving trains and flashes of lightning. For general relativity, he considered a person falling off a roof, accelerating elevators, blind beetles crawling on curved surfaces.

Shannon worked much the same way, feeling his way forward from an intuition. Although friend and colleague to such computer age giants as Alan Turing and Von Neumann, Shannon humbly said of his process, "I try to get a feeling of what's going on. Equations come later." Like Einstein, he was something of a Trickster. His biographers describe "a life spent in the pursuit of curious, serious play… He worked with levity and played with gravity; he never acknowledged a distinction between the two."

What drove this tinkerer was anomalies, or, as he put it, "constructive dissatisfaction" or "a slight irritation when things don't look quite right." Shannon needed homeostasis—the "steady state" where things look and feel right and where his thinking could flourish—which neuroscientist Antonio Damasio argues motivates all life. Such homeostasis, according to Damasio, is driven by embodied emotions. (More on Damasio in a moment.)

But, imagine: fire without lightning? How do you get the ingredients together to make fire when you don't know what the ingredients are? Unless you're Zeus—or Einstein—lightning bolts aren't ready to hand. But what if someone happened to notice while making a spear point, say, that striking flint and iron ore produced a spark? What if that spark reminded our ancestor of the sparks that rose from fire? What if she connected the two?

Once known, fire-making can be taught by means of structured, sequential thought: *You do this, then you do that.* But the original discovery, how to make fire, takes "unstructured thought." It takes a leap. Consider that it was Hermes, ever alert to the present moment, who invented fire. Prometheus just stole it. But Prometheus is an improviser too. His name means "before-thought." Stealing fire, whether Hermetic or Promethean, is an act of pre-consciousness: Hot Cognition. Both god and titan capture the role of unstructured thought in our mental life and culture.

But the sparks of innovation cannot be taught. There are no steps, only leaps. It's what's happening when we speak of our mind taking flight. It is

THREE: *Eureka!—Improv, Invention, and Paradigm Shifts*

why the Greeks imagined Hermes wearing winged sandals and helmet. It's Perkins's breakthrough thinking. It's the illogical leap of *metaphor*—throwing across, linking one thing to another. Along with its privileging of "nature" and "natural," celebrating that kind of unstructured thinking is another of improv's springboards, proof, improvisers say, of their authenticity. In a sense such thinking *is* natural, but no more natural or authentic than is Cold Cognition. We need both. Both are "natural" functions of the brain. Cold Cognition is the *natural* site where reasoned artifice emerges. Hot Cognition is the *natural* site where non-linear, creative, intuitive leaps are made.

That impulse, to stretch reason, is at the heart of the creative enterprise. It is the culture of spontaneity's gift to civilization, the gift of innovation and renewal when rigidified system has set in. Every creative act is an effort to roll back the dominance of the purpose-driven rationality that is driving us now to the brink of extinction. But often the rhetoric of spontaneity reminds us that at times the rational mind needs to cede its high-status, power-driven dominance and authority so that innovations can emerge. Sometimes the rhetoric of spontaneity persuades us to let go of our reasoning mind when we need it most, and a demagogue takes charge. Primed by most instances of improvisation to expect benign innovation, we need to know when an improvisation is driving us toward chaos.

Embodied Emotions That Underlay Reason

Neuroscience is confirming the crucial role of embodied emotions—the basis of our instincts and intuitions, what some call the brain's supercomputer—in our cognitive life.

Antonio Damasio, head of the Brain and Creativity Institute at USC and a rock star among today's neuroscientists, champions affect, the role of feeling and emotion he believes central in constituting, not just affecting, our cognitive life. An early campaigner for embodied mind, he believes cognitive science has leaned too far toward René Descartes's mind-body duality. Descartes's *cogito ergo sum*—I think therefore I am—not only separated mind from body but dismissed the body's role in our mental life.

In his recent book, *The Strange Order of Things: Life, Feeling, and the Making of Cultures* (2018), Damasio doesn't just explain the emergence of consciousness but also of life as we know it. He offers a grand vision of life, driven all along the way by affect—emotion—even down to the cellular level. Human culture emerges from the same impulse—the imperative to maintain homeostasis—that drives all bio-evolution, from single, unnucleated cells up the evolutionary tree. It's a moving and persuasive vision. And, like improvisation, it starts with spontaneity. Bio-evolution too is spontaneous, but scripted, orderly disorder, routine unruliness. It re-engineers culture.

What drives bio-evolution is affect which is the result of the instinctive need for homeostasis ("steady state"), the underlying imperative *felt* by all life to maintain the conditions to sustain itself and to flourish (i.e., to reproduce). "Homeostasis," according to Damasio, "has guided, *non-consciously and non-deliberatively, without prior design,* the selection of biological structures and mechanisms capable of not only maintaining life but also advancing the evolution of species to be found in varied branches of the evolutionary tree." Homeostasis "is the powerful, *unthought, unspoken* imperative [that] has been the pervasive governor of life in all its guises" (my emphases). Feelings, *affects,* are born of the balance or imbalance of homeostasis. Responding to imbalances, they come *"unthought, unspoken…non-consciously and non-deliberatively, without prior design"*: life begins with and maintains itself by means of improvisation. Cold Cognition need not apply.

Nobel laureate British physicist Francis Crick (with American biologist James Watson) first deciphered the DNA double helix. But how it emerged from the primordial soup was for Crick "one of the great unsolved mysteries of science." Resorting to extraterrestrial explanations, Crick explained it as "Directed Panspermia": some distant cousin of ET purposefully sowed DNA to the interstellar winds. We are the happy result. Damasio argues we need not venture so far into the universe (or fantasy). Genes and the neuronal systems that became mind emerged in response to life's imperative to homeostasis.

Even the roots of the evolutionary tree, single cell, unnucleated, "unminded" bacteria, are governed by the imperative of homeostasis, keeping in balance so they thrive and flourish. Bacteria can't "feel," and yet, argues Damasio, "all living creatures are equipped with the regulation devices that were precursors to feelings." Charged by the imperative of homeostasis with metabolizing energy to sustain life, bacteria sense when the internal conditions for life are out of balance. They sense where in

THREE: *Eureka!—Improv, Invention, and Paradigm Shifts*

their environment they might find an organism to metabolize to right the imbalance they "feel." Such feelings necessarily are the precinct of Hot Cognition: Cold Cognition evolved millennia after the neuronal picture-making Damasio is describing.

These "unthought, unspoken" responses to internal states and to the environment underlie all life. Homeostasis is life's response to disorder (entropy/unlife). Any *felt* imbalance results in just that, in *feelings,* feelings that motivate the organism to act. *I'm feeling low on energy and I'm sensing an organism nearby that I can metabolize. Let's shimmy on over there.* I speak metaphorically: bacteria aren't self-aware of their feelings. They can shimmy but they have no "I" directing the motion. Nonetheless, they shimmy and get the fuel they need to stay alive.

Damasio makes this leap from bacteria to humanity based on this fundamental connection: the longing for homeostasis shapes all life. The conditions that led to and regulate life—from bacteria to you and me—start with *feeling* and lead ultimately to human culture: "Feelings, as deputies of homeostasis, are the catalysts for the responses that began human cultures." What "jump-start[s] the saga of human cultures [is] feelings, from pain and suffering to well-being and pleasure."

In 1986, the computer graphics programmer Craig Reynolds fashioned the artificial life program "Boids" that showed that simple algorithms could generate complex behavior. To get cyber "boids" to behave like a flock of birds on a computer screen, all you needed was a simple three-step algorithm:

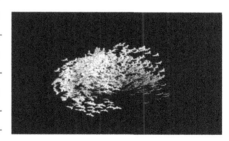

"Boids" (Yeeng Park © 2023)

    separation: steer to avoid crowding local flockmates
    alignment: steer towards the average heading of local flockmates
    cohesion: steer to move towards the average position
                      (center of mass) of local flockmates.

For Damasio, all life *emerges* from an even simpler algorithm: if your homeostasis "feels" out of balance, steer toward a source that can right that imbalance.

The algorithm that drives all comedic improvisation is also simple. In 1957, Ted Flicker's Compass improv group in St. Louis—Flicker, Del Close, Elaine May, and Mike Nichols—"became the first ensemble devoted to cracking the 'how' of improvisational comedy." They "mixed potions like mad scientists" till an algorithm, the secret sauce, emerged. Sam Wasson describes the moment:

> Flicker and May found that improvisers, to ensure scenes of dramatic integrity, had to establish a who, where, and what (as in, what are they doing?). To help players achieve and develop such scenes, they wrote, after weeks of breakfasts, what would be known as the Westminster Place Kitchen Rules. There were three:
> - Don't deny. If [a player] says he has a bunny in his hands, he has a bunny in his hands.
> - Whenever possible, make a strong choice. The less obvious the better.
> - You are you. What you think of as your "character" is really just a magnified piece of you. Therefore, onstage, be you.

The secret sauce. Later, *Yes, and...* refined "Don't deny." "Strong choice...the less obvious the better" anticipates improv's dependence on anomalies, the surprising. "You are you" embraces the player's subjectivity as both springboard and goal.

We think of human culture as the crowning glory of mind. It was rational intellection we imagine—Pythagorean mathematics—that conceived the golden rectangle and built the Parthenon. But the golden ratios that underly the golden rectangle (1.618...) are found in nature in the Fibonacci se-

Fibonacci sequence

quences visible in many organic forms from pinecones to chambered nautiluses. The golden ratio underlies human sex appeal: the ratio of chest to torso to hips is subconsciously read by males as a sign of fecundity, and we shimmy on over there. Females register the appeal of a man's shoulders that are 1.618 times his waist. Thus, the golden ratio could have been discovered by intellect or as a subconscious response to embodied experi-

THREE: *Eureka!—Improv, Invention, and Paradigm Shifts*

ence. *"I see it feelingly,"* says Gloucester to Lear, two aristocrats, their entitlement and arrogance finally humbled.

An anointed king gets his crown and glory from above, hence, according to the Great Chain of Being, his "divine right." The God-given crown ignores the body that supports it. Reason, Will, and Judgment think that they are our most god-like faculties and that the lower, animal faculties should fall in line or fall silent. I wouldn't deny the mind its crown

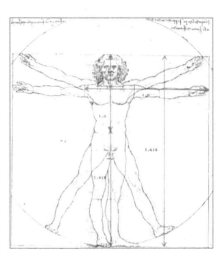

Da Vinci's *Vitruvian Man*

and glory, but what makes it so comes from below, bottom-up not top-down, from the base of the evolutionary tree (bacteria) and from the body that evolved from them. The mitochondria that fuel our cells and that have their own genome may have evolved from bacteria. Bacteria are not just a part of our gut's biome but of our cells.

Damasio comments on the dramatic irony of the mind dismissing the body:

> When a living organism behaves intelligently and winningly in a social setting, we assume that the behavior results from foresight, deliberation, complexity, all with the help of a nervous system. It is now clear, however, that such behaviors could also have sprung from the bare and spare equipment of a single cell, namely, in a bacterium, at the dawn of the biosphere.

"Strange," Damasio concludes, "is too mild a word to describe this reality." And yet that is the reality that improvisation taps.

Spontaneous, unthought images are so fundamental to the bio-evolutionary tree that, as Damasio explains, in multicell organisms (*metazoa*) a kind of proto-image creation precedes not only the bodily equipment for sight (eyes, retina, cornea, etc.), but even a nervous system and mind. "Unminded" multi-cell organisms have "the ability to map the objects and events they sense. This meant that rather than merely helping detect stimuli and respond suitably, nervous systems literally began drawing maps of the configurations of objects and events in space, using the activity of nerve cells in a layout of neural circuits...The maps," Damasio continues, "are the basis for the integration that makes images possible, and those images as they flow in time are the constituents of minds." Which is to say, images derived from any of the senses constitute story which, for Damasio, constitutes mind. Think of Proust: one taste of that madeleine and a whole world fills his senses. It takes a novel heavily strewn with emotions and sensations, images and metaphors, to recover it.

Like metaphor and analogy, image and narrative are fundamental to improvisation. There is no improvisation without them. Even comedic improv is built on the bones of story, not joke-based comedy, as Keith Johnstone signals in the title of his second book, *Impro for Storytellers*. As Johnstone remarks, "The improviser who does not tell stories is chained to the treadmill of always needing a 'better' joke."

Damasio accentuates the involuntary nature of these actions: "*unthought, unspoken...non-consciously and non-deliberatively, without prior design, unminded.*" Such terms are the kind of "code-word substitution[s] for the absence of reason" that Henry Louis Gates calls attention to in his study of the disruptive rhetorical structure of African American Trickster art, the "trope of tropes" Gates terms *signifying*. The mainstream (in Gates's case, white culture) uses such words to dismiss anything outside the pale of reason (or whiteness). Gates adds "accidental, unconscious, or unintentional" to Damasio's list of code words. All such substitutions are put-downs; they code as low status. The improviser *signifies* right back: *yes indeed, I have no control over this. Ain't life grand?* Even better: *free of reason? please don't throw me in that briar patch!* Freedom from reason's constraints is the improviser's royal road to transcendence. It is by means of Hot Cognition that we get from embodied affect to the glories of mind.

Trailing clouds of images, desire leads to story—*I'm not feeling well, I think I need to metabolize some of that...let's go over there*—which takes us to the heights (and depths) of human culture. Damasio's unitary vision describes a process whereby, with no help from Reason (or ET), through direct evolutionary leaps, feelings (affects) become maps, maps become images, images

THREE: *Eureka!—Improv, Invention, and Paradigm Shifts*

become story, story becomes mind, mind becomes human culture. At the imagined apex of that trajectory stand life forms (you and me) who lend high status strictly to "foresight, deliberation [and] complexity." We call it Reason. Which then turns upon and dismisses the role of embodied desire, the actual bedrock and engine of our reasoning faculties.

In periods of paradigm shifting, improv has functioned like those unnucleated bacteria to help redefine rationality. Feeling an imbalance in Reason's dominion over mind, improv prioritizes behavior that is unthought and undeliberated. Improvisation broadens rationality's toolkit by metabolizing "lesser," non-cognitive human faculties: instinct, intuition, and embodied emotion. Improvisers are called to this enterprise of redefining rationality because Cold Cognition behaves dismissively to "lesser" faculties and cuts them off at the corpus collosum. Reason rules the roost. Improv seeks to knock that cock right off.

We like to think rational decisions shape our lives but, in fact, instincts, appetites, and accidents have an equal role. We may marry for prudential reasons, but lust or greed, or hopefully that most irrational emotion, love, is part of the story. Why marry him and not another? Yes, he's attractive but who put him in your way on the street that day? *Accident.* What of that man who inhabits the next street but whom you haven't met? *Should you wait for another accident?* Unthought, unspoken, unbodied desire—longing—will help you decide.

"Everything changes," quipped French polymath Paul Valéry, "except the avant-garde." Ever making us modern, an avatar of the avant-garde, improvisation arises from the imbalance between Reason and desire to return us to homeostasis. It seeks to balance Reason and Unreason, the mind's imagined objectivity and the body's largely ignored subjectivity. In improvisation, "unthought and unwilled desire" take a poke at "intentionality, judgment, and self-consciousness" that imagine they are the whole ball of wax, and, with Hot Cognition, melt them to proper size. A strange loop, indeed, by which culture advances, paradigm shift by paradigm shift, advancing by returning us to life's starting point, spontaneous feeling.

CHAPTER FOUR

The Rhetoric of Spontaneity:
Serious Man vs. Rhetorical Man

> Don't forget, what we do is oratory, it's rhetoric.
> —George Carlin to John Stewart

Francis Bacon, the father of empiricism, founded the inductive scientific method as a wholesale challenge to Aristotelian deduction, a brand-new "doctrine of a more perfect use of reason." Deductive reasoning moves from general statements (premises) to specific conclusions. If heavy matter falls to the center of the universe, and the earth does not fall, then the earth is the center of the universe. *What could go wrong?* Bacon argued that we must reason the other way around, starting from particular pieces of evidence and working inductively toward general conclusions. Bottom-up, not top-down. Galileo sees the moons of Jupiter, and the heliocentric paradigm emerges.

So much is well known. Less often noted was Bacon's notion of how the scientist came to know particular pieces of evidence. For Bacon, the scientist was the direct, unmediated recorder of nature. In *Of the Wisdom of the Ancients* (1609), he imagines Nature as the god Pan, whose spouse, the scientist, is Echo. Science *"echoes most faithfully the voice of the world itself, and is written as it were from the world's own dictation."* It is *"nothing else than the image and reflection of it, which it only repeats and echoes, but adds nothing of its own."* As Nature's secretary, the scientist merely transcribes the raw data of nature: unadulterated, unmediated by mind, artifice, or the desire to persuade.

You might dismiss Bacon as very old school with little currency today. *He wrote some essays, didn't he?* But the notion of unmediated objectivity that underlay induction had staying power, fostering science's cult of objectivity. "Human communications ought to be like the United Parcel Service," modern master of rhetoric Richard Lanham vividly explains, "an efficient mover of information boxes from one destination to the other." Scientists "think they are merely stating facts, not making audiences," writes Deirdre

FOUR: *The Rhetoric of Spontaneity*

McCloskey, a member of the late Milton Friedman's deeply conservative University of Chicago Economics Department. McCloskey's title—*The Rhetoric of Economics*—throws a gauntlet down to her colleagues. Economists and social scientists, who model themselves on 19th-century physical sciences, prize objectivity—raw data—and deny the rhetorical, or persuasive, nature of their discourse. But, as Stanley Fish, literary critic and public intellectual, points out, "the 'motor' by which science moves is not verification or falsification, but persuasion."

What's rattling around in this teapot about the value of rhetoric are crucial differences about the nature of truth and how you find it. Science, Reason's handmaiden, takes the *serious* position that truth is something foundational: it's out there for us to discover. Lanham calls a person who adopts this position *homo seriosus*. The Serious Self envisions truth as ontological: *Truth is. We can find it if we refine our experimental techniques and instruments.*

The Serious Self posits an authentic identity, of which there is necessarily only one. The Rhetorical Self knows we wear many masks. In this regard it is worth recalling the masks worn by the readers of *Choose Your Own Adventure* books. Called branching-path narratives or gamebooks, these were meant for readers ages 9-12. They are improvisations in which the reader determines what happens next. They sold more than 250 million copies between 1979 and 1998 when they were superseded by hypertext fiction and electronic games. They still sell a million copies annually. As Leslie Jamison argues, "a *Choose* book proposes a conception of character that differs from that of traditional novels." Defined by the choices they make, characters in *Choose* books—as in life—are defined by "a range of possibilities, rather than as a series of inevitable decisions." The Serious Self is natural, hence authentic. Acknowledging that its many selves are constructed or adopted, the Rhetorical Self questions "natural" authenticity.

This is one inflection of that dangerous word "natural": because *dictated* by Nature, says the scientist, my findings are natural, hence authoritative. We stumble here on the paradox that both the lower-faculty-driven improviser and the higher-faculty-driven scientist fly the flag of being "natural." Freedom from the mind's mediation is such a powerful trope, everyone wants a piece of it.

Thomas Kuhn used the Gestalt drawing of the rabbit-duck to explain paradigm shifts. Framing it as a duck, the eye focuses toward the left and sees duckbill rather than rabbit ears and ignores the rabbit's nose, seeing it as perhaps just the artist's mistake, mere noise in the signal. The rhetorical purpose of the rabbit-duck figure is to call attention to the powerful role of frames—or paradigms—in mediating what we see. Look for a duck, you see a duck; look for a rabbit, you see a rabbit.

Rabbit or Duck?

This paradox of both scientist and anti-scientist making the claim of unmediated experience calls to mind the *New Yorker* cartoon where two medieval armies both fly a rabbit-duck pennant as they enter a field of battle. The caption: "There can be no peace until they renounce their Rabbit God and accept our Duck God." Playing on the wars of religion fought over the proper way to be inspired by Holy Script, the cartoon captures our fetish for direct, unmediated experience, free from interpretive frames.

What we see depends on what we go looking for, the conceptual hypothesis we pursue. We see light as a particle or a wave depending on the experiment we submit light to. Light is real, an objective fact; our experience of light, however, is contingent on context. As Kant memorably put it in *The Critique of Judgment*, "Thoughts without intuitions are empty, intuitions

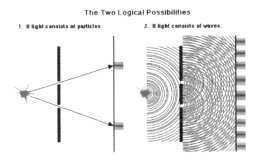

Particle or Wave?

without concepts are blind." Concepts—*rabbit or duck?*—shape what we see. Subjective intuitions choose the hypothesis—*I think light is a particle*—that shapes the experiment that yields "objective" data. But the experiment subjectively determines in advance *which* objective data it will find.

Science needn't have waited for quantum physics and the Heisenberg Principle to learn of the contingent nature of reality. It needed only to listen across the aisle to the improvisers who have always hammered this theme home. The high-status of the "rhetoric of reason" in post-Enlightenment culture is part of Reason and Science's sales pitch: not, *did I ever steer you wrong?* but, rather, *did I ever steer you?* Reason's objectivity is like the *Odyssey's metic* Phaeacian ships—more about those later—which need no steersman or rudder. Think what you want to know, and a Phaeacian ship brings the data, Lanham's UPS packages. Meanwhile *almost* truly rudderless, the improviser happily puts himself at the mercy of the winds—or her subjective whims.

Basing truth on anything but objective facts is, for the Serious Self, frivolous and wrong-headed, a slippery slope that leads to relativism. As Stanley Fish points out, "there is always just beneath the surface of the antirhetorical stance a powerful and corrosive elitism." Fish adds, "What serious man fears—the invasion of the fortress of essence by the contingent, the protean, and the unpredictable—is what rhetorical man celebrates and incarnates." It is just what drives improvisation: the contingent, the protean, and the unpredictable, that is, anomalies.

Where Serious Self promises Truth, Rhetorical Self promotes pleasure, inviting the reader to luxuriate in the text. The Sophists invent rhetoric, i.e., the art of persuasive speech. They win contests by giving us the pleasure of well-spoken language. They invite us not just to enjoy what is beneath the surface (meaning) but its texture. Text and texture come from the Latin *texere,* to weave. Serious Self believes Truth lies beneath the woven surface of Reality that he alone through mastery can penetrate (the masculine pronoun seems appropriate). Rhetorical Self finds pleasure in the texture of truths that lie on the surface, shaped by our subjective, embodied experience. For the abstract colorist Robert Motherwell, "the business of painting is the skin of the world."

The Serious and Rhetorical Selves both claim unmediated experience, but improvisation is aware that such claims are artificial, a mask the improviser wears for the moment. The improviser knows our mask shapes how we perform, and what we experience. Immediacy, the freedom from mediation, in an improviser's hands is an extreme trope that pounces on the Serious Self's lack of irony. Such tropes are expressive fictions—masks, lies—that get us to subjective truths. Understanding knowledge and truth as contingent, improvisers offer their "immediacy" with a wink. Well, most of them.

Kerouac, who told Robert Giroux that his spontaneous kickwriting in the *On the Road* scroll was dictated by the Holy Ghost, might demur.

Of course, winks are not always so charming. Sometimes the wink's irony is so cynical that it poisons civil discourse.

The rhetorical gestures of improvisations are "natural" signs, where the scare quotes are performative, part of their ironic wink. Like Louis Armstrong's famous grin and "effortless" playing as he wipes away profuse sweat, they are "natural" signs of the "natural"—complete with scare quotes. Hardly unmediated, they are a metaphor for an idea. Huck Finn is an innocent, "natural" child, one of the wild children that the nineteenth century fetishized. But Mark Twain stands grinning behind him, as we'll see in the next chapter, challenging the moral value of Huck's spontaneity.

Improvisers' extreme promises in Black culture read as signifying: an ironic wink that points to the dominant culture's irony-free promises of unmediated authenticity and power. The signifying wink seeks to undermine white culture's power. Thus, improvisations acknowledge, however subtly, the artificial status of their immediacies and point to Reason's failure—like McClosky's economists—to acknowledge their artifice. This ironic distancing prevents improvisation's lapsing into decadence. Drunk with its high status, science is susceptible to hubris, one reason the improviser must drag Reason down from its high perch. The other is the improviser's quest to embrace all of life, what Reason with its selectivity and its penchant for hierarchies ignores or leaves out. Know-it-all Reason's not just wrong, it's half-blind, doesn't hear so well, and ignores its embodied senses.

Suddenly it appears that the Rhetorical Self speaks for, or at least leans toward, democracy. Every voice should be heard. She prefers the plural and lower case. She seeks truths which are made not *found,* because all truths are contingent upon subjective framing. The act of perceiving always adds its bit to what is perceived. Posing as natural, the improviser makes naturalness part of her artifice. Competition between subjective points of view—call-and-response—keeps the subjective element honest and the mind alert. Its default status is not high. No voice has a lock on truth. Every voice should be heard.

In fact, as Lanham, and Jung's analytic and James Hillman's archetypal psychology all argue, we each ourselves have many voices, and sometimes competing voices within us speak different truths. The Rhetorical Self, believing that truths emerge from the to-and-fro of converse, speaks to an audience, even if the audience is just another of her selves. In its embrace of the indeterminate and contingent nature of truth, improvisation anticipates the latest avant-garde, postmodernism.

Although the profit motive can influence the data in the laboratory, charging scientists with an element of subjectivity is not meant to accuse scientists with fudging their data. Hunger can corrupt, but it is the best seasoning. Improvisation—Trickster—accepts this as a fact of life. With her eye on the articulations, Dr. Karikó was as natural a Trickster as she was a biochemist. She sought funding to study mRNA and a life-saving vaccine emerged—along with a well-earned promotion. Lord of the marketplace, Trickster has an ear both for merchants and for thieves. The archetypal embodiment of our appetites, she champions our desires.

But facts don't tell, they must be told, and sold. It's been pointed out that the sentence "We need new sources of energy" is hard to argue with. But what you are agreeing to is contingent upon the context. If the speaker is Exxon's CEO, the contingencies in play are depleted oil fields, the profit motive, and the need to cancel government restrictions. If the speaker leads Green Peace, the contingencies are more restrictions and more solar and wind farms.

Lanham's Rhetorical Self helps us understand improvisation and the rhetoric of spontaneity. This quarrel between philosophy and rhetoric, between Socrates and the Sophists, is played out in the battle between the culture of Spontaneity and the culture of Reason, between Hot and Cold Cognition. The battle is constant, Fish writes, "continually presenting us with the (skewed) choice between the plain unvarnished truth straightforwardly presented and the powerful but insidious appeal of 'fine language,' language that has transgressed the limits of representation and substituted its own forms for the forms of reality." Largely unacknowledged, improvisers have carried on the quarrel in these very terms: "plain unvarnished truth" vs. "fine language." The opponents represent our two kinds of attention, what neuroscientists now acknowledge are central to mental life. The clash between Hot and Cold Cognition is part of our evolutionary baggage.

In both fields, philosophy and the applied arts, more is at stake than the aesthetics of a pretty surface. What hangs in the balance are the reigning paradigms and the new paradigms that battle to replace them.

Changing paradigms, how we know the world, is heavy freight for an improv troupe's *Yes, and...*, or a jazz combo's simple call and response. And yet that is what I am claiming, that there is an essential form and theme to the discourse of improvisation. Improv shadows and challenges, as in a double helix, the growing dominance of Rationality. Improv's thematic purpose—for, yes, it has a purpose—is as important as its formal gestures. Behind the rhetoric of spontaneity stands Hot Cognition vying to be heard.

CHAPTER FIVE

"I'm Going to Slop You Up":
The Rules for Rule-Breaking

> Authenticity is such a monster marketing tool.
> —Anya von Brentzen, *Around the World in Search of Food, History, and the Meaning of Home*

Advice from Johnny Vidacovich and Frans Hals

There's a story in the New Orleans music world about one of our great drummers, Johnny Vidacovich. Johnny has played with everyone: Bobby McFerrin, Willy DeVille, Mose Allison, Johnny Adams, Professor Longhair, James Booker, and Alvin Tyler, among others. In New Orleans music—a tradition as saturated in great drummers as it is great trumpet players—he's the real deal.

So, the story goes, a student comes for his first lesson. Johnny listens. He says, *hey man, you're a very proficient drummer. My job is going to be to slop you up...*

Johnny Vidacovich © Skip Bolen

To slop you up. That verb captures improvisation's appeal: while much of the world values craft and virtuosity, there is also a value in apparent artlessness. There is a charm and a sense of authenticity, and hence authority, that comes from the apparent freedom from the meddling mediation of artifice. To *achieve* effortlessness is the oxymoron at the heart of improv. This charm and its promise of authenticity is the power behind the rhetoric of spontaneity.

If Vidacovich's student exemplified a virtuosic attention to drumming's received rulebook, slopping him up, aspires to something else. That something else is suggested by Johnny's comments during the 2019 Improv Conference New Orleans drum panel ("Drum Improv: Organized Chaos?"). Speaking with local drum greats Stanton Moore, founding member of the funk band Galactic, and Shannon Powell, known as "The King of Treme," Vidacovich was the last to address the question, what does improv in drumming mean to you? He explained:

> VIDACOVICH: When you're improvising, you're constantly coming up to forks in the road… So, improvising is making a quick decision, or trusting your spirit, or trusting the Holy Ghost to tell you what to do next…
>
> SHANNON POWELL: [appreciatively] come on now!
>
> VIDACOVICH: … to tell you what to do. And that's your best bet, because if you try to think about it and control it, you're going to get too academic, or too technical or too cold, or you're just not going to have the depth of prayer that you would have if the Holy Ghost is telling you, go on, swing hard right now…
>
> SHANNON POWELL: You know, that's what I want to see, John. Thank you.
>
> VIDACOVICH: So opening your heart and your soul, surrendering yourself to the music, the spirit will guide you.

Later in the panel, Vidacovich explains that he seeks

> to bypass my brain. I'm trying to achieve it in my stomach, and in my throat and in mouth. I'm going to try to make that come out on the drums… I'm not going to ask my brain to put any restrictions or any, "this is good and that's bad." I'm going to ask my brain to have nothing to do with it so the Holy Spirit can come to me easy.

Coming from New Orleans—a Catholic city but with an infamous commitment to embodied experience—Vidacovich seeks both the incarnate (The Holy Ghost) and the carnal, "whatever is in my stomach, and in my throat and in mouth." From whatever source, Johnny seeks a kind of naturalness, free of artifice, in sum, embodied emotion delivered directly to the drumskins.

Naturalness

To understand how such "naturalness" is "achieved," consider seventeenth-century Dutch painter Frans Hals. Painting after Netherlands declared independence (1581) from Spain and its Catholic repression, Hals was influenced by the frenetic energy released in Dutch sciences and arts. But at a time when visible brushstrokes were still thought a flaw, Hals was, according to the *New Yorker* art critic Peter Schjeldahl, "the first virtuoso of the visible brushstroke." Wallace Stevens celebrates Hals's brushstrokes as he paints

Frans Hals
The Gypsy Girl, c.1628
Musée du Louvre, Paris

the "weather... Brushed up by brushy winds in brushy clouds." Hals used the technique called *alla prima,* painting directly on the canvas, instead of the Renaissance technique of laying on a background layer first. No preparatory drawings by Hals have been found. A major influence on Monet, Hals was applauded in his day, as he is in ours, for "imbu[ing] his paintings with such force and vitality that they seem to breathe and live."

I don't know if Hals had Holbein the Younger in his crosshairs, but Holbein's carefully crafted, brush-free portraits from a century earlier exemplify what Hals is pointedly not doing. His exquisite portrait of a Dutch merchant (*A Member of the Wedigh Family*) is as static as Hals's portraits are dynamic. The inscription giving the year (1533) and the merchant's age (39) fixes it, makes it a timeless icon. Holbein extensively used preliminary drawings, which he would transfer to canvas. Egg yolk tempera were then

Hans Holbein the Younger
A Member of the Wedigh Family, 1533
Staatliche Museen zu Berlin, Gemäldegalerie/
Jörg P. Anders Public Domain Mark 1.0

layered with tiny brushes so carefully that no brushstrokes are visible. By means of such careful method Holbein the Younger leaves behind his father's Gothic portraiture and helps usher in the Northern Renaissance, of which, like Hals, he is a key figure.

And yet Hals's achievement is the result of a *method,* too, a system of artifice Hals used that even had a name. His mentor Karel Van Mander, the first theoretician of the great Dutch Mannerist school, distinguished between the "neat" style—exemplified by Holbein—and the "rough" or "coarse" style's broad, loose brushwork. In the rough style the splashes of color, seemingly dashed on using the "wet-on-wet" method, achieve the effect of being true to life-in-the-moment, a performance that expresses the subject's and the painter's own *joie de vivre*. Van Mander's job was to *slop* Hals up.

Hals's *The Gypsy Girl* needs no slopping up. Titled centuries later, the subject—wanton woman? tavern girl?—has been captured in a disruptive, coarse style. Hals has caught her in the moment, complete with sideways leer and generous cleavage. Curators' probes reveal that Hals repainted her decolletage to make it more seductive.

Hals's maiden is surely not a member of the rising capitalist class, not among those likely to commission portraits to display their wealth. What does that say about her portraitist and how he spent his time? Apparently, he didn't curry favor at court among the decorous, orange-sashed courtiers his near-contemporary, Rembrandt, famously painted. Had he been a century earlier, Hals might have been found at the local tavern with Rabelais and his rowdy, carnivalesque readers, whom he addresses as "illustrious drinkers and you, precious syphilitics." Whoever bought Hals's paintings sought not merely to display a representation of their wealth but of life as it is lived richly in the moment, free from Spanish oppression.

FIVE: "I'm Going to Slop You Up"

But, for all this deliberate disruptiveness, counterintuitively—and here's the key point—Van Mander recommended the rough style, a cultivated aesthetic and method, to those *late* in their career *because it is harder to achieve*. Hals may strike us as a primitive, but, like many contemporary "folk artists" today, he is an absolute virtuoso of the rough style. Improvisers embrace a rough style in dialogue with the "neat" or refined style they reject. They present themselves as *less* structured. The rough style, loose and suggestive, is a cultivated affect, a rhetorical gesture, a performance. Its deep structure is to appear unstructured.

Not only the subject of the portrait but also the presence of the artist is embodied in its apparently loose brushwork and *joie de vivre*. Because of Hals, loose brushwork becomes a peculiar quirk of seventeenth-century Dutch painting. And yet this rough style, by whatever name, is shared by improvisations since classical times. I offer a taxonomy of improvisation's stylistic and thematic tropes—the "decorum of indecorousness" in *A Taste for Chaos*. A quick list will serve here. Art is "artless" when the artist frames her art as:

  a. careless or without effort
  b. directly and dramatically transcribes experience
  c. writes by chance
  d. offers a found object
  e. writes in an intimate, unthreatening situation
  f. writes in an inconvenient situation, or
  g. is inspired, drunk, drugged or otherwise affected by some external power

In jazz, it is the sound of surprise, the syncopated rhythms that Vidacovich plays around the beat. During his Harvard lectures on "Music as Metaphor," Wynton Marsalis defines syncopation as "accenting off the beat and coming back at unexpected times. It's like you offer someone something and then when they reach for it, you snatch it back. Syncopation is playing a rhythm on the opposite side of the beat." Warming to his theme, Marsalis continues:

> That's exactly what Jonas Salk was talking about when he said giving you a virus could keep you from getting it. It's what Mark Twain did

in *Huckleberry Finn* when he used Huck's embarrassment in having shown humanity to the nigger Jim, a man who we know is less than human, to elicit the opposite reaction in his reader. Syncopation is the daring application of dexterity, jocularity and timing to challenge the common grid, the common way of doing things the accepted way. It is the masterful challenging of convention, the element of surprise that makes a punch line funny.

Decorous drumming, staying on the beat, the 1-2-3-4, 1-2-3-4 of military marches—the metronome—is based on the rule book. Syncopation *signifies*—again, Gates's term—on the norm. To syncopate or to listen to syncopation is to "expect the unexpected." Slopping it up, it is Van Mander's "rough style."

Syncopation is then double-voiced, a matter of call and response. On *Fresh Air*, New Orleans musician Jon Batiste reflected on the union of simplicity and complexity in Bach's *Two-Part Invention* he had just played:

> But it's just two voices. You see...the simplicity of how he makes something that is just two melodies playing in conversation, asking questions, responding, sometimes they're talking at the same time. Other times, it's call and response. Sometimes it's in harmony. Sometimes there's dissonance. Just...that's life. That's our journey exemplified in a simple piece that he wrote for his kids. That's amazing.

"That's life": there is something fundamental in call and response, the taproot of innovation. Innovation comes in response to some need. According to Sidney Bechet, it is born from the longing for "a place where they all used to be happy once." Building community, its *Yes, and...* gives voice to both our individuality and our shared humanity.

Vidacovich's syncopated drumming is *impromptu*, establishing the beat, keeping time, but once established, playing against it in response to his players, or as a call to send them in a new direction. Sometimes it is to accompany the players (comping), sometimes a break, a solo where he goes his own way.

No doubt, like the New Orleans drummers on the improv conference panel, Hals so completely learned Van Mander's lessons in roughness that the moment of execution was embodied: muscle memory. He wasn't thinking a coarse method. For drummer Stanton Moore, you have to master, "all that cerebral stuff, but on a gig when it's time to play a shuffle, I ain't thinking about it anymore...You have to do all that conceptual thinking, but when it comes time for the gig, it's got to be neck down." Uniting cerebral and muscle memory, improvisers promise *immediacy*: art in the present tense, unfiltered by meddling from the frontal cortex. While the great artists of the Italian and Dutch Renaissance were looking back to the rediscovered genius of Greek and Roman Antiquity for the skills to render *ideal* beauty, improvisers like Hals create with bravado. Improvisers seek no training. Antiquity and its decorous muses be damned. Like Rabelais one hundred years before, Hals seeks the essential marrow of life. Like James Joyce three hundred years later, he finds it in life in the streets.

But improvisation's promise of "naturalness" is one of its white lies. For Raymond Williams "nature is perhaps the most complex word in the language." George Orwell lists "natural" among his "catalogue of swindles and perversions" that corrupt the English language. C.S. Lewis calls such naturalistic talk "philosophically...scandalous."

John Stuart Mill, admitting that Wordsworth's nature-drenched lyrics saved him from the depression Bentham's Utilitarianism had sunk him into, nonetheless condemns

> the vein of sentiment so common in the modern world (though unknown to the philosophic ancients) which exalts instinct at the expense of reason, an aberration rendered still more mischievous by the opinion commonly held in conjunction with it that every feeling or impulse which acts promptly without waiting to ask questions is an instinct. Thus, almost every variety of unreflecting and uncalculating impulse receives a kind of consecration.

Mill is wrong about the philosophic ancients who in fact indulged in such primitivist talk as much as we do. (See Arthur O. Lovejoy and George Boas, *Primitivism and Related Ideas in Antiquity*). The first pastoral poems, which celebrated the pure, natural life, were written by Theocritus, a Syracusan who may have been the head of the great library of Ptolemy II in Alexandria. The good librarian's pastorals, based on the trope of naturalness, were great poems. But Theocritus didn't hail from Edenic Arcadia like his shepherds and shepherdesses (and like Hermes). He portrays low naturalness through high artifice.

These big guns, Orwell, Lewis, and Mill, attack the rhetoric of spontaneity, in some ways a Romantic legacy, because its use is so prevalent and its power over us so great. In principle they caution against the slippery slope that leads to demagoguery. Hitler's longing for an Aryan race was a longing to recover the natural. Miscegenation, the mixing of races, was "unnatural." We've seen this in real time: *My gut knows more than many brains.* Much of right-wing judicial "originalist" constitutional theory, according to Thomas McAfee, a Professor of Law at the University of Nevada, Las Vegas, depends on the theory of "natural law...a kind of general trump card." Writing in 1995, McAfee's pun is accidental but prescient. McAfee reminds us, "justice is a human enterprise." Justice doesn't flow from nature; it is a social construct, artificial. One of humankind's rarest but highest achievements.

Toni Morrison eschews the word "natural" in her characterization of Black art, perhaps because African Americans have long been stigmatized as "primitive." Instead of, "it must look effortless" she could have said, "it must look natural." Effortless—the opposite of labored, painstaking, purposeful—is one of the things we think of as natural. Morrison clarifies, "If it makes you sweat, you haven't done the work."

That something is "natural" is what Gregory Bateson refers to as an "explanatory principle" which explains nothing but which we agree to deploy as if it did. Bateson offers the example of Molière's depiction of a medical student who, when asked to explain how opium works on a patient, says, "'Because there is in it a dormitive principle.'" Bateson's playful point is that such explanations are dormitive in the second sense: they put the mind to sleep just when it needs to be awake. Like "dormitive," "natural" and the like—"instinct," "intuition"—are "explanatory principles" that the audience will fill, guided by a given improviser's personal preferences. They are inherently ambiguous "but," Bateson concludes wryly, "one thing is certain: that explanatory principles must not be multiplied beyond necessity."

Wisława Szymborska, too, asks us to accept life's transitory nature by allaying our fears with the charming naturalness of the "fleeting day":

> Why do we treat the fleeting day
> with so much needless fear and sorrow?
> It's in its nature not to stay:
> Today is always gone tomorrow.

To think so, that life should be easy and natural, is compensatory: we know too well that only through effort will we get through the day. Hovering just above this *carpe diem* poem, unspoken, with grace and a light touch, is another hard truth that the poem compensates: if the day is fleeting, so, too, are our lives.

But that's only natural, so I guess it's ok.

Blue Jeans Wars

Trickster Hermes is Lord of the Marketplace, patron of both merchants and thieves. Little surprise then that he has a heavy hand in marketing.

In 1980, a 15-year-old Brooke Shields's ad, shot by high-fashion photographer Richard Avedon to promote Calvin Klein's new line of super-tight jeans, was meant to make a stir, or to stir the blood. The tag line? "What comes between me and my Calvin's? Nothing." The scandal chased the ad off ABC and CBS. Klein did not back down. "Jeans are sex," he remarked. "The tighter they are, the better they sell." Naked beneath her jeans and just 15 years old, Brooke Shields is as *au naturelle* as we dare imagine.

J. W. Davis, inventor of the five-pocket, riveted blue jeans, sold them as long-wearing work pants at his dry goods store in Reno, Nevada, to the mining community (note the pickax in the patent application). Unable to afford the patent office fee, Davis approached Levi Strauss, his denim cloth wholesaler in San Francisco. In return for half interest, Strauss, a German-Jewish immigrant born in Bavaria, funded the patent. Improved by man's artifice—rivets—the origin jeans were anything but natural.

"What comes between me and my Calvin's? Nothing."
(Retro AdArchives/Alamy Stock Photo)

J.W. Davis's patent application, mining pick and all, emphasizes the work in work pants

Hollywood (James Dean and Marlon Brando) and the countercultural movement eventually made Levi's a fashion statement that accented its unstuffy naturalness, a far cry from the businessman's worsted wool.

Then along came designer jeans. European designers saw they could emphasize not durability but high design. Brooke Shields's Calvin's was an effort to take back the mantle from Girbaud and other European designer jeans. Calvin Klein jeans' sales boomed sevenfold in one year. According to the *New York Times*, Klein himself "told Shields in a recent interview that the commercial put the company on the map."

Levi's response came in 1984 with the launch of their 501 Jeans. Marketing emphasized their retro button fly, and, where designer jeans emphasized tight fit, 501s promised "shrink-to-fit"—meant to appeal to American individualism. But the main theme of the ad campaigns was roughness, as opposed to Avedon's studio slickness. Levi's countered with washed out, overexposed, now familiar shaky-camera shots pairing blues/roots music with scenes of young people enjoying life. The award-winning ads—saturated in

James Dean rocking his Levi's (Album/Alamy StockPhoto)

FIVE: *"I'm Going to Slop You Up"*

naturalness—helped launch the careers of several actors, from Bruce Willis and Stanley Tucci to Jason Alexander.

The Levi Strauss site recalls how the TV spots were recorded. Shooting in New York's Meatpacking District, hardly the glam spot it is today, director Leslie Dektor told the actors to take a break while they reloaded the camera. Meanwhile a long lens from across the street caught the young actors just hanging out and having fun. If Keats "hate[d] poetry that has a palpable design upon us—and if

Jason Alexander (center) selling Levi's 3 years before *Seinfeld* launches

we do not agree, seems to put its hand in its breeches pocket," these regular guys literally don't have their hands in their pockets, trying to sell you something. Dektor's unconventional method allowed him to capture young people acting naturally. Audiences connected with it.

Jeans-wearers favor brands in part because of different tastes. But many products are just commodities essentially no better than their competitors: natural gas, wheat, most cattle (but not my mom's, served at Ruth's Chris, which relied on corn feeding so unnatural it requires heavy doses of antibiotics). Carrying the legacy of hunter gatherers, we are conditioned to notice difference. Because much of television is now recorded on DVRs, advertisers face the problem of the fast-forward button. They solve it, in part, with off-kilter narratives and avatars used to capture

Selling dog food

our attention. The *New York Times* reports that "ads are sometimes most successful when they are eye-catchingly terrible." The ad above is meant to sell more nutritious dog food. Be assured, lemons aren't part of the new diet. Yellow lemon, red tongue, and the incongruity of lemon-licking puppies grab clicks. Besides, they're adorable.

Ever wonder why so many advertisements feature stupid mini-narratives? Stupid sticks out as well as saber-toothed tigers once did. Outrageously stupid? All the better. We pay attention. Anomalies, the next best thing to things natural, sell.

It was not always so. As Peter Brook points out, in the age dominated by radio, the singing commercial ruled the day. Radio used catchy image, melody, and rhyme to get our attention:

> I'm Chiquita Banana and I've come to say
> Bananas have to ripen in a certain way—
> And when they're flecked with brown and have a golden hue
> Bananas taste the best and are the best for you…

When advertisers switch to television, they switch to narrative mode. The talking, dancing banana grabs our attention, telling the story that explains to American consumers how best to enjoy the unfamiliar fruit.

Advertisers selling commodities rely on story to hook and pull you in. The goal is not to compete on quality or value. The unexpected triggers Hot Cognition—exactly where "top of mind" resides. "Top of mind," however, is a misnomer. Our impulse buying lives not in the prefrontal cortex but in the amygdala, deep in the brain's cortex, the seat of our emotions and memory. When you need insurance, Geico might come to mind because the anomalous gecko CGI character is a bit nutty (low status). Goofy narratives rule. A highly verbal gecko with a vaguely Australian/Cockney accent make Geico unforgettable. The Geico gecko in 2005 was voted America's favorite advertising mascot.

Geico spends over a billion dollars a year on its little Trickster who made his debut in 1999. The gecko is easily more appealing than the corporate moniker he stands in for: Government Employees Insurance Company. Geico is owned by the brilliant Warren Buffet who once said he would spend $2 billion on Geico if he could. There was nowhere left to place the ads. (Mr. Buffet got his wish: by 2021 Geico spent $2.07 billion).

If Madison Avenue exploits the new findings of neuroscience and uses the rhetoric of spontaneity to shape carefully crafted ads, you know it is a powerful device. When something presents itself as off the cuff, watch your wallet.

The Marlboro Man Gets Roughed Up

Like Frans Hals portraits, advertising relies on *seeming* rough. This Madison Ave Marlboro cigarette advertisement plays upon themes native to improv. The Marlboro Man is caught at the decisive moment, lighting up. We should smoke these coffin nails because this "natural" man, this Man Alive from the high plains, smokes them. Shortened from Marlborough, where dukes apparently live, the trademark is unpretentiously American.

I served for a short time as marketing director for a national company, so I can say with some authority—*see how the "rhetoric of reason" works?*—that advertising always attacks the product's greatest negative by leading with its opposite. *If X is the worst thing about what we're selling, then we are going focus our campaign on non-X.* At Ruth's Chris Steak House, price is the sticking point: why spend $46 for a slab of filet? As

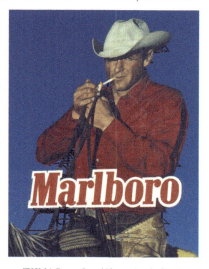

(ZUMA Press, Inc./Alamy StockPhoto)

United Fruit did for bananas, my mother, Ruth's Chris's founder, educated the marketplace about "Prime beef" with the headline, "Why only 2% of the beef sold in America is good enough for my customers." Arnie Morton, scion of the Morton's Steak family, once told me, "your mother created the prime steak business." It surprised me: the Morton's family started in Chicago in the 1920s. He meant she educated the marketplace to appreciate the value of prime.

If lung cancer is cigarettes' greatest negative, ads must promise health and naturalness. Promise a red-meat kind of guy in a romanticized American landscape. Here the "Marlboro Man" sits tall on his horse as "proof" that cigarette smoking will not kill you. (It did kill Marlboro model Clarence Haley Long, known as Marlboro Patient Zero, but never mind that little detail). That Marlboro, the largest selling cigarettes in the world, still in 2017 had 40% of market share suggests how powerful and long-lasting the rhetoric of naturalness can be. Such rhetoric is the target of Mick Jagger's rock and roll anthem, "Satisfaction": "he can't be a man because he doesn't smoke the same cigarette as me."

Wildly successful, still, *as an improvisation* the ad misses the mark. If the first test of an improvisation is the claim of spontaneity—it's "naturalness"—the Marlboro ad fails the second test, to persuade us that its formal means—its stylistic devices—share the rough immediacy or the naturalness its image promotes. Like the Calvin Klein ad, the Marlboro Man fails—as improv—because it is slick. It wears its slickness on its eye-catching red sleeve and white Stetson. As they say in Texas: the ad, as improv, *is all hat, no cattle.*

Here is a more successful ad *as improv.* Flint was a French cigarette that launched in 1973, claiming that it was "the cigarette that's not for the pretty cowboys." The ad out-naturals the natural man. Not just the slogan challenges Marlboro's pretty cowboy, the style also challenges slick Madison Avenue. Note the grainy black-and-white photo and the setting—a galley kitchen in an urban setting far from the high plains.

(RiskyWalls/Alamy Stock Photo)

Finally, the model in T-shirt and old jeans wipes his eyes from cutting onions: this casual, unassuming dude may wear jeans and even a cowboy buckle on his belt, but he is anything but rugged. If he is primitive, he shares rather in the urban primitivism of his jazz *confrères*. Perhaps as his T-shirt suggests, he joins those sophisticated primitives at one of the several jazz festivals on the beautiful (and once natural) *Côte d'Azur*. "Flint," runs the tag line, "it's good, that's all."

The Flint ad employs an artifice of the inartificial, presenting its art as artless, more direct, hence more real, authentic, and trustworthy. The dude plays low status beside the authority-drenched Marlboro Man, which in the end lends the Flint ad high status and more authority. *Smoke Flint. You'll be cooler than the Marlboro Man.*

Notice, too, that the Flint ad doesn't attack Marlboro's worst negative, that smoking them will kill you. Smoking Flint will kill you too, so it can't very well seize on that argument. No, what's wrong with Marlboro is that its ads are too slick and manipulative, says an ad, that in its own anti-slick and anti-manipulative way—"It's good, that's all"—slyly manipulates us.

Not sly enough for you? One of the campaign's salient features is the English name. To use an English name is 1970 is hip/disruptive, pushing back against the Royal Academy's distaste for *franglais*—the use of English in contemporary French, an affront to national pride after the war. Confronted with an English word in the media, inevitably the French public sought out the translation. The answer: "flint" in French is "silex." Subliminally, Flint is selling SEX to the sex-obsessed French.

A lot of money was at stake in the launch of this product in a saturated marketplace. It's safe to assume that the agency behind this ad went through several creative sessions, refining it and gauging its impact on focus groups. The agency executives were probably far more chicly dressed than the model they chose and carefully styled. Despite their efforts, the cigarette fell from the marketplace within a few months.

Innovations like Flint's roll-out are one sure-fire way to challenge the dominant authority, in this case the product that dominates the market. Yet innovations, like Flint, always have their eye cast back on the thing they have come to replace. Thus, improvisations are always in artful dialogue with some dominant discourse they wish to supplant.

The great Russian literary theorist Mikhail Bakhtin celebrated such "dialogic texts" as "polyphonic" and "heteroglossic." They are polyphonic because there is more than one voice, the unassuming chef responding to the cowboy's call. Heteroglossia, like code-switching, uses multiple languages to reflect varying ways of knowing and experiencing the world. Bakhtin's great exemplars are the carnivalesque, festive world of Rabelais, and the radical subjectivity of Dostoevsky's novels. In dialogic discourse, tradition and objective consciousness is not ignored. It is referenced or satirized, the irony putting in relief its flaws and limitations. At bottom, both dialogic polyphony and heteroglossia are forms of *call* and *response*. In its unspoken dialogue with Marlboro, Flint signifies on Marlboro, attempting to upend its power in the marketplace.

Huck Finn's "Free and Easy" Raft

Such rhetoric, the gesture of careless, spontaneous composition, has been deployed to sell blue jeans and coffin nails. It has also been used to powerful, humane effect. Mark Twain's famous notice to *Huck Finn* jokes tongue-in-cheek that "Persons attempting to find a motive in this narrative will be prosecuted; persons attempting to find a moral in it will be banished; persons attempting to find a plot will be shot." The joke nostalgically invokes the pastoral world of Huck's journey where like shepherds, Huck and his sidekick Jim loll about without purpose because none is needed. The river and the great American continent it drains will provide. Such rhetoric initiates us into Huck's world where he and Jim drift "free and easy" down the Mississippi. Huck's ready improvisations get him out of trouble again and again. Like Trump, Huck boasts he goes "a good deal on instinct."

But the great improvisers like Mark Twain know that careless spontaneity is as much problem as solution. Drifting lands Huck and the enslaved father figure Jim deep in slave territory. Tom Sawyer's reappearance at the end of the novel illuminates the dark side of improvisation. "Free and easy" offers little guidance, little ground upon which to take a reasoned moral stand. Huck goes along with Tom's romance-driven improvisations and Jim is made to suffer in the name of "Walter Scott with his enchantments" which, Twain writes in *Life on the Mississippi*, sets "the world in love with dreams and phantoms; with decayed and swinish forms of religion; with decayed and degraded systems of government; with the sillinesses and emptinesses, sham grandeurs, sham gauds, and sham chivalries of a brainless and worthless long-vanished society." Within the novel we learn from Huck that the steamboat *Walter Scott* has sunk—Twain's little revenge against the arch-romantic who did so much, in his view, to inspire the brutality of the Civil War.

Things get so dark that many readers feel Twain lost control of his narrative. But Twain couldn't have been clearer about his feelings for "jejune romanticism." Going "a good deal on instinct" is not always a good moral guide. Jim suffers.

Once you have opened the doors to the inspiration of external or instinctual forces, dampening reason's ability to judge, you never know who will take the helm, whether the force steering you will be divine or demonic, healthy or pathological, democratic (little D) or demagogic (big R). Hitler is the most monstrous example. In analytic psychologist Carl Jung's report, Hitler "listens intently to a stream of suggestions from a whispered source and then acts upon them." How do you judge once you've dismissed judgment?

The great improvisers, like Twain, deploy the rhetoric of spontaneity to explore the tensions and contradictions in our longing for "the natural" and the authentic. Trump does so to manipulate his base. Weave a circle round him thrice...

That Trump's administration failed quickly to produce and disseminate a scientific test for coronavirus should not surprise. To test is to measure, a rational exercise. Better to measure by hunches and imaginary numbers that his base finds easy to swallow and that support his fragile ego. The quants of Wall Street found hunches less appealing and the DOW tumbled. Without tests we have no tools of rational measurement, flying in the dark without instruments.

It is not just that the Trump administration was slow to produce enough tests, or that he lied again and again that enough tests were available. It is also that, citing regulations, state and federal authorities shut down an early and effective testing program in Washington state, at the time one of the most infected. When Governor Inslee tweeted that "our work would be more successful if the Trump administration stuck to the science and told the truth," Trump called him a snake. He was. The governor's research team sought to eat from the Tree of Knowledge through science.

CHAPTER SIX

What the Neuroscience of Psychedelics Tells Us about Improvisation

Only connect...
—E.M. Forster

To them, the snuff was nature's ultimate medicinal tool: it allowed them direct access to the spirit world, where all healing originates.
—Mark Plotkin, *The Shaman's Apprentice*

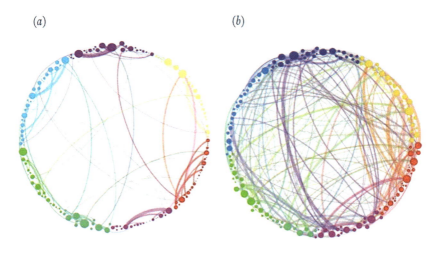

(*a*) your brain on placebo; (*b*) your brain on psilocybin
PETRI ET AL./PROCEEDINGS OF THE ROYAL SOCIETY INTERFACE

This diagram was the solution to the problem I faced when I moderated a dream panel on "Psychedelics and Improvisation" at the 2019 Improv Conference NOLA: A Festival of Ideas.

The first member of the dream panel was the distinguished writer Michael Pollan. Best known for his books that explore the socio-cultural impacts of food, Pollan had recently published *How to Change Your Mind: What the New Science of Psychedelics Teaches Us About Consciousness, Dying,*

SIX: *What the Neuroscience of Psychedelics Tells Us*

Addiction, Depression, and Transcendence. The above diagram was in his new book, but I hadn't yet connected the dots.

The dream team's second member was fellow New Orleanian Mark Plotkin, author of *Tales of a Shaman's Apprentice,* a book so compelling I once missed my stop on the A train by forty blocks trying to finish it. Mark, with a PhD from Tufts, did research under the father of ethnobotany, Harvard's Richard Evans Schultes.

Mark Plotkin collecting samples in the Amazon

Ethnobotany is the study of plants used by indigenous peoples. With chemist Albert Hofmann, the discoverer of LSD, Schultes co-authored *The Plants of the Gods: Their Sacred, Healing, and Hallucinogenic Powers* (1979), which is still in print. Schultes was the first non-native individual to academically examine ayahuasca. But his examination of this now famous Amazon Basin hallucinogen was not entirely academic. Neither was it for Mark. As Mark said during the panel, the difference between an anthropologist and an ethnobotanist is that, when offered hallucinogens in the bush, the first declines: *oh, no, I'd lose my objectivity.* The latter replies: *yeehaw!*

Fearing that shamans and their lore were disappearing, Mark completed a handbook for the Tiriyó people of Suriname detailing their medicinal plants—the only book printed in Tiriyó other than the Bible. Many of those plants are medicine for the soul: psychedelics. He is the co-founder of the Amazon Conservation Team that does important work supporting indigenous tribes. His podcast, *Plants of the Gods: Hallucinants, Healing, Culture, and Conservation* brings his work to a wide audience.

I was not alone in thinking this was a dream team. Loyola's Louis Roussel Hall was full. I once listened to Miles play there—with his back to us—and once heard Allen Ginsberg chant *Howl,* his finger cymbals chiming. Seven hundred New Orleanians awaited our revelation: how improv and psychedelics were connected.

The problem was this: that there was a connection between improv and psychedelics was just my intuition. I'd read their books and made copious

notes that seemed to support the intuition. Mark and Michael seemed to agree with my intuition. But something scientific that we could point to and say, *here's how they connect?* That, none of us were ready or able to do.

That problem was compounded by two others, problems of a personal nature. First, the conference team had been understaffed. I had spent the last two months spending way too much time on matters like fundraising rather than preparing to moderate the panel. Those matters demanded Cold Cognition—*whom do we approach? How do we make our ask?*—that drained away my attention to the subject matter. By the time the panel began, I was fried but my mind—Hot Cognition—hadn't been cooking. I had seen the diagram in Pollan's book but hadn't understood how it solved the problem I was burning to solve.

The other personal problem is a bit, well, personal. There was an abstract quality to my intuition. It was purely theoretical. Here I had been studying for 50 years a kind of art that claimed to present direct experience, on the fly, unmediated by the ego. I knew from the neuroscience I had studied that this unmediated experience was an empty boast, a scientific impossibility: the mind always shapes experience. Suddenly in Mark's and Michael's books I was reading about substances that induced the death of the ego, enabling direct, unmediated experience.

I started college in 1968 so I was among the legions of once-long-hairs who had tried psychedelics. But the notion of "heroic doses" as the avenue to unmediated experience was not something we knew about or sought. In my narrow experience psychedelics had been what Pollan describes as "a low-dose 'aesthetic experience,' rather than a full-blown ego-disintegrating trip."

So, I felt that in preparation for the panel I owed it to myself to try a heroic dose. I did. A massive dose of psilocybin suspended in chalky choco-

SIX: *What the Neuroscience of Psychedelics Tells Us*

late obtained from a friend in California. Within fifteen minutes of ingesting it, I turned to my guide, and asked in horror: you mean *I'm going to feel this sick for four hours?!?* It turned out to be five. Unable to sit still, I carried around a basin all afternoon, hoping for relief that never came. It became clear that, at least in this case, when you're suffering intense nausea there is no unmediated experience, no death of the ego. My experiment had been a dismal failure. I went into the conference panel with an intuition that had no basis in experience.

Some friends said nice things about the psychedelics panel. But I came away frustrated. We circled around but didn't put our collective finger on the connection.

What the Diagram Shows

After a well-earned rest, I returned to Pollan and Plotkin's books and the books by Aldous Huxley and others that Pollan had relied on.

The ego is the "I," our everyday, walk-around, conscious self. It is who we think we are. It denies those things we may not like about ourselves. The ego, the seat of self-awareness, is who's conscious of thinking when we think. It's who gets things done, our "executive" function that performs what the reasoning mind decides needs to be done.

Freud's tripartite theory of the mind placed the ego in a space between the subconscious id and the moralizing super-ego. In neuroscience, the present thinking is that the ego inhabits the Default Mode Network (DMN), a tightly linked set of structures in your brain that connect the pre-frontal cortex to older, deeper centers of memory and emotion. The DMN was discovered only in the last twenty years with the advent of fMRIs. Before asking subjects to perform some task to see what parts of the brain would light up, to get a baseline scientists would ask them to do nothing: *not* to think. But rather than the brain growing impassive—dark on the fMRI—this particular network would light up. The anomalous DMN was born.

And so, neuroscientists started studying the DMN. On the panel, Pollan explained what they learned:

> it really is the network in your brain that's active during certain mental functions, including self-reflection, time travel, the ability to

think about the future or the past, which is, of course, very important to the creation of an identity. You can't really have a self without a sense of past and future, what's called the autobiographical memory...

If the ego, the self, can be said to have an address, it appears to be this network. Within the brain, it's kind of a top-down controller. The brain is a hierarchical system and at the top is this Default Mode Network that is kind of this communications hub. One of the neuroscientists I interviewed described it as the orchestra conductor or the corporate executive or the capital city.

The unconscious also makes us do things, but without passing through the oversight of the DMN or the reasoning brain. Such unconscious, impulsive behaviors sometimes harm the ego, our sense of self, which therefore denies such impulses. The id or unconscious is a chaotic realm where free associations are made seemingly willy-nilly, chaotically but with their own inner logic. If your professor unconsciously reminds you of your overbearing father, it may hurt your performance in class, not something your conscious mind seeks. The ego does its best to keep things orderly by keeping the unconscious unconscious. *Let the id stay hid.* The goal of Freud's analytic method was, *where id was, there shall ego be.* Freud wants unconscious urges to become conscious. Once conscious, they have less power over us.

The ego, residing in the DMN, thus functions as what early psychedelics advocate Aldous Huxley, under the influence of Harvard's Schultes, called "a reducing valve." Ego's reducing valve brings order to the chaos of the present moment by responding only to familiar details useful in forming predictions—Cold Cognition. The reducing valve, for efficiency's sake, silences what American psychologist William James, characterizing the consciousness of an infant, called a "great blooming, buzzing confusion." The ego is utilitarian, purpose driven. Blind to anomalies, how the present moment is unlike any other, Cold Cognition looks instead for the familiar, how the present moment is enough like the past to inform behavior. It registers only what counts in the moment to know what needs to be done. Anomalies, things Cold Cognition can't notice or predict, are the business of the Hot Cognition, so who cares?

By promising immediate and unmediated experience, the improviser's spontaneity also challenges the ego's reducing valve. Improvisation tries to

SIX: *What the Neuroscience of Psychedelics Tells Us*

deny and to overcome the reducing valve's hard reality. But hard reality it is. I can't emphasize enough that the brain's reducing valve *almost* inescapably comes between us and raw experience.

Neuroscientists confirm filters are deeply inscribed in the nature of the brain. In *On Knowing: Essays for the Left Hand* (1962, hence roughly contemporary with Huxley), the early cognitive psychologist Jerome Bruner, while seeking to bypass science's "self-imposed fetish of objectivity," nonetheless admits that the brain presents its own constraints on freedom:

> We know now ... that the nervous system is not the one-way street we thought it was—carrying messages from the environment to the brain, there to be organized into representations of the world... Selectivity is the rule and a nervous system... is as much an editorial hierarchy as it is a system for carrying signals.

Although his language (left and right brain) is now outdated, Bruner employs the aesthetics of improvisation on the one hand (*Essays for the Left Hand,* i.e. from the "right brain") to urge a freeing up of the rational mind. Intuition, he urges, not just rational experiment, needs to inform science. And yet, on the other hand, while employing this "left-handed," more open and spontaneous writing, he acknowledges the hardwired limits of the mind's freedom—limits which neuroscientists forty years later will confirm with fMRIs. Semir Zeki, a professor of neurobiology at University College London, for example, reports that although the brain employs one-third of its mass to sight, that "it distills, or abstracts, the essence of what it sees—like a caricature does—because of its limited memory system." Such tensions between the longing for unmediated experience and the recognition that, short of mystical experience, it is beyond our reach, are ever at the heart of improvisation.

And yet, momentously, neuroscience is beginning to explain how psychedelics seem effectively in some measure to open the reducing valve to give us bottom-up, raw data of experience. The mystic's experience of raw immediacy, once accessible only by heavenly intervention or strict spiritual discipline, now is within reach—a pill or cup of tea. Under the influence of psychedelics we are in *now* time, unconcerned with utility, with what needs to be done, attending to things with the unfocused, gestalt consciousness of an infant. Pollan writes:

> The efficiencies of the adult mind, useful as they are, blind us to the present moment. We're constantly jumping ahead to the next thing. We approach experience much as an artificial intelligence (AI) program does, with our brains continually translating the data of the present into the terms of the past, reaching back in time for the relevant experience, and then using that to make its best guess as to how to predict and navigate the future.

With psychedelics, the reducing valve open, chaos ensues. We are present tense. Hot Cognition takes the wheel.

Confronted by this chaos, the psychonaut and the improviser say with the ethnobotanist: *yeehaw!* Sometimes chaos, acknowledging anomalies here and there, is what the reigning system—the metronome—grown rigid with its predictive algorithms, needs. Although classical physics says all matter devolves to entropy, emerging Chaos Science has called attention to how turbulence, a form of entropy, can spontaneously order itself.

For Gonzo Journalist Hunter S. Thompson, LSD was "the Studebaker of the drug market." In the words of LSD's inventor Albert Hofmann, psychedelics open a crack "in the edifice of materialist rationality," that is, in scientific positivism. "Heroic doses" of psychedelics—enough to dissolve the ego—take the predictive mind beyond what Pollan calls "italicized" experience. Dissolving the ego achieves what Emerson declared our "insatiable desire…to forget ourselves." Emerson, almost anticipating psychedelics, saw in "Dreams and drunkenness, the use of opium and alcohol…the semblance and counterfeit of this oracular genius, and hence their dangerous attraction for men."

What matters for the psychonaut, as for the improviser, is being present—like an infant—to that "great blooming, buzzing confusion." Who knows what thing we will be next called upon to say *Yes, and…* to? *What is it about those trees?* And because the mind is a pattern-making machine (one of the engines of predictive consciousness), it freely makes connections by association: hallucinations, stories, visions, none of which are objectively true, but which might lead to subjective insight, to meaning.

Psychedelics help us understand Hot Cognition's role in improvisation. If free association, the leap of analogies and metaphors, is central to impro-

SIX: *What the Neuroscience of Psychedelics Tells Us*

visation, then that single fMRI image speaks a thousand words. I had not experienced anything to support my intuition. As a psychonaut, I was a failure. Nonetheless, the science is there to support it. There, in Pollan's book, the second time through, I managed to connect the dots.

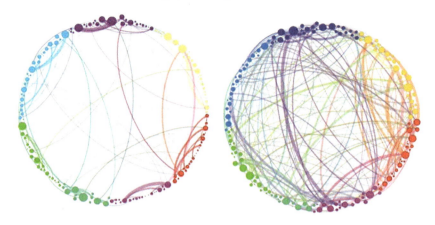

On the left, in normal brain activity, connections are mostly made *within* the brain's various networks (differentiated in the original image by color) with a few outliers that leap to other brain networks. On the right, with the DMN now quieted, the reducing valve opened, the brain on psychedelics makes thousands of new connections, "linking," as Pollan explains, "far-flung brain regions that during normal waking consciousness don't exchange much information... The brain appears to become less specialized and more globally interconnected, with considerably more intercourse, or 'cross talk,' among its various neighborhoods."

Pollan had all but said it at the 2019 Improv Conference:

> So, your sense of smell might be communicating directly with your vision: synesthesia. And suddenly you're seeing smells. And so dots are connected in whole new ways. And that may account for a lot of the kind of spontaneous insights that people have. And arresting imagery. I mean, if your emotion centers are talking to your visual cortex, you're going to see your fears or see your wishes.

Under the influence of psychedelics—or in the improvising mind of Robin Williams—the patterns and connections come fast and furious. All will not prove valuable—or get laughs—but the psychedelic experience and the improviser both assert that those connections are all worth considering. The connections you make are based on your subjective experience, not necessarily empirical fact. The patterns, imperfect and contingent, that emerge are *your* patterns. From them, meaning emerges.

Tracking blood flow in the brain with fMRIs confirms that subjectivity and story are deeply implicated in improvisation. Charles Limb at Johns Hopkins and Dr. Allen Braun at the NIH together confirm the analogy of improvisation to psychedelics. With fMRIs at the ready, they challenge pianists and freestyle rappers first to play or speak rote, memorized passages, then to improvise freely.

Limb and Braun found that improvising deactivates the orbitofrontal prefrontal cortex (LOFC) which monitors goal-directed behavior—purpose. Improvising also deactivates the dorsolateral prefrontal cortex (DLPFC) which monitors and adjusts sequences of learned behavior. These areas are adjacent to the DMN areas—site of the ego. Together the LOFC and DLPFC "are thought to provide a cognitive framework within which goal-directed behaviors are consciously monitored, evaluated and corrected." Deactivating the DLPFC allows "unfiltered, unconscious, or random thoughts and sensations to emerge." In sum, improvisation appears like psilocybin to deactivate control centers to allow interconnectivity between brain regions. Improvising jazz riffs or spitting verses opens the reducing valve. "Spitting" is the hip-hop term for improvising.

When memorization ends and improvising begins, the fMRIs show an increased level of activity in the medial prefrontal cortex (mPFC). Research suggests the mPFC enables us to add subjective intentionality separate from our main technical goal, in this case improvising piano or "spitting" verses. The mPFC is involved in expressing, for example, emotion independent of technique. "The association of mPFC activity with the production of autobiographical narrative," Limb

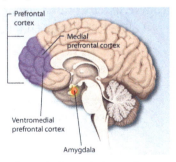

Improvisation activates emotion independent of mPFC

and Braun write, "is germane in this context, and...one could argue that improvisation is a way of expressing one's own musical voice or story."

In the climax of Pollan's first heroic dose of psilocybin, he is in his writing house and has a more than "italicized," heightened experience of the vegetative life outside his window. Pollan, who has spent his life exploring the human relationship to plants, finds his voice and story:

> It seemed to me these were the most beautiful leaves I had ever seen. It was as if they were emitting their own soft green glow. And it felt like a kind of privilege to gaze out at the world through their eyes, as it were, as the leaves drank up the last draughts of sunlight, transforming those photons into new matter. *A plant's-eye view of the world*—it *was* that, and for real!...
>
> I felt as though I were communing directly with a plant for the first time and that certain ideas I had long thought about and written about—having to do with the subjectivity of other species and the way they act upon us in ways we're too self-regarding to appreciate—had taken on the flesh of feeling and reality.

Pollan seems to echo John Clellon Holmes celebration of Kerouac's *On the Road*: "Somehow an open circuit of feeling had been established between his awareness and its object of the moment."

Pollan's intersubjective gaze turns to two trees that he had years earlier carefully sited his writing house to take advantage of. He is saddened to see how they've grown old and worn:

> As I gazed at the two trees I had gazed at so many times before from my desk, it suddenly dawned on me that these trees were—*obviously!*—my parents: the stolid ash my father, the elegant oak my mother. I don't know exactly what I mean by that, except that thinking about those trees became identical to thinking about my parents. They were completely, indelibly, present in those trees.
>
> And so I thought about all they had given me, and about all that time had done to them, and what was going to become of this prospect, this place (this me!), when they finally fell, as eventually they would. That parents die is not exactly the stuff of epiphany, but the prospect, no longer distant or abstract, pierced me more deeply than it ever had, and I was disarmed yet again by the pervasive sense of poignancy that trailed me all that afternoon.

Areas of Pollan's brain usually not connected here connect: *trees = parents* is a surprising, anomalous connection. His story becomes his aging parents' story. So anomalous is the connection that Pollan explains parenthetically: "(Do I need to say that I know how crazy this sounds? I do!)" But entertaining that hallucinatory, metaphoric connection elicits a deeper understanding of his relationship to his aging parents and his fear of losing them. The thought of their loss "pierced me more deeply than it ever had." Meaning emerges. He is moved. As was I.

The Quest for Meaning

Promising to embrace *all* of life, improv, limited by the brain and sensorium's inherent filters, instead delivers *more* life. Opening the reducing valve, psychedelics say *Yes, and...* to bottom-up raw experience—or as raw as it can manage. Aldous Huxley, under the influence of mescaline gazing upon a small vase of flowers, saw "what Adam had seen on the morning of his creation—the miracle, moment by moment, of naked existence...flowers shining with their own inner light and all but quivering under the pressure of the significance with which they were charged." But as with improv, there are inherent governors limiting how far psychedelics can open our reducing valve. In the world of psychonauts, these governors are known as set and setting.

Stanislav Grof, a Czech-born psychiatrist, calls psychedelics "unspecific mental amplifiers." What they amplify is set and setting. "Set" Pollan explains, "is the mind-set or expectation one brings to the experience, and setting is the environment in which it takes place. Compared with other drugs, psychedelics seldom affect people the same way twice, because they tend to magnify whatever's already going on both inside and outside one's head." Depending on your internal and external environment, where and when you take them, and what your expectations are, you will have a substantially different experience.

This "expectancy effect," Pollan explains, is "such that patients working with Freudian therapists returned with Freudian insights (framed in terms of childhood trauma, sexual drives, and oedipal emotions), while patients working with Jungian therapists returned with vivid archetypes from the attic of the collective unconscious, and Rankians with recovered memories of their birth traumas." Literate in both English literature and Eastern philosophy, Huxley experiences not naked existence but something clothed in

SIX: *What the Neuroscience of Psychedelics Tells Us*

the language of Milton and Blake (Huxley's title comes from *The Marriage of Heaven and Hell*) and Eastern mysticism.

The psychedelic experience is raw and yet constructed by the user: cooked. Pollan's experience of the dissolution of his ego, for example, was a cloud of Post-it notes that burst and "spilled onto the ground." It was a dissolution "appropriate for a writer," he explained to the audience, a bit abashed,

> but I beheld this. I observed this phenomenon, but from a perspective that was completely unfamiliar to me, that was completely untroubled by, you know, I had perfect equanimity about this catastrophe, I was gone... Consciousness without self.

Asked from the audience about the animal spirits that often emerge under the influence of psychedelics, Pollan again referenced set and setting.

> It's funny, I find I have those kind of feelings about plants. My plant spirit kind of speaks to me more than my animal spirit. So it just may depend on your orientation.

Pollan's career had largely been plant-based. Such meaning is subjective, low status to the reasoning brain where objective knowledge alone has high status. But isn't all meaning necessarily subjective?

The scientific method seeks not meaning but statistical truth. For Enlightenment encyclopedist Denis Diderot, godfather of scientific positivism, "Facts of whatever kind, constitute the philosopher's true wealth." The cognitive psychologist Steven Pinker seems to agree in his recent "triumphalist" celebration of the results of Enlightenment rationality. Reason and its disciple, technology, Pinker rightly argues, have brought millions of the earth's billions out of poverty and illness. Committed to utility—the greatest good for the greatest number—Pinker dismisses arguments for the value of subjectivity: because proponents of subjectivity use logical arguments, they "refute themselves"—an incredibly thick-headed argument. As if, if you mention $E=mc^2$, you can't speak of subjectivity in the same sentence. Pinker's discussion of meaning settles for a utilitarian argument. Clearly a member of the usurping servant's party.

I met Pinker during a Vancouver TED talk in 2018 between sessions in a lounge area. I looked up, and there he was. *All that hair, so perfectly coiffed!* It was too good an opportunity to pass up. I offered that the father of the Enlightenment Denis Diderot believed facts were the philosopher's true wealth, but that nonetheless in his experimental novels *The Nephew of Rameau* and *Jacques the Fatalist*—both self-styled improvisations—Diderot not only devalorized facts but also made a case for the value of subjectivity in finding meaning and in advancing culture. Pinker didn't see the point. I felt like an apple debating the virtues of crispness with an orange. The conversation was soon over.

Maybe like Diderot we should be ambivalent too. After all, there are two ways to take Diderot's idea that facts are the philosopher's true wealth. Yes, it is the springboard for science's high regard for objectivity. But remember what Diderot and the Enlightenment were laboring to replace. For the Enlightenment, facts were a kind of wealth that could buy our way out of a world where myth and tradition—Church and King—were the only coin of the realm.

I have cast the Enlightenment, along with Descartes, as the villains in my allegory. Descartes will be the target of many of the improvisers (and of the neuroscientist Damasio) who, champions of embodied cognition, will attempt to disrupt the Cartesian method and to break through the mind-body split Descartes advanced. Nonetheless, like Renaissance improvisers (e.g., Montaigne and Bacon), Descartes conceived his *Discourse on Method* as a widening of reason's powers beyond the constraints of the scholastic method. His first-person autobiographical narrative answered the scholiast's appeal to authority. First-person grounds his method in lived life. Maurice Blanchot celebrates not only the Method's "freedom of form" but that "this form is no longer that of a simple exposition (as in scholastic philosophy), but rather describes the very movement of research that joins thought and existence in a fundamental experience." Improvisation's binary—our Hot Cognition vs. their Cold—is always a matter of degree. Improvisers leapfrog one another time after time. They assert they are more unmediated and direct, more rough or sloppy. Another paradox of improvisation: the Enlightenment was in many ways an improvisation which, becoming the dominant rationality, got set in its ways. In the nineteenth century, Enlightenment's heirs buy into the model of science and systematic Scientific Positivism becomes improv's target.

But, in his mind-body split and commitment to certainty Descartes takes two seriously wrong turns. While the Enlightenment's utility has

SIX: *What the Neuroscience of Psychedelics Tells Us*

been significant—who can deny it—Pinker mistakes facts' usefulness for meaning. Steven Colbert's sendup of Pinker's commitment to what Colbert called "truthiness" came early and often. Pinker appeared three times on *The Colbert Report*. Responding to Colbert's challenge to Pinker's book, *The Better Angels of Our Nature,* Pinker replied, "We do have inner demons. We have a lot of motives that erupt in violence." To which Colbert zinged:

> Right, I'm fighting the urge to punch you right now.

Pinker's broad brushstrokes don't reach down to the granular level to contemplate the encyclopedists' own ambivalence about their rationalist project. At such a level, anomalies begin to show themselves. Pascal, too, inventor no less of calculus, nonetheless distrusted reason: "Reason's last step is the recognition that there are an infinite number of things which are beyond it. It is merely feeble if it does not go as far to realize that." For Pascal, "the heart has its reasons of which reason knows nothing."

As T. S. Eliot muses in *Choruses from the Rock* (1934) in a line that resonates profoundly today, "Where is the wisdom we have lost in knowledge?/Where is the knowledge we have lost in information?" Jungian Murray Stein puts his finger on where this loss began to trickle through our fingers: "The Age of Enlightenment left a legacy of facticity without meaning."

Meaning is an order of wealth different from facticity and truthiness. Psychedelics and improvisation—both promising *raw* experience but settling for *more* connectivity—are two possible roads to pursue it.

Improvisation makes the case for individual subjective experience rather than the statistical. Science's quest for the statistical average ignores the exceptional, the anomalous. As Carl Jung writes, "One could say that the real picture consists of nothing but exceptions to the rule, and that, in consequence, absolute reality has predominantly the character of *irregularity*." Like Mandelbrot's fractals, experience is nothing but anomalies that nonetheless fit a nonlinear pattern—anomalies that, seen as part of a pattern, aren't anomalies after all. Every event is the first of its kind and part of a pattern perhaps we alone are able to see: our myth. As the American artist Edward Hopper quietly remarks: "More of me comes out when I improvise." Improvisation seizes not only more of the life around us, but also of our embodied selves.

Winging It

Improvisation, like psychedelics and like psychoanalysis, privileges subjective truth based on experience in the present. The novelist Henry James suggests in *The Art of Fiction* that the novelist's role is to "Try to be one of the people on whom nothing is lost." In a short story, "The Figure in the Carpet," he urges upon all of us that we discern "the figure" in our life's "carpet." It's there for us to find if we pay attention. Improv and psychedelics, by opening the reducing valve, allow us to find meaningful subjective patterns based on anomalous connections. They bring chaos into our lives—*more life!*—that invite meaningful patterns and narratives to emerge.

Exploring improvisation's tensions and contradictions is clearly the figure in my life's carpet. What improvisation wants to add to Reason's toolkit is Pollan's experience of those parental trees, subjective consciousness that we access by intuition, inspiration, instinct, embodied emotion, accident, spindle cells, or drugs. All three—psychoanalysis, psychedelics, and improvisation—have a profoundly invested *taste* for chaos. They aren't suggesting we swallow chaos whole. Improvisation argues that Reason sometimes needs an infusion from our "lower" faculties. An openness to chaos leads to new meaning and to a new order.

In André Breton's first *Manifesto of Surrealism* (1924), for example, his purpose is to broaden the boundaries of reality by opening to art the *surreal* realm of dreams that Freud's new "discoveries" have made accessible. Breton was an early French supporter of Freud's work. The wild excesses of Surrealism are well-known: automatic poetry; dreamscapes in many media—poetry, sculpture, painting, and film; mixed-media collage; and other apparently anarchistic formless forms that exploit the element of surprise, unexpected juxtapositions, and *non sequitur,* all drenched in illogic that make little everyday sense. And yet his stated purpose is "the future resolution of these two states, dream and reality, which are seemingly so contradictory, into a kind of absolute reality, a *surreality*" (his emphasis). Breton's goal is not unreality or unreason. By wedding the two, Reason and Unreason, he seeks transcendence: *sur* = over = *über*. The echo of Nietzsche suggests Breton's *surreality* is an echo of *Birth of Tragedy*'s wedding of Apollonian and Dionysian. Will dream take charge of this new surreal land? No. Breton writes,

SIX: *What the Neuroscience of Psychedelics Tells Us*

> If the depths of our mind contain within it strange forces capable of augmenting those on the surface, or of waging a victorious battle against them, there is every reason to seize them—first to seize them, then, if need be, to submit them to the control of our reason.

As Freud said, "where id was, there ego shall be"—a far cry from the Dadaist anarchism Surrealism emerged from.

Meanwhile, unquestioning, MAGAland trusts in Trump's unfiltered Tweets which seem to have no purpose but which cannily re-engineer our democracy. However meticulously prepared, Trump's social media will always have the appearance of his reducing valve flowing unchecked.

CHAPTER SEVEN

Improv's Bravura Performer: Charisma's Starring Role

In simplest terms, charisma is the self-confidence an improviser must have—in improv comedy, jazz, or hip-hop, to name a few—to improvise without a net. Lin-Manuel Miranda, who had a career in hip-hop before Broadway, points to such moments as an "adrenalized unsafe situation." The improviser must trust that, despite the considerable challenge confronting her, some answer to the *Yes, and . . .* will come in time, that the needed rhyme or musical chord will appear and make sense, and that this next first thought will be not only a way forward but the best way forward. To have the self-confidence charisma embodies is to be in the state of flow, which Mihaly Csikszentmihalyi, co-founder of the field of positive psychology, defines as optimal experience "in which people are so involved in an activity that nothing else seems to matter; the experience itself is so enjoyable that people will do it even at great cost, for the sheer sake of doing it." Charisma is embodied presence in the flow of the moment.

But despite its boast of focused presentness, charisma also casts its eyes over its shoulder. It has a target. Charisma is a power not for direct but for indirect confrontation. Rather than battling Reason on its own turf through logic and argumentation, charisma insinuates itself into our pleasure zones. "Insinuate" comes from Latin, *insinuare,* "to creep in,

Matt Wuerker © 2019 | POLITICO

intrude, wind one's way into" and comes to mean "entrance through a narrow way." This is exactly what Trickster is best at. She is the lord of the crossroads and the threshold—liminal spaces. Master of *aporia*—the rhetorical figure meaning "no pore," or "no portal"—she finds a way where there is no way, a key for the door's lock, or a door where there is no door. Trump is Lord of the Dog Whistle, saying what can't be said, challenging the woke culture that cancels those who say the unsayable. And gets away with it by gaslighting: *I was just joking. Don't you have a sense of humor?* Like improv, charisma has both a light and a dark side.

When Zeus and Apollo confront Hermes for stealing the cattle of the sun, Hermes makes them laugh which opens the door to reconciliation. Jocularity, as Wynton notes, is intrinsic to syncopation. However rageful, signifying is usually seasoned with twinkle. Aspiring to a seat on Olympus, this day-old baby clutches his baby blanket like an uptown matron her pearls, but with a wink:

> As he spoke, Hermes of Kyllene, the slayer of Argus, winked and clutched his baby blanket tightly in his arms. Zeus laughed aloud at the sight of his scheming child so smoothly denying his guilt about the cattle. And he ordered them both to come to an agreement and go find the cattle. He told Hermes the guide to lead the way and, dismissing the mischief in his heart, to show Apollo where the cattle were hidden. Then the son of Kronos nodded his head and good Hermes obeyed, for the will of Zeus, who holds the shield, persuades without effort.

Zeus, who "persuades without effort," is the ultimate improviser. But not before laughter creates community. The future guide of souls becomes for a moment a guide of the gods.

It is Trickster's charisma that charms us into embracing the moment and taking joy in meaning-making through story and figuration: the play of language and mind. On improvisation's conceptual map, Reason and Unreason battle for dominion. Controlling the corpus callosum, Reason displays all the palpable and imperial power, or rather *force*. *Force* is Simone Weil's term: power used for utility, when we make people into things. The improviser deploys instead the impalpable but nonetheless powerful weapon of charisma. Charisma in Trickster's hands is *power* not *force* because, in many ways a mere pose or mask, it doesn't diminish or treat the audience as lower in status or as object. If improv was just out for laughs with the next, better joke, it would be treating the audience as object. No, it invites the audience to find its own emergent meaning in the narrative that emerges. The goal is not laughs but gasps of recognition.

Winging It

Charisma, as if despite itself, achieves Martin Buber's "I-Thou" relationship, eschewing the "I-It" relationship inherent in its pose. Rather, inviting the audience to join in the improviser's game builds community, all together for the moment fully embracing the flow of life. To be in the flow is a creature and creation of the moment and inevitably momentary. No one can sustain such presentness, yet the appearance of full and constant presence is essential to improv.

"Charisma" is rooted in "grace, beauty, kindness." *Charis* was the name of one of the three Graces, attendants of Aphrodite. Both are related to a root meaning "to rejoice at." Joy and desire: We are back to single cell bacteria and their homeostasis-driven desires. In action, charisma is a kind of charm, a spell cast upon us. Sociologist Max Weber gave charismatic leadership a secular definition: "'Charisma' is the personal quality that makes an individual seem extraordinary, a quality by virtue of which supernatural, superhuman, or at least exceptional powers or properties are attributed to the individual: powers or properties that are not found in everyone and that are thought to be the gift of God or exemplary, rendering that individual a 'leader' (*Führer*)." The trope's religious roots are never far. For the apostle Paul, the Holy Spirit bestows charisma; charisma is a direct result of grace. "Charity," the basis of much of the community we achieve, is related.

Etymologies help stake out the territory I describe, but charisma is far better appreciated and understood in action. In the *Odyssey,* Athena dresses *metic* Odysseus in his charisma when he needs to attract Phaeacian Princess Nausicaa to help advance his scheme. Shipwrecked, tossed by the waves, he is cast on the beach shorn of his clothes, naked, as if reborn. He needs help from King Alcinous, the princess's father, to get home. How can this naked flotsam find his way to the royal court and home?

In a word, he relies on his quality of being *polytropos*: many-turning, ever cunning—"a complicated man" in Emily Wilson's new translation.

Nausicaa, brought to the beach by Athena's promptings, provides him the wherewithal to clean and clothe himself, then Athena finishes the job:

> But when he was all clean and richly oiled,
> dressed in the clothes the young unmarried girl
> had given him, Athena made him look
> bigger and sturdier, and made his hair
> grow curling tendrils like a hyacinth.

SEVEN: *Improv's Bravura Performer*

> As when Athena and Hephaestus teach
> a knowledgeable craftsman every art,
> and he pours gold on silver, making objects
> more beautiful—just so Athena poured attractiveness
> across his head and shoulders.
> Then he went off and sat beside the sea;
> his handsomeness was dazzling. The girl
> was shocked.

Charisma is an inner state here represented outwardly. Athena almost literally gilds the lily, pouring golden charisma on Odysseus's already argentine character. His charisma is both secular and divine. In charisma we stand taller, our chest expands, our shoulders square. Nausicaa doesn't stand a chance.

Nausicaa's Phaeacians are a *metic* race. They are a race of improvisors and share the cunning intelligence prized by the Greeks that produces Odysseus's effortless, polytropic response to challenges. Their king, Alcinous, means "mighty mind," mighty because it is *metic*. The front doors of Alcinous's palace are symbolically flanked with two dogs made of silver and gold, constructed, we learn, by Hephaestus, one of the *metic* gods (along with Athene and Hermes). The Phaeacians' ships have Hermes's ability to unite thought with deed—the immediacy that is Zeus's special gift and the essence of charisma. Characteristically, the Phaeacians often welcome the gods as visitors: direct, unmediated experiences of godhead. The ships need no steersman or rudder. Think where you want to go, and a Phaeacian ship takes you there. A vehicle with a kind of charisma of its own, fit for the *metic* great-grandson of Hermes headed home to Ithaca. Odysseus has cast up right where he needs to, just as improvisers always do.

To turn to another wanderer: Walt Whitman's first self-presentation in the frontispiece of *Leaves of Grass* is saturated, like his *Song of Myself*, in the same charisma. No buttoned-down Manhattanite, this guy. The cocked hat, open shirt *sans cravat*, casual stance with slanted hips all say, *flâneur*, the idler or lounger who embraces the city's crowds or the open road, at once detached and engaged. Like the improviser, the *flâneur* is not driven by purpose. The portrait says: *Come with me.* Even before his opening, "I celebrate myself, and sing myself," insinuates itself into your longings, you're ready to tag along. Charisma.

With Hollywood's help, the *flâneur* became part of popular culture. But it was first celebrated by French poet Charles Baudelaire. As industrialization made traditional art inadequate to describe the dynamics of modern life, the *flâneur* becomes the artist immersed in the metropolis' spectacle. Baudelaire seems to anticipate Csikszentmihalyi's *Flow* as he describes the *flâneur*:

> The crowd is his element, as the air is that of birds and water of fishes. His passion and his profession are to become one flesh with the crowd. For the perfect *flâneur*, for the passionate spectator, it is an immense joy to set up house in the heart of the multitude, amid the ebb and flow of movement, in the midst of the fugitive and the infinite...The lover of life makes the whole world his family.

"In the midst of the fugitive and the infinite," Baudelaire's *flâneur* seems to have found the still point of the turning world, the eternal present, that crossroads that Trickster rules, joining matter and spirit, present, past, and future. We in our metronome-bound time live in what the Greeks called *chronos,* clock time. The improvisors inhabit *kairos,* the opportune moment.

Long the province of men because of women's restricted normative role, transgressive *flâneurie* has recently been explored from the woman's point of view. Lauren Elkin's fascination with walking the streets of Paris, she writes, had "to do with the utter, total freedom unleashed from the act of putting one foot in front of the other." Such pointless wandering could be utterly, well, pointless. Unless, as in Elkin's case, it is sheer joy. Enjoyment, an end in itself, depends upon the charismatic state of mind, open and engaged in the passing scene.

Charisma takes Hollywood

A Whitman-like charisma informs the nonchalance and elegance that becomes a mainstay of Hollywood stars: the *flâneur* persona of Cary Grant or Fred Astaire. Astaire's characters, unassuming, taking life as it comes,

SEVEN: *Improv's Bravura Performer*

embody Trickster's characteristic bravado and nonchalance. Astaire is often compared to Gene Kelly whose persona is far more earnest and purposeful. For the great French dancer Leslie Caron, who partnered with both, Astaire

> was just made for dancing. You could see him walk in the streets and it was almost like he was dancing. There was a swing to it and a rhythm to it... And he heard the music; he played with it, he danced with it, he understood it so well... Everything was easy for him... He also had fun ideas—I think he's the dancer who made fun of himself the most. He would goof around and the result is lovely.

By contrast, Caron adds, Kelly "was very demanding and very professional. He didn't think dancing was fun. He really thought it was hard work." For commentator Jennifer Walsh, tellingly, Kelly "inspires a person to think that if she just tries hard enough, she might be able to do what he does. Fred's dancing says, 'Pfft. Forget it. You'll never be this good.'" Astaire's dancing embraces and privileges unstructured, embodied emotion. Kelly is all about structure, Perkin's structural thinking. *Hey, you can do that. First, you...*

The only duet Astaire and Kelly danced, "The Babbitt and the Bromide" from Ziegfeld's *Follies* (1946), is aptly set up by a dialogue where Astaire disguises their hard work and Kelly calls attention to it:

> Astaire: Say, why don't we ad lib something together then.
>
> Kelly [laughing]: Whip it up right here on the spot? Like the one we've been rehearsing for two weeks?

Everyone testified to Astaire's obsessive rehearsing. Yet, he was so determined to give the impression of being unrehearsed that hired guards kept his rehearsals private.

Many of the narrative lead-ins to Astaire's dance routines work hard to give the impression of not working hard at all. In *Royal Wedding* (1951), he "improvises" the famous hat rack duet when his dancing partner (Jane Powell) doesn't show up for their planned rehearsal—just to kill time, just for fun. Astaire rehearsed with more than 30 commercially available hat racks before insisting the prop department build one he could work (or play) with.

According to *Life* magazine, just as jazz was America's original musical form, tap along with the Lindy Hop were our "only native and original dance form[s]." In *Swinging the Machine,* American Studies scholar Joel Dinerstein argues that tap dancing emerged as a "rhythmic organization of industrial noise."

Visiting New York in 1935, the great modernist architect Le Corbusier heard things unheard in Europe: "New sounds...the grinding of the streetcars, the unchained madness of the subway, the pounding of machines in factories." Le Corbusier adds, "[f]rom this new uproar [African Americans] make music." Like jazz, tap brought under control that "irritable, nervous, querulous, unreasonable" world that Henry Adams had seen in industry's dynamos. Jazz and tap humanized modern industrial life, the world that Cold Cognition built. It made "natural" what was unnatural. Tap has its repertoire of steps, just as machines do. But where a machine is locked into its steps, in tap, innovation is key. For the tap icon John W. Bubbles, "creating new steps is the only worthwhile challenge and achievement in the art." As that other icon of Modernism Ezra Pound demanded, "make it new."

Sally Sommer, a leading expert on dance in American popular culture, distinguishes between African-derived tap dancing and European-derived ballet aesthetics: "one expresses the self, the other perfection." Seeking perfection privileges those linear, step-by-step, structured human faculties that enable us to achieve mastery. Ballet's endless hours of repetitive training and exercise at the *barre* come to mind. Learning tap of course, is no less arduous. But seeking to express the self privileges non-linear, unstructured human faculties by which the self can be known: intuition, instinct, the unconscious. Eleanor Powell and Fred Astaire, two dance masters, both often dreamed their dance routines.

Ballet has a long tradition of innovation (think Balanchine), but its goal is to participate in and to confirm the European tradition of artifice. The tap tradi-

SEVEN: *Improv's Bravura Performer*

The Rites of Spring, 1913

tion predates Igor Stravinky's *The Rite of Spring* (1913), but his modernist ballet anticipates how American dance, jazz's tap and swing's Lindy Hop, named for Charles Lindberg's first "hop" across the Atlantic, would come to transform industrial noise. Stravinsky's dissonant *The Rite of Spring* pushed the envelope of ballet (and of music) so far that, like rock and roll in its day, it caused a riot.

Commissioned by famous impresario Serge Diaghilev and danced by his Ballets Russes, Stravinsky's score for *The Rite of Spring* contradicted every rule about what music should be. The sounds are often deliberately harsh, right from the Lithuanian folk melody opening, played by the bassoon in its highest, most uncomfortable range. For Anglo-American poet T.S. Eliot, who was at the premiere that night in May, 1913, Stravinsky's music, a puzzling combination of the primitive and the modern, seemed to transform "the rhythm of the steppes into the scream of the motor horn, the rattle of machinery, the grind of wheels, the beating of iron and steel, the roar of the underground railway, and the other barbaric cries of modern life; and to transform these despairing noises into music." Together, Eliot and Stravinsky foresaw the "rhythmic organization of industrial noise" effected by modern dance: tap and swing.

Appropriating machine rhythms fulfills the first two criteria Toni Morrison sets for "Black art": "it must have the ability to use found objects, the appearance of using found things." Those accustomed to classical dance often dismiss tap because tap dancers make it look effortless—fulfilling Morrison's third criterion: "it must look easy." In the spirit of improvisation, effortlessness conveys a freedom from outmoded conventions, conventions to which ballet is dedicated. Amy Brinkman of Milwaukee's Danceworks reports, "I once had a student tell me that she thought tap dancing was going to be really easy. When I asked her why she thought that, she said, 'When you see ballet dancers with their leg up by their ear you think, wow! That's hard. But when you watch tap dancing, it looks so easy and effortless.'" For dancer Chuck Green, "Tap is all about freedom." Those qualities—effortlessness, freedom and innovation—are improvisation's signatures.

Busby Berkeley's highly stylized routines displayed battalions of identity-less young women dancing in geometric, kaleidoscopic lockstep. These, too, were a response to mechanization. But Berkeley routines identify, as it were, with the oppressor. Plenty of fun to watch, nonetheless Berkeley's *response* was just a repetition of the machine age's *call*. Berkeley's routines do not transcend the machine, do not leap into freedom. What made the difference? "Astaire and George Gershwin's parallel rhythmic sensibilities," writes Todd Decker, "are generally understood to come from black jazz players and dancers."

Astaire dances to "Slap that Bass"
(Allstar Pictures Library Ltd./Alamy Stock Photo)

In *Shall We Dance* (1937), the famous "Slap that Bass" number—written by Gershwin—is a rich example of Astaire's leaps to freedom and their source. Astaire plays a ballet dancer, where, to secure his star status in an artistic world decidedly Eurocentric, he is billed as the "Great Petrov." Down-to-earth "Petrov," however, is happy to declare his all-American name, with a wink, almost tap dancing with his tongue: "Pete P. Peters from Philadelphia PA." Petrov/Peters has fallen for a music hall dance star, the equally all-American Linda Keene (Ginger Rogers).

To the ballet world, Keene's tap dancing is déclassé. As the film opens, Peters' tonier but bumbling British manager, Jeffrey Baird (Edward Everett Horton), is shocked to see Peters practicing his dance steps to a "hot" jazz recording—"hot" codes as Black. The script reads:

> "[Horton] opens the door: then recoils as he is greeted by a blast of hot swing MUSIC. As [Horton] enters and stands petrified with astonish-

SEVEN: *Improv's Bravura Performer*

ment. A portable talking machine is blaring out a hot tune. Petrov is tap dancing!"

Shocked, Baird responds "That's not art." In an early draft, Peters replies with feeling:

> Pete: Maybe not. But it means dancing to 100,000,000 American hearts. I have a marvelous idea, Jeffrey. Suppose we could combine the technique of the ballet with the warmth and passion of jazz!
>
> Jeffrey (shocked): Jazz! You're not thinking of being a jazzer!!
>
> Pete: Why not!—Dancing to jazz has so much more meaning. Why— it's the skyline of New York, and the dust bowl of the Middle West— and the roar of the Mississippi—and the sun of California.
>
> He bursts into a newer and bigger enthusiasm.
>
> Pete (cont.): It's Broadway, Jeffrey—and Main Street—all at once and together—It's—why, it's tap dancing.

Besides, Pete Peters wants to capture not just Broadway and Main Street but Linda Keene's heart. He longs for this new art, but embodied desire drives the plot. Peters follows Keene from Paris to New York to woo her. During the trans-Atlantic passage, his manager Baird watches a ballet rehearsal on deck, surrounded by a bevy of scantily clad young women. Meanwhile, Peters is below decks in the engine room appropriating some new licks.

As Decker writes, "Habitual Hollywood practice and fear of protests from Southern distributors normally prevented blacks and whites from getting too close to each other on-screen." Astaire listens to the engine crew perform a song—Gershwin's—that promises to cure the world's Machine Age problems: "If I can only get me/Someone to slap that bass/Happiness is not a riddle..."

Astaire then does them one better, transforming their rhythms to dance. He tops their song, but the dance steps are, of course, theirs, appropriated, like the Boyoyo Boys that Paul Simon admired, at once improvised and derivative.

With dance, Astaire doesn't just point to the flaws in orderly systems but surpasses them—as improvisation always does, call and response. A machine repeats itself over and over building the modern world. But like most systems, it is rigid. It cannot veer off in new directions. To do so is just to throw a rod, break a cog, or run off the rails. Improv, with its elasticity (and irony) instead creates something new (or, considering its derivativeness, newer). Either way, it codes as freedom. It is the signifying *response—Yes, and…—*to mechanization's rigid call. "Slap that Bass"—free in another sense—is among the first Hollywood studio system scenes to mix Black and white performers. The scene represents Hollywood's slow awakening.

Astaire's on-screen persona here and elsewhere is pure Trickster. *Vanity Fair* in 1928, discussing four iconic tap dancers (including Astaire), speaks of them as "clowns of extraordinary motion." Cagney once remarked, "you know, Freddie, you've got a touch of the hoodlum in you"—as does Hermes. In *The Barkleys of Broadway* (1949), dismissing a stuff shirt, Astaire announces, "Aw, that fellow brings out the gangster in me." Especially in the early Ginger Roger vehicles *Shall We Dance* and *Swing Time*, Astaire always plays the outsider, a Trickster who playfully challenges the received decorum and hierarchies.

In *Swing Time* (1936), Lucky Garnett (Astaire), an inveterate gambler (Hermes is the god of chance), he scowls ironically at the dance studio's slogan where he meets and begins to woo Penny Carroll (Rogers). It reads:

> To Know How to Dance Is
> To Know How to Control Yourself

Pausing at the threshold, Astaire dismisses this chestnut with a knowing smirk. Like improvisation's Trickster figure, lord of gateways and portals, Astaire is in no need of the constraints self-control demands and that gateways mark.

Astaire's persona, needing no character development—again like Trickster—seems to leap fully-formed onto the screen, tuxedo-clad. In the *Homeric Hymn,* the *metic* Hermes, just born, leaps from his cradle ready to invent, trick, lie, steal, break norms, and cajole. By contrast, in Kelly's *Singing in the Rain* (1952), the narrative twice recounts (once in a flashback, once as a story within a story) how Don Lockwood (Kelly) melodramatically claws his way to Hollywood through rough-and-tumble touring vaudeville acts.

For Joel Dinerstein, "'Slap That Bass' encodes a classic primitivist framework. Astaire goes to the 'lower' classes—the less-evolved, folk, primitive cultures—for the raw, instinctive passion lacking in 'civilization.'" Here

SEVEN: *Improv's Bravura Performer*

marred by race, this primitivist framework is characteristic of improvisation, inscribed in the gesture of spontaneity: *this is good because it's "natural," innocent of hard work, artifices, and sophistication.* Hermes's birthplace is Arcadia, traditional setting for the pastoral, the genre where shepherds woo shepherdesses during apparently work-free endless summers—like Huck and Jim on their carefree raft. Aspiring to Olympus from Arcadia, Hermes is essentially a rube, a country bumpkin trying to get to Broadway. But he's not one to give such hierarchical distinctions any mind. I won't make too much of Astaire's lifelong choreographer's stage name: Hermes Pan. Pan, another Trickster god, was a shortened form of the choreographer's impossibly long Greek surname, Panagiotopoulos. Pan, also Arcadian, is Hermes's offspring, equally lascivious. Surely as a Greek the award-winning choreographer must have settled on goat-footed "Pan" with a wink worthy of Astaire's partner in crime.

Improvisation reaches back to a time well before democracy took root. But the spirit of democracy is deeply inscribed in improv. Improvisation's affirmation of vitality—any and every *Yes and...* will do—tends to level hierarchies, which makes improvisation throb with a democratic impulse. Mixed-race (god and nymph) Hermes's effort to gain Olympus, Wordsworth's celebration of the peasantry, Whitman's celebration of, well, *everything*: all anticipate the leveling of hierarchies that followed World War I which aristocrats and the upper-classes did so much tragically to muddle. Jazz, with its commitment to hearing what every voice has to say, even if it's "rotten fruit," is the greatest democratic expression, apart from American democracy itself, when it works. Thumbing his nose at the normative, Astaire projects Bakhtin's carnivalesque "realm of community, freedom, equality, and abundance."

Charisma is not hard to exemplify in Black performance where it is the heart of the matter, commanding center stage. Consider the ever-rhyming, -smiling, and -gorgeous Muhammad Ali. But being from New Orleans and of a certain age, I offer instead the example of Jessie Hill's great 1950s rhythm and blues anthem, "Ooh Poo Pah Doo" (1960). Produced by the legendary Allen Toussaint and recorded at the equally legendary Cosimo Matassa's J&M Studio, birthplace of rock and roll, Hill's song embodies Trickster's charisma in one of the leanest, most direct and economical lyrics in rock and roll history. The song is a true anthem, having been recorded by Ike and Tina Turner, The Shirelles, Etta James, The Righteous Brothers, Mitch Ryder and the Detroit Wheels, Wilson Pickett, New Orleans's Tommy Ridgley, Taj Mahal, the Steve Miller Band, and Hill's own nephews, Troy (Trombone Shorty) and James Andrews. What's its magic?

Other than the many expressive shouts and scat-like lines that play on and around the title, the lyric boils down to a constant iteration of this:

> Baby, they call me the most...
> And I won't stop tryin' till I create disturbance in your mind.

Hill's simple but emphatic boast, "they call me the most," and his promise to "create disturbance in your mind" are the essence of Trickster's transgressive charisma, the embodiment of Gates's *signifying*.

Half of rock and roll seems to consist of songs that celebrate charisma; the other half are of songs of heartache when charisma deserts or can't be found.

But this one is about seduction, a *carpe diem* song. As one wag explains on Songfacts forum:

> I think it's pretty obvious... "I won't stop trying till I create a disturbance in your mind" = Until you can't stop thinking about me, As well as "a disturbance in your mind" being a nice way of saying "Until you're so hot for me you can think of nothing else."

Yes, the sought-for disturbance is sexual, but it also can be read politically, the charisma not just hormonal but in part compensatory. Emerging out of the dehumanization of enslavement, Jim Crow, world wars, and the Depression, Blues charisma signifies on power. After World War II, such charisma is appropriated by mostly working-class whites who mount the British invasion that brought Black signifying into mainstream culture for good.

There's nothing so second-hand in Hill's lyric. Native to Treme, the first free Black neighborhood in America, Hill, his nephew James Andrews tells me, had Mardi Gras Indian connections. Hill's opening moan,

> Yo-o-oh!
> (Yo-o-oh!)
> Yo-o-oh!
> (Yo-o-oh!)
> Ooh, yeah!
> (Ooh, yeah!)

SEVEN: *Improv's Bravura Performer*

could have Indian roots, as may his eponymous lyric, Ooh Poo Pah Doo. We may never know. In Mardi Gras Indian culture, the central gesture is charismatic: "I won't bow down."

A similar braggadocio will be a mainstay of urban rap and hip-hop. At its braggadocious extreme—as for example the 1990s phase known as gangster rap—rap exemplifies charisma's dark side or Jungian Shadow, where women and bling are equally objectified, forced to feed the braggart's narcissism. Again, compensatory: gangster rap compensates for the inner city, redlining, failed desegregation, and the new Jim Crow. Mayhem, like the murders of Tupac Shakur and The Notorious B.I.G., ensued. Hardly an ideal community, but nevertheless community is one of its key tropes. Us versus Them.

The paradox of benevolent charisma (as opposed to the malignant variety that we cannot ignore in hip-hop or in Trump's behavior), is that while it asserts the improviser's specialness, nonetheless it builds community. I'm sure I didn't understand Jessie Hill's lyrics when it was part of the soundscape of our weekend dances at F&M Patio or when I snuck into the members-only Uptown spot, The Valencia Club. Nonetheless, those dances gave me my teenage years' most potent sense of community, dancing with friends and strangers to the hits by Irma Thomas, Benny Spellman, and Deacon John's Jump Blues. Community is not only in the lyrics but in the syncopation, which had us all favoring the heavy backbeat and had us singing along, call and response: *ooh poo pah doo,* all equally clueless about what it meant, its roots in resistance to white power, but not caring.

A psychologist once defined a charismatic for me as a person who completely identifies with his grandiosity. He was describing malignant charisma. Where the malignant charismatic person identifies with his grandiosity, the benevolent charismatic understands it is a momentary pose, a persona. With roots in Greek theatre, persona refers to the actor's mask or role-playing. She disappears into the role and yet is not fully identified with it. This is one of the truths understood by Rhetorical Man, that we have many roles, many selves. The role is assumed only while on the stage or in a given situation. The charismatic person ignores for the moment but does not deny her many, inevitable moments of self-doubt and hesitancy.

Charisma draws upon what neuroscience calls the salience network (SN) which avoids the pointless rumination the default mode network (DMN) sometimes condemns us to. DMN uses less brain energy, happy to spend our time using little glucose to daydream about all our faults and failures or to imagine how those faults and failures will doom our next endeavor, so why try? The high energy SN, called to make the most of this present moment with its many salient, anomalous stimuli, enables the improviser to negotiate the aporia she faces. *What is the next rhyme word? What metaphor will I weave into the story I hope to advance?* You must be in a charismatic state that will allow the *metic* rudderless ship to take you there.

Each answer that comes is an epiphany, a sudden appearance of the charismatic, the divine spark in us. Self-doubt will come, but let it come backstage. Self-doubt would break the flow of optimal experience that brings that rhyme word, metaphor, or linguistic play just in time.

Trickster knows charisma is just one of his poses. Sometimes he's *Compère Lapin*, Br'er Rabbit, cowering and pleading not to be thrown into that briar patch (while the audience knows well who's in charge). Where malignant charisma's grandiosity destroys community, healthy charisma alchemically transforms the audience/crowd into what the Puritans would call a community of saints. Embracing her pride, the charismatic improviser invites us to embrace our own charisma and, by following the flow, to join the community the improviser is forming. Following the improviser's metaphoric and poetic leaps baptizes us into the community of improvisers.

That charisma's braggadocio has a Shadow side need not infect the appropriate pride—the rejoicing in being alive—that charisma embodies and expresses. We must appreciate charisma on its own terms, as one pose or posture among many that we assume in the pageantry of life. *All the world's a stage...* Appropriate pride, inviting an interactive, call-and-response process, creates what Toni Morrison calls "an indelible hand of agency"—restoring what was stolen by enslavement. Through that shared sense of agency, call and response creates a flourishing community. The Shadow side of braggadocio's malignant narcissism at best creates a cult leader surrounded by followers who invest their aggrieved alienation in the cult and are willing to die—or murder or commit insurrection—for their charismatic leader. Hard to acknowledge but impossible to deny, Trump's charisma promises agency to his followers, an agency of which they feel long deprived.

As Jung knew, everything solid casts a shadow. Charisma's dark side, alas for the Republic, is a measure of its power to constellate community.

CHAPTER EIGHT

Norm Breaking and Vigilantism: The Dark Side of Intuition and Instinct

Life in the present moment. Having no purpose. That is what improvisation proposes as the solution to our existential ills. Improv models and instills the heroism of being vigilant, just watching. Improv primes us to expect the best from such vigilance. But sometimes vigilance slides over into vigilantism—extrajudicial justice—norm breaking at its most dark and extreme.

In *The Death and Life of Great American Cities* (1961), urbanist Jane Jacobs anticipated the Chaos Science that Benoît Mandelbrot with others would soon develop. She celebrated the "organized complexity" of the city streets of the pre-grid Greenwich Village, rhapsodizing over "the daily ballet of Hudson Street"—her home. The virtue of this "ballet" is that it has spent no time practicing at the *barre*. No, the ballet of Jacobs's Village is improvised.

According to Jacobs, conventional modern city planning blunders by offering top-down, planned solutions. Urbanists mistake the "organized complexity" of cities as "problems of simplicity" and "problems of disorganized complexity," which need, they argue, only a healthy dose of their rationality to rectify. The Radiant City of the French architect Le Corbusier gets rid of all that irrationality with high density, rectilinear glass towers and adjacent parks. Louis Mumford's urbanist vision, *The Culture of Cities* (1938), is for Jacobs largely "a morbid and biased catalog of ills." His "Decentrist" solution, the

Le Corbusier's Ville Radieuse, 1933

Garden City, was enabled by President Eisenhower's interstates and by Jacobs's nemesis Robert Moses's parkways. The solutions of Le Corbusier, Mumford, and Moses were all top-down approaches. Their systems would solve all those urban problems, top down, and bring about a modern utopia. *Trust us.* Jacobs offered instead an ironic mash-up of Le Corbusier and the Decentrist: "The Radiant Garden City Beautiful." She satirized the couched-as-rational rage for urban renewal (polite for "slum clearance") as motivated less by reason than by a rage for racial purity. In Robert Moses's hands, the urbanists did much to decimate the city and impoverish the lives of its marginalized—mostly its people of color. She put her trust elsewhere.

Chaos Science would soon discover how a "strange attractor" could spontaneously order chaos or turbulence. For Jacobs, what made the chaos of New York City not only livable but full of vitality was simple: "eyes on the streets." That is, given enough density, urban streets promised enough observers to keep streets safe, bottom up. No visible hand devised that density. It was improvised by the invisible hand of the marketplace, driven by desire and the longing to flourish. The lack of eyes on the streets and parks that surrounded the Corbusian high rises and the pedestrian-free suburban tract developments illustrated their deep human failures. The strange attractor that lay behind "eyes on the street" is trust. The trust that emerged on high-density streets is unthinkable if you conceive the city as "a morbid and biased catalog of ills." Without trust, how does community emerge? The streets and sidewalks may be a chaos of unplanned events, moment by moment. A horror to the rationalist. But with a modicum of trust, order emerges, life flourishes. Jacobs's "eyes on the street" became Dan Biederman's "eyes on the park" concept in Bryant Park's renewal (1988-92). Biederman lowered the park so people could see into it. Trust reduced crime in the park by almost 100%. Biederman had been vigilant.

In 1807, the New York State Legislature—less trusting—appointed a commission to provide for the orderly development of Manhattan between 14th Street—above Jacobs's beloved Greenwich village—and Washington Heights. The 1811 Commissioners' Plan instituted the grid loved today by developers and hated from the beginning by naturalists like Frederick Law Olmsted, who designed many of the America's most beautiful parks, and urbanists as diverse as Mumford and his opponent Jacobs.

EIGHT: *Norm Breaking and Vigilantism*

The grid's most colorful opponent, surely, is Timothy "Speed" Levitch, a fast-talking former tour guide for New York's Grey Line bus tours. Levitch was once described as "a psycho-geographer for the unloved, the unseen." In Bennett Miller's 1998 documentary, *The Cruise,* Levitch sets "anti-cruising," or what he thinks of as "commuter consciousness," against his vision of improvisational city living: "cruising."

This contrast comes to a climax in the film during Levitch's walk from 34th street toward 23rd street, deep in the grid. Levitch notices a homeless person's bedding on the street and recalls a conversation he had with a "fastidious" woman, clearly an anti-cruiser, about the grid. "Everyone," she insisted, "likes the grid plan." You can almost hear Robert Moses behind her yelling at Jacobs in the late 1950s during a public hearing on the Washington Square controversy: "There is nobody against this—NOBODY, NOBODY, NOBODY but a bunch of, a bunch of MOTHERS!" Moses's sexism rivaled his racism.

To Levitch, "the grid plan is puritan, it's homogenizing, in a city where there is no homogenization available, there is only total existence, total cacophony, a total flowing of human ethnicities and tribes and beings and gradations of awareness and consciousness and cruising." Levitch tells us that the fastidious woman's remark, "everyone likes the grid," seems not to include "whoever that is under the white comforter, cuddled up on 34th and Broadway." Nor, he notes, does it include Levitch himself. Levitch waxes visionary as he imagines that the homeless person is "probably much more on my plane of thinking, ... which is, let's just blow up the grid plan and rewrite the streets to be much more a self-portraiture of our personal struggles, rather than some real estate broker's wet dream from 1807."

Hardly a solution to appeal to urbanists, Levitch's impulse to chaos—a vigilante's fantasy—deserves a hearing. Or at least his voice should be noted. Improvisation would have it so. The first step surely is to recognize that the counter-impulse, to control and to rational order, is deeply inscribed in urbanist methodologies as well as in the urban planning philosophies that have done so much to decimate New York Black communities as did the Cross Bronx Expressway (1948–61). Urban planning shapes the "powerful and corrosive elitism" that Stanley Fish points to in the anti-rhetorical stance. Urban planners with their Cold Cognition predict a rosy future that usually have the ear of the planning boards. The technologies that make building possible—AutoCAD, AI—speak so loudly they threaten to drown out every objection, obscure every alternative. Coldly objective, such technologies ignore the lived lives, mere noise that greatest-good-for-the-greatest-number urban planning decimates. Nonetheless, "the still, sad music of humanity"—like the voices of New York City's homeless—continue to demand a hearing. What's an urbanist visionary burning with Hot Cognition to do?

Let's put a pin in the phenomenon that makes Jane Jacobs's beloved Greenwich Village safe: "eyes on the street." For Jacobs, it is urban density that creates this spontaneous self-protection. Informed by experience, instinct, and intuition, the butcher on the corner knows who belongs, whose kids those are, and who doesn't belong. Wary eyes bring spontaneous, effortless safety.

But "eyes on the street" is at least cognate with a phenomenon that haunts improvisationland: vigilantes, literally "watchmen." Benign for Jacobs, "eyes on the street" nonetheless have a dark side that will emerge to our delight in the Marvel Comic Universe and to our horror on January 6 when tens of thousands believed they were following a higher law. Historically, vigilance committees kept informal rough order on the U.S. frontier or in other places where official authority was imperfect. For Jacobs

> the brains behind the eyes on the street, an almost unconscious assumption of general street support when the chips are down—when a citizen has to choose, for instance, whether he will take responsibility, or abdicate it, in combating barbarism or protecting strangers. There is a short word for this assumption of support: trust. The trust of a city street is formed over time from many, many little public sidewalk contacts.

Trust may be a short word. But the slippery slope from Jacobs's vigilance to vigilantism can be both short and quick. Improv's commitment to disrupting norms—and laws—can grease the skids. Trusting in someone's gut that knows better than many brains can lead to insurrection.

Let's be clear. Jacobs's norm-breaking civil disobedience never rose to the level of vigilantism. Jacobs did face inflated charges for organizing the fight against Moses's Washington Square plan: inciting a riot, criminal mischief, and obstructing public administration. These charges were surely driven by Moses's strongman, power broker hand. After months of trial the charges were reduced to disorderly conduct. Washington Park was saved.

Jacob's disorderly conduct anticipated the unrest of the 1960s at the heart of which lay Mario Savio's call during the Berkeley Free Speech Movement to resist the machine:

> There is a time when the operation of the machine becomes so odious, makes you so sick at heart, that you can't take part! You can't even passively take part! And you've got to put your bodies upon the gears and upon the wheels…upon the levers, upon all the apparatus, and you've got to make it stop! And you've got to indicate to the people who run it, to the people who own it, that unless you're free, the machine will be prevented from working at all!

Since Thoreau, it would be difficult to find a more cogent and sympathetic call to civil disobedience. And yet, soon the Weather Underground will blow up a building on a quiet street in Jacob's beloved Greenwich Village. Vigilance, alas, stands on a slippery slope.

Significantly, vigilantism—improvised, extra-judicial justice—is the soft moral underbelly of cop shows. Spend enough screen time with charismatic cops and soon you sympathize with the corners they cut, each one quietly nibbling at our constitutional rights and freedoms. "Copaganda" it's called, a portmanteau of "cop" and "propaganda." You understand their need to get around the chief detective's protocols. Using unconscious body English you help them pick those locks.

If improv in many ways dominates contemporary culture, according to *The Hollywood Reporter* in 2020, "Crime shows outnumber every other drama subgenre (family dramas, medical shows and the like) on the broadcast nets, and have for some time, and they're among the most-watched series on TV." How to explain this dominance? Violent crime, according to Pew Research Center, has been steadily declining since the 1990s. But Americans are afraid because violent crime saturates daily print and broadcast news: "If it bleeds, it leads." And *Fox News*? *Fuggedaboutit!* The Fourth Estate's promotion of violence comes out of the same toolkit that fine-tunes your Facebook algorithm. Fear and rage ratchet up engagement. Eyeballs reap advertising dollars. (We'll get to social media's exploitation of fear and rage in Chapter 10). We're afraid for our lives and need compensatory narratives that show violent crimes being solved, one way or another.

Vigilantism is a solution that sometimes rises to the level of problem. The Marvel Cinematic Universe is rife with vigilantism. Spiderman, favorite of the MCU, coaxes us with his ready quips to forget he seeks to avenge his beloved Uncle Ben. Ben's death at the hands of a petty criminal—whom Spider-Man had the chance to apprehend but chose not to—incites almost all versions of Spider-Man's origin story. Few of the bad guys Spidey nails get their day in court. The MCU has far worse: Daredevil, Hawkeye, Punisher, Luke Cage. For what does all this extra-judicial justice compensate?

Amazon Prime's series *The Boys* (2019-20) interrogates the MCU's vigilantism directly. The Boys, a group of hardcore vigilantes, set out to take down corrupt superheroes—the Supes—who, vigilantes themselves in the pay of a corrupt corporation, abuse their superpowers.

There's nothing soft about the vigilantism that broke out on January 6, 2021, spurred on by our improvising president whose super costume could sport a big orange "V." I'd bet many of the Oath Keepers and Proud Boys had DC or Marvel subscriptions in their teens. Videos of their march on the Capitol show men and women clearly awash in their self-righteous charisma, charged with the "high confidence" that Daniel Kahneman warns us does not correlate with accuracy. Despite the mask of spontaneous moral outrage, they followed pre-arranged orders from somewhere above. How far above is the question. As congressional sleuths and Jack Smith, Special Counsel for Trump Inquiries, slowly ferret out justice for that nation-shaking disruption, we continue to stream police procedurals that promise that it's okay to cut corners to nail the bad guy. Many regret the attention to protocols that slowed the January 6 inquiry to a crawl, while Trump ignores every congressional and judicial demand at lightning speed. We long for justice, for a narrative that makes sense. We're willing to consider extra-judicial justice even if it doesn't fit the American narrative, equal justice for all.

Private eyes, cop shows, and superheroes all interrogate the normative, routine, procedural world that leaves us longing for something freer, something new. They also interrogate the problems that longing may lead to.

EIGHT: *Norm Breaking and Vigilantism*

Sleuths and Super-Sleuths

Police procedurals do not have the form of improvised discourse. And yet their structure pits Cold Cognition against Hot, a planner against an improviser.

Perhaps it is no surprise that E.A. Poe not only invented detective fiction, but set the pattern of conflict between sleuth and super-sleuth that is the heart of such narratives. In his time, metropolises were a new thing and police forces were too. Like today, people worried about the rise of violent crime. The Parisian metropolitan police force was among the first. It was led by Eugène-François Vidocq, the father of modern criminology, who inspired not only stories by Poe but also by Victor Hugo and Honoré de Balzac. Vidocq was a criminal turned criminalist, the start of a detective fiction trope, that there is a thin line between cops and criminals. Which means both that there are a lot of dirty cops, and that it takes one to catch one. Ignoring proper procedure, Poe's super-sleuths will be a little bit dirty, a little bit out of place.

We can think of the sleuth, an archaic word cognate with sloth, as the slow, plodding detective who pours over the crime scene with Sherlock Holmes's magnifying glass. All that science-based evidence didn't exist before the scientific revolution. Bacon's inductive method and the Enlightenment he inspired made possible Arthur Conan Doyle's "deductive" method—Doyle's misnomer. In *A Study in Scarlet,* the first appearance of Sherlock Holmes and Dr. Watson, we read what constitutes detective fiction's Enlightenment manifesto:

> I then walked slowly down the garden path, which happened to be composed of a clay soil, peculiarly suitable for taking impressions. No doubt it appeared to you to be a mere trampled line of slush, but to my trained eyes every mark upon its surface had a meaning. There is no branch of detective science which is so important and so much neglected as the art of tracing footsteps. Happily, I have always laid great stress upon it, and much practice has made it second nature to me.

If that moment of "detective science" is the alpha of macho sleuthing, its omega might be the moment in *Chinatown* (1974) when director Roman Polanski himself steps forward. Polanski plays a punk working for the criminals Jake Gittes (Jack Nicholson) pursues. So diminutive Gittes calls him

Jack Nicholson in *Chinatown*, 1974
(Photo 12/Alamy Stock Photo)

"midget," Polanski places a switchblade to Nicholson's nose and comments on his detective work,

> You're a very nosy fellow, kitty cat. Huh? You know what happens to nosy fellows? Huh? No? Wanna guess? Huh? No? Okay. They lose their noses.

At which point the punk slices Gittes's nostril. Sleuthing can be rough on noses.

Chinatown is a masterpiece of self-reflexive detective fiction, as much a commentary on the genre as it is an embodiment of its tropes and figures: the fast-talking charismatic super-sleuth, the ditzy dame, the cynical villain. One trope casts the super-sleuth as a bloodhound who follows wherever his nose leads: Sherlock Holmes sometimes tracks using his bloodhound, Toby. The slicing of Gittes's nose is meant to mark the end of his macho detective persona, and, generically, the end of heroic sleuthing. Or should have: *CSI: Crime Scene Investigation* and its forensic-lab kin will have a long future.

His nose bandaged for much of the movie, super-sleuth Gittes nonetheless persists in ignoring not only diminutive punks but also standard protocols. The original crime behind the complicated plot is rape and incest, which produced Evelyn Mulwray's daughter/sister Katherine. Power-mad, her father, Noah Cross, wants possession of Northwest Valley's water rights

EIGHT: *Norm Breaking and Vigilantism*

to develop his property in Los Angeles. He also wants possession of his daughter/granddaughter Katherine. Gittes slaps Evelyn Mulwray to get these dark truths about Katherine to emerge, breaking protocol, to say the least:

Jack Nicholson in *Chinatown*, 1974
(Moviestore Collection Ltd./Alamy Stock Photo)

> "She's my daughter."
> SLAP
> "She's my sister."
> SLAP
> "She's my daughter."
> SLAP
> "She's my sister AND my daughter…"

With Gittes's help, Mulwray later tries to escape with Katherine from their Chinatown hideout to Mexico. Confronted by her father on her way to her car, she wounds him. The police know SOP is to protect the powerful. A police volley guns Mulwray down. Cross takes possession of his daughter/granddaughter. The film's sleuth, Lieutenant Escobar (Perry Lopez), famously explains to Gittes: *"Forget it, Jake, it's Chinatown."* Hot Cognition is not always a match for the dark forces of moneyed power.

Poe's Super-Sleuth

Begun in 1841, Poe set the world's first detective series in Paris. Poe's detective stories follow this pattern: an anomalous event—some crime outside the normal range of experience—takes place. The methods and protocols of the Prefect of Police prove ineffective. The super-sleuth is called in. Clues—anomalous data—emerge, each a call either to forensic science or to intuition. How will Poe's detective, Chevalier C. Auguste Dupin, follow the trail to determine what happened, with Hot Cognition or with Cold?

Remembering Poe's "Philosophy of Composition"—where Poe crows that his famous poem "The Raven" was premeditated from start to finish—and primed by Conan Doyle's tributes to Poe as "a model for all time," many would reply that Dupin's method is emphatically rational: cold reason. (Cue Francis Bacon, proudly polishing his nails). Poe's heir Sherlock Holmes, master of footprints and much else, heir to the Enlightenment, declares himself free of emotion ("I am a brain, Watson"). Much of the British tradition of sleuthing, and much of the *CSI: Crime Scene Investigation* police procedurals that dominate the small screen, depend on coldly scientific methods: fingerprinting, autopsy, CCTV, computer wizardry, chemistry, DNA sampling—the works. Scientific methods and forensic technicians in their lab coats take up much of police procedurals' airtime and the audience's attention, assuaging our fears. The chief detective who oversees the detective assigned the case insists that strict protocols and procedures, all the routines of due process, must be followed: negotiating the legal system, putting the criminal in jail, and making the audience feel safe from violent crime.

But another narrative arc shadows all that Cold Cognition. The super-sleuth always passes through doorways she should not. Her pocket always contains the criminal's tool of choice, the lock-pick. Like Hermes and his Trickster brethren, super-sleuths know how to get through aporia that cold reason cannot.

In Poe's hands, from the beginning, the detective novel is about reason's limits. It's about life on the margins, the extremes. It's about life—the detective's—experienced as pure presence, one moment, one clue at a time. It is improv. If we were left uncertain whether Poe meant it without irony when he said that "The Raven" was premeditated down to the last jot-and-tittle, what is certain is that the tension between the rational and the intuitive is the systole and diastole constantly beating in Poe's narratives, both in his grotesques like "The Tell-Tale Heart" and in his detective fiction.

Chevalier C. Auguste Dupin's method is adamantly anti-rational and anti-system—improvisation's *bêtes noires*. Dupin's archaic title "Chevalier" introduces another trope that will dominate hard-boiled detective fiction. Dupin is a "knight" from a long-lost feudal system that has collapsed, a knight-errant who has no king and hence no legal system to direct his idealistic pursuit of justice. The knight errant, having internalized the system's now foundationless ethical code, is a force for good—usually. Such knights-errant people the hard-boiled detective fiction of Dashiell Hammett (Sam Spade and his nameless predecessor, the Continental Op), Raymond

EIGHT: *Norm Breaking and Vigilantism*

Chandler (Philip Marlowe), and in Japan the great samurai/*ronin* films of Kurosawa (like *Seven Samurai* and the Hammett-inspired *Yojimbo*). Hard-boiled knights-errant have free-wheeling hearts of gold, sometimes.

Poe's narrator (the model for Doyle's pedestrian Watson) describes Dupin's "Bi-Part Soul," and amused himself, "with the fancy of a double Dupin—the creative and the resolvent." Here "resolvent" is a term drawn from mathematics, denoting a function introduced to reach a solution. It is Dupin's rational, but not his only, side. "Creative" and "resolvent" are Hot and Cold Cognition, intuition and rationality.

Toshiro Mifune wears his sword on his shoulder and his big heart on his sleeve
(Allstar Picture Library Ltd./Alamy Stock Photo)

In "The Purloined Letter," a letter from the queen's lover has been stolen from her boudoir by the unscrupulous Minister D—. The Minister saw the letter and switched it for another. He has since been blackmailing the queen. The Minister hid the queen's letter in plain sight where the methodical police are sure not to look.

Poe launches his attack on rational system from the get-go. His epigraph, translated from Latin, reads, "Nothing is more hateful to wisdom than excessive cunning." "Cunning" here is not the *metic* intelligence that intrigued the Greeks but instead denotes systematic rationality. In Poe, "cunning" is the forensic rationality of the official police force that Dupin will surpass by means of his truly *metic* cunning.

The police, seeking the stolen letter, are frustrated. The Prefect explains: "'We divided its entire surface into compartments, which we numbered, so that none might be missed; then we scrutinized each individual square inch throughout the premises, including the two houses immediately adjoining, with the microscope, as before.'" Dupin satirizes their efforts: "The measures adopted were not only the best of their kind, but carried out to absolute perfection." Chaos scientist Benoît Mandelbrot would be pleased at Poe's satire of measurement. The Prefect's sleuths did their job well, they just chose the wrong tools.

Their hyperrational method lacks Dupin's intuition and empathy, "an identification," Poe writes, "of the reasoner's intellect with that of his opponent." Dupin's explanation of how he achieves empathy seems to employ what twenty-first-century neuroscientists will call embodied emotion and mirror neurons. It's a game he played at with his school chums:

> "When I wish to find out how wise, or how stupid, or how good, or how wicked is any one, or what are his thoughts at the moment, I fashion the expression of my face, as accurately as possible, in accordance with the expression of his, and then wait to see what thoughts or sentiments arise in my mind or heart, as if to match or correspond with the expression."

Christian Keysers at the Netherlands Institute for Neuroscience uses fMRI and transcranial magnetic stimulation (TMS) on subjects as they witness others' actions. He states, "Very rapidly, we got this unifying notion that when you witness the states of others you replicate these states in yourself as if you were in their shoes, which is why we call these activities 'vicarious states.'"

Dupin's vicarious empathy puts him in Minister D—'s shoes. It's how the super-sleuth, in the words of thriller novelist Lee Child, "sees things five seconds before the rest of the world." Child's hero Jack Reacher, a former Army Military Police (MP) major explains: "Years and years, I hunted deserters and AWOLs. You train yourself to think like them, and you usually find them." How? By being totally in the moment. By using the supercomputer of embodied emotions that intuition taps. Reacher is an improviser who unites Hot and Cold Cognition. But he breaks protocol—and bodies—all over the place, vigilante-style.

What's at stake in the Dupin stories is more than an intuitive super-sleuth outshining the plodding, methodical police. Showing himself as able a mathematician as he was a poet at Jefferson's just-founded University of Virginia, Poe then trained for a short time as an engineer at West Point. As a

EIGHT: *Norm Breaking and Vigilantism*

journalist he followed closely the debates about the creation of the universe and pre-Darwinian debates about evolution. D. H. Lawrence considered Poe "almost more a scientist than a poet."

William Blake, *The Ancient of Days*,
from *Europe a Prophecy*, copy K, 1794
Fitzwilliam Museum, Cambridge University

Just as Emerson had charged poets to stop imitating European culture to create an *American* literature, American scientists were doing their best to rival continental science. If Bacon, Galileo, and Kepler helped launch the paradigm shift that became the Enlightenment, it was the task of the nineteenth century to work out the details. Doing so, the first half of the nineteenth century became, according to Thomas Kuhn, "the second scientific revolution." What made it revolutionary were advances in precise methods of quantification and measurement. William Blake, archenemy of the Enlightenment, saw the problem coming, challenging the calipers that would measure reality anew. "On an unprecedented scale," Poe's biographer John Tresch writes, "science was on the march, gathering up facts and placing them within a stable, all-embracing picture of the world."

As Tresch sums up, "The promise of the Enlightenment—to use observation, experiment, and reason to place the world within a uniform grid of quantification and classification—seemed to be coming true." Taylorism, the careful measurement of every movement on the assembly-line floor to push workers to their limits, lay in the future.

Whitman, too, had doubts about the best ways to advance science:

> When I heard the learn'd astronomer,
> When the proofs, the figures, were ranged in columns before me,
> When I was shown the charts and diagrams, to add, divide,
>   and measure them,

> When I sitting heard the astronomer where he lectured with
> much applause in the lecture-room,
> How soon unaccountable I became tired and sick,
> Till rising and gliding out I wander'd off by myself,
> In the mystical moist night-air, and from time to time,
> Look'd up in perfect silence at the stars.

Poe's police, like Whitman's "learn'd astronomer," are masters of measuring within a Cartesian grid. Dupin represents Poe's newer science which pushes back against mere induction and deduction.

Poe's objection to this second revolution was the same that improvisation has long registered, the overreliance on system. *Eureka*, Poe's difficult and visionary scientific manifesto expresses his ultimate pushback.

Eureka's Challenge to the Measurers

Eureka (1848) is a nonfiction work Poe sometimes called "An Essay on the Material and Spiritual Universe." Adapted from a lecture he had presented at the Society Library in New York in the same year, *Eureka* describes Poe's intuitive conception of the universe. Poe offers little scientific data to support his conclusions. It was, as his subtitle announced, "A Prose Poem."

Poe begins with a bang, a letter from 2848—a thousand years in the future—retrieved "corked in a bottle and floating on the *Mare Tenebrarum*" (the Sea of Darkness). In this letter, a future philosopher-scientist expresses bemusement at the nineteenth century when scientists believed there were only two possible roads to truth, the inductive and deductive, the "Aristotelian and Baconian." You can begin with axioms, self-evident truths, and then sleuth out facts to support them; or you can begin with evidence and sleuth your way to the truth. For the letter writer, this is a laughing matter because by 2848 everyone knows "the progress of

EIGHT: *Norm Breaking and Vigilantism*

true Science...makes its most important advances...by seemingly intuitive leaps"—what in our day David Perkins of Harvard's Project Zero will call "breakthrough thinking." Hot Cognition.

Most laughable for Poe is the idea of axioms, self-evident truths that scientists seek to build Truth upon. By 2848, it is "the now well understood fact that no truths are self-evident." There is always a subjective element in what we know. "The simple truth is," the philosopher-scientist from 2048 reports, "that the Aristotelians erected their castles upon a basis far less reliable than air; for no such things as axioms ever existed or can possibly exist at all."

One of Poe's targets for this nonsense of axioms is John Stuart Mill's utilitarianism. Mill's posthumous *Autobiography* (1873) is twenty-five years in the future. There Mill will explain how Wordsworth's intuitive nature poetry saved him from the depression Benthamism led him into. But writing in 1848, Poe sees Mill as an unreconstructed utilitarian. Poe satirizes Mill's utilitarian axiom that, "'Contradictions cannot *both* be true—that is, cannot cöexist in nature.' Here Mr. Mill means, for instance—and I give the most forcible instance conceivable—that a tree must be either a tree or *not* a tree." Which leaves little room for metaphor or for myth. Nor, for that matter, does it leave room for Michael Pollan's experience under the influence of psilocybin when for a moment two trees were his aging parents. Sometimes trees are trees and not trees. When we allow trees not to be trees, meaning emerges, life grows richer.

Unsupported by scientific evidence, Poe offers *Eureka* as a species of poetry meant for "dreamers and those who put faith in dreams." For "the Soul...loves nothing so well as to soar in those regions of illimitable intuition which are utterly incognizant of '*path*.'" The wandering improviser makes his own path. Intuition is achieved though empathy by imitating, the narrator writes, "the *only* true thinkers...the generally-educated men of ardent imagination...The Keplers, I repeat, speculate—theorize—and their theories are merely corrected—reduced—sifted—cleared, little by little, of their chaff of inconsistency—until at length there stands apparent an unencumbered *Consistency*...an absolute and an unquestionable *Truth*."

Using intuition, Poe depicts a "universe," writes Tresch, "beginning with a single particle and exploding outward in a rapid flash...spookily reminiscent of the 'big bang' theory advanced in the twentieth century—the mathematically grounded cosmogony that took into account the constraints of relativity." Poe can imagine a macrocosmic big bang and big collapse because in his own microcosmic way he's personally experienced them both. For Poe, who faced great successes and great failures, expansion and contraction, hope and despair, are the human condition. Intuitions emerge from such embodied experience. Tresch concludes:

> Instead of a dead machine, this cosmos was alive with thought and passion, known through leaps of intuition and sympathy. It would never be fully tamed by analysis, tables, or grids; at best it might be followed and extended along routes suggested by nature itself. Though shot through with the aesthetics of design, it offered no naive return to Edenic harmony. Poe affirmed disorder and destruction at the core of existence, and the fragile enmeshment of human ideas and actions with the world.

For Poe, mere data collection and measurement is not science. It is Cold Cognition used in the service of utility and bent on profit. It is, in the words of the Jungian Murray Stein, the Enlightenment's "legacy of facticity without meaning." The result is the rapidly expanding Industrial Revolution, which uses force to treat its workers as things. As in the poet William Blake, such Urizenic reason, promising utopia, can have but one result, which Poe describes in *The Colloquy of Monos and Una*: "Huge smoking cities arose, innumerable. Green leaves shrank before the hot breath of furnaces. The fair face of Nature was deformed as with the ravages of some loathsome disease."

Utilitarian rationality is the "loathsome disease" the nineteenth century suffers from.

Dupin's Dark Empathy

Understanding *Eureka*'s commitment to intuition and empathy underscores what's at stake in the Dupin stories. Just as *Eureka* builds its vision on intuitive empathy, so, too, does Dupin his super-sleuthing. Poe shows himself a thorough-going Romantic, committed to the imagination. But, no surprise, there is in Poe's Romanticism an acknowledgment of the imagination's dark side. In Leslie Jamison's "The Empathy Exams" we hear that, "empathy is always perched precariously between gift and invasion." Just as the world

EIGHT: *Norm Breaking and Vigilantism*

is our doppelgänger—"the fragile enmeshment of human ideas and actions with the world"—so, too, Poe's heroes and villains double one another. Our doppelgängers are sometimes gifts and sometimes invasions.

In the big reveal of "The Purloined Letter" we learn that Dupin and Minister D— share a dark history. "D—," Dupin reports, "at Vienna once, did me an evil turn, which I told him, quite good-humoredly, that I should remember." His revenge in "The Purloined Letter," nabbing D—, is his dish best eaten cold. So, while Dupin first presents empathy as morally neutral—a schoolboy's pastime—it becomes clear that darker emotions factor into the insights empathy produces. Dupin's intuition is not a neutral tool but a weapon used in service of revenge.

The names hint at another, darker possibility, that the letter's thief, Minister D—, anticipating Arthur Conan Doyle's Moriarty, is one of Poe's tales' many doppelgängers. Not only double himself—"bi-part"—Dupin has an outward double. Empathy is no more neutral a perceptual tool than is normative science's rules and measures. Cold Cognition depends on light to take its measurements. But it is by embracing our dark side, the "disorder and destruction at the core of existence," that intuitive empathy finds its way through the aporia we face, the lonely gap between Nature and our humanity. So much for Dupin's heart of gold.

Let's remember, the goal of such intuitive science is a reconciliation of Einstein's unfaithful servant and sacred gift, reason and intuition. Poe finds that marriage in the history of science, in "the *only* true thinkers...the generally-educated men of ardent imagination" like Kepler who "discovered his laws in part through a dream," writes Tresch, "followed by intuitive and imaginative leaps."

Such dreamers peopled the nineteenth century's "second scientific revolution" too. Though it lay years after his death, Poe would have appreciated the "unencumbered Consistency" that got sifted from the chaff as scientists searched to explain how the elements, gases and metals, related. First sketched in the eighteenth century, the Periodic Table of Elements took shape in the mid-nineteenth century, initially ordered according to whether the elements were metals or gases. The work of many hands, the modern table finally was formulated by Dimitri Mendeleev. A man of his time, Mendeleev wrote of the need for system: "The edifice of science requires not only material, but also a plan, and necessitates the work of preparing the materials, putting them together, working out the plans and symmetrical proportions of the various parts." His Cold Cognition was stumped.

Mendeleev's breakthrough in 1869 came to him in a dream. After three days of nonstop effort to organize the elements, missing a train, Mendeleev fell asleep: "I saw in a dream, a table, where all the elements fell into place as required. Awakening, I immediately wrote it down on a piece of paper." Mendeleev combined metals and gases in a single framework according to atomic weight (how many protons and electrons each element measurably had). Measurement met intuition. Mastery and mystery combined to create an image that reflected the order of the universe. The image had oracular force: it predicted which elements would and wouldn't react to one another. It predicted the properties of elements not yet known to science (e.g., germanium, gallium, and scandium). It corrected measurements. Prior to Mendeleev's work, uranium was supposed to have atomic weight of 120. Mendeleev realized that it did not fit in his periodic table and doubled its atomic weight 240 (close to the modern value of 238). Intuition had prophetic power.

Improvisation primes us to trust our instincts and intuitions, but much work has been done in recent years on the many evolution-based cognitive biases that corrupt our instinctive or intuitive choices. The problem with intuition and instinct—like Reason itself—is that their mask of neutrality is hollow. Behind the mask sometimes lies narcissism. Funny how Trump's gut, which knows more than many brains, so often chooses self-aggrandizing options that seek to destroy his opponents. Vigilantism, after all, shares with Trump's malignant narcissism the right to abrogate other citizen's rights and civil norms. The two—vigilantism and narcissism—merged on January 6, both charged with aggrieved trauma narratives.

CHAPTER NINE

Hamilton as Signifying Trickster: America's Experiment in Exceptionalism

Jeffersonion [*sic*] Democracy...

Twenty or so years ago, the late Julia Reed, contributing editor at *Vanity Fair* and *Garden and Gun,* was having a party at her home in New Orleans's Garden District. Julia, who wrote books about Southern grace in entertaining, was famous for her parties. The glitter- and literati were sure to be in attendance. I wasn't going to miss it.

I didn't share Julia's politics, which leaned right, but I shared her love of Southern entertaining. I headed straight for the dining room where, instead of the generous spread of exquisite finger foods I expected, Julia's sublime gesture was an heirloom silver punch bowl mounded with Crabmeat Maison, a cornucopia that was repeatedly refilled—gallons and gallons of lump blue crabmeat in homemade mayonnaise with minced scallions and capers to be spooned on thin slices of New Orleans French bread. I elbowed my way in.

When I took a break from this ambrosia, I turned to find on the near wall this painting by Mississippian Bill Dunlap. I knew Julia's father had founded the Mississippi Republican Party. Primed with that background, I responded to the sight of Monticello at the base of which four Treeing Walker Coonhounds ate watermelon. The caption I took to read, "Jeffersonian Democracy." I was shocked by what looked both

William Dunlap
Jeffersonion Democracy: A Work in Progress, 2005

racist and anti-democratic. This was no way to treat the ideological hero, for Southerners, of the American Revolution. I left the party, Crabmeat Maison be damned.

What I missed was the irony that suffused the painting. Closer inspection revealed, for example, the proper title: "Jeffersonion." Dunlop had painted in a small blue "A." Was Jeffersonian Democracy an onion, not so sweet to bite into as those watermelons the hunting dogs feasted on? I've gotten to know the artist and was pleased to find him the ironic portraitist Jefferson deserves. His title reads in full, *Jeffersonion Democracy: A Work in Progress*. "Democracy," I later noticed, seems to be fading to black. Was that the progress Jefferson envisioned for his vaunted democracy? Would shedding the blood of patriots and tyrants—draining the swamp—refresh the tree of liberty or plant seeds of demagoguery?

A few years later, Lin-Manuel Miranda's *Hamilton* schooled me in how well-deserved Dunlap's ironies were. I had to let go of my schoolboy crush on The Sage of Monticello.

Hamilton as Improvisation

Hamilton an improvisation? Yes, this Broadway blockbuster borrows from hip-hop the impression of spontaneity at lightning speed. Based on Ron Chernow's 2004 biography, *Hamilton* casts non-white actors as the Founding Fathers of the United States as they improvise the birth of a nation. Miranda described *Hamilton* as about "America then, told by America now." It is the story of a revolution waged against the metropole's norms by an incorrigible, unstoppable, charismatic Trickster. It explores improv's central themes: the challenge to authority and decorum; the tension between Reason and Unreason; and the embrace of instinct and the appetites.

Like other improvisations, *Hamilton* is about charisma. Different kinds of charisma compete in the birthing of an exceptional, that is, charismatic nation. Portraits of Hamilton and Washington offer mostly positive examples of charisma. Burr and Jefferson offer versions of charisma gone wrong. Hamilton's credit plan—a key plot point and crucial to the union's creation—relies, as we shall see, on a kind of charisma, as does the American experiment, its "errand into the wilderness." A play about revolution, *Hamilton*

NINE: *Hamilton as Signifying Trickster*

means to inspire another. It proposes to refresh the tree of liberty not with Jefferson's vigilante threats of bloodletting of patriots and tyrants, but with the power of verbal and dramatic signifying.

The gesture of improvising signifies on the high status a culture gives to careful, premeditated composition. That gesture has always depended at least in part not on the *fact* of composing in the moment but, rather, on creating the *impression* of improvisation: its rhetoric of spontaneity. Obviously, a major Broadway play with millions of dollars at stake leaves little room for the impromptu. What the performers recite may be rote, and yet hip-hop's common self-characterization as "spitting verses" suggests the indecorous texture and feel of what we witness on the stage. Some editors, for example, exclude *The Hymn to Hermes* from *The Homeric Hymns* because of its "impiety" and indecorousness. Jazz, to offer a more familiar example, emerged from music said to be "ragged." Early jazz took apart popular songs—like the woof and warp of a rag—and put back together in syncopated fashion: ragtime.

In first drawing the central conflict, the play itself associates "spitting verses" with Hamilton and his friends' rush to revolution, not with cautious Burr. Asked by Hamilton's friend Laurens to "Give us a verse, drop some knowledge," Burr demurs: "Good luck with that: You're takin' a stand. You spit. I'm 'a sit. We'll see where we land." The revolution imminent, Hamilton drives the point home: "If you stand for nothing, Burr, what'll you fall for?" Hamilton's impetuous commitment to revolution contrasts again and again with Burr's temporizing. Hamilton leaps; Burr waits for his main chance.

While improvisation presents itself as unlike anything you've ever seen or heard before—pure innovation—*Hamilton,* like the hip-hop it is derived from, samples from hip-hop and musical theatre. *Hamilton*'s extensive use of sampling might challenge Goldilocks's narrow definitions of improvisation. Sampling is the reuse of a portion (or sample) of a sound recording—its rhythm, melody, or lyrics. Hip-hop itself emerged from sampling "breaks"—the intense drum solos an MC would rap over to maximize intensity on the dance floor. Rather than insist on his play's radical innovation, Miranda's marginal notes in the published *Hamilton* libretto shout out again and again to his "rap gods"—Miranda's term—and to musical theatre greats. Tinkered from these many samples, the production had to pay royalties for each sample. Biggie Smalls's "Ten Crack Commandments" lends its shape to "Ten Duel Commandments"—to offer only one example. A full page of these samples in 8-point type is acknowledged in the book of the libretto, each "used by permission." The formal and figurative allusions form an inextricable part of the meaning. They underscore that something just like this *has* been heard before. Fighting a duel in Weehawken is like slinging crack on a street corner. Somebody eventually is going to throw his life away.

Improvisation's rhetorical insistence on pure innovation is at most a bold front, a pose, part of improv's bravado and charisma. Improvisation knows that beneath that pose it builds on the detritus of its precursors. It samples and signifies no less than The Great Tradition of English poetry does, each poem of which is a weave of allusions, a collage of shout-outs. Wordsworth's *The Prelude* is a swerve from *Paradise Lost,* which calls and responds to Dante, who takes off from Virgil, who passes it forward from Homer—each claiming to improvise, inspired by their version of the muse. Harold Bloom explained this as the anxiety of influence—an aspiring author's Oedipal, psychological struggle to overcome the influence of her literary antecedents. For Bloom there are no original poems: every new composition builds upon a misreading or misinterpretation of its precursor. But Bloom's "swerves" can also be explained as improvisation's need to challenge those whose too-systematic and hence incomplete ways of knowing the world need challenging. Miranda's marginalia in the published libretto gives the impression that, in his eyes, hip-hop and American musical theatre need take no back seat to T.S. Eliot's Great Tradition or Bloom's Western Canon.

Hamilton inevitably presents itself as having roots in a special kind of hip-hop known as freestyle in which the artists "spit verses" totally impromptu as prompts are thrown their way. In 2004, Miranda and Anthony Veneziale created *Freestyle Love Supreme* (*FLS*) where performers rap and beatbox, backed by keyboards. As in Johnstone's Theatresports games, *FLS* audience prompts are picked out of a bucket or shouted from the audience—*oysters!*—to inspire the largely impromptu theatre evening. Using the same game formats nightly—What Y'all Know, On the Fence, True, Foundations of Freestyle, Pet Peeves, Home, Second Chance, Deep

NINE: *Hamilton as Signifying Trickster*

Dive—provides a rule-bound counterpoint. In one game, "Day in a Life," an audience member is brought on stage to recount her day. After returning her to her seat, the players with sympathy and humor then rap and dance her day—just moments after hearing her account without conferring, just *Yes, and*-ing...along. Humbly started in the Drama Book Shop basement on West 39th Street with audiences in the low two digits, *FLS* in 2022 filled Broadway's Booth Theatre with audiences of nearly 800.

As Miranda remarks in the documentary about *FLS*, *We Are Freestyle Love Supreme*, "I'm a dork when it comes to rhyme." He is long-studied in rhyming dictionaries and the hip-hop catalogue. *Hamilton* audiences may not know about *FLS*, but Miranda's street cred as hip-hop artist able to improvise spontaneously was part of the play's promotion. *Hamilton*'s performers may recite Miranda's well-studied and long-composed libretto, but that halo of street cred informs our experience of *Hamilton* as improv.

In the *We Are Freestyle Love Supreme* documentary, Miranda speaks of the high adrenaline spitting rhymes in the moment induces:

> Our stomach doesn't know that we're good at this. It goes, what the fuck are you doing, there's no script. Your reptile brain understands that we're going into an adrenalized unsafe situation. You can't tell your stomach, hey we've done this a million times, something will happen and it will be fine.

As Daniel Levin Becker points out, "the point of rap...is the pleasure of finding words that aren't just transparently informative but challenging to use, surprising to hear, satisfying to say." That pleasure—the sound of surprise—is shared by artist and audience alike.

Just as *Hair* had done using rock and roll, in adopting the ethos of rap, *Hamilton* challenged the musical theatre tradition. *Hamilton* challenges American history as it is traditionally taught—Hamilton biographer Ron Chernow calls it "American history for grown-ups."

Hamilton even became a challenge to how Broadway does business. Though unquestionably Miranda's composition, *Hamilton* was co-created by many hands over the course of many years. The performers had such an extensive role in shaping the libretto and staging that twenty-two original cast members challenged the producers and Miranda to acknowledge their contribution:

> There was undeniable genius on the pages we were given at the start. And once this well-chosen assemble of artists was assembled, we all witnessed something *else* too: there was a collective emotional intelligence at work almost immediately. There was a collective genius in the *approach* to the material. That is what we brought, that is why we were chosen.

Miranda's improvisation created community. Winning a slice of the financial pie—1% of the net profits and 0.33 percent of profits from future U.S. road productions—those original cast members reshaped how Broadway will function. Most of the signees have now left the show but will continue to profit from their collaboration.

Challenging tradition and re-engineering culture is improvisation's way forward.

Embodied Cognition in *Hamilton*'s Hip-Hop

Samuel Taylor Coleridge famously explained the pleasure we get from imagined stories (like his "Rime of the Ancient Mariner") through "the willing suspension of disbelief for the moment which constitutes poetic faith." Neuroscientists now explain poetic faith through a brain function called simulation.

Studying *How Emotions Are Made,* neuroscientist Lisa Feldman Barrett walks us through the many bodily functions involved with biting into an apple: the motor neurons that fire for us to seize it; the sensory neurons that experience the taste, crispness, sweetness, and smell; the neurons that fire in order to make your mouth water to begin digestion, etc. Her point is that just the word or image "apple" has much the same effect. "Simulation," she notes "happens as quickly and automatically as a heartbeat." Barrett adds,

> Simulations are your brain's guesses of what's happening in the world. In every waking moment, you're faced with ambiguous, noisy information from your eyes, ears, nose, and other sensory organs. Your brain uses your past experiences to construct a hypothesis—the simulation—and compares it to the cacophony arriving from your senses. In this manner, simulation lets your brain impose meaning on the noise, selecting what's relevant and ignoring the rest.

Through such simulation *Hamilton*'s audience completes the play's impression of improvisation. The impression is hammered into us by the speed with which the verses are delivered. Daveed Diggs as Lafayette set the musical's Bonneville Salt Flats speed record. An online site ScreenRant reports,

> Diggs raps at 6.3 words per second during the quickest verse of *Hamilton* Act 1 performance of "Guns and Ships." For context, Eminem holds a Guinness World Record for rhyming the most words (1,560) in a hit single ("Rap God"). In that particular 2013 song, the man known as Slim Shady averages 4.28 words per second over six-plus minutes.

Miranda's marginal notes to "Guns and Ships" point to Diggs's speed:

> Doesn't hurt that Daveed is one of the most technically gifted rappers I've ever met, so I knew I could build him tapestries. It was actually his idea to rap this "resilience/brilliance" rap in a triplet rhythm, which is perfect.

The singers may not be improvising, but following the rapid flow of the narrative and trying to catch their often impossible-to-anticipate rhymes—resilience/brilliance—makes us improvisers. We leap with them to stay up, sometimes jolted by metaphors anachronistically slammed together from different epochs, Revolutionary and contemporary.

What drives us as we watch imitations of improvisation is the echo of ordinary experience. Barrett's neuroscience points to our need to escape the inescapably "ambiguous, noisy information" of every moment. We need to impose meaning on the noise. We need to determine what the right next step is, the step we are meant to take that shapes the best, right future. Improvisers, ever the audience's avatar, enact this dangerous, decisive moment. Jazz historian Stanley Crouch captures the texture of the challenge the improviser faces:

> What the improvising artist did was something different: he experienced time at the tempo of emergency, when the consciousness understood that in order to survive—as in an accident, or when facing the threat of death—your perception had to be sharp enough to recognize every significant detail and put it to use.

Trauma—the threat of death, real or metaphoric—is improv's springboard. The improvising artist experiences time at the tempo of emergency because she is hyperalert, ever determined not to be again surprised. How American history turned out is more or less in the history books. How this "American history for grown-ups" will turn out in "every significant detail" is not.

Spitting verses "at the tempo of emergency" requires not worrying where the next verse and rhyme will come from. It takes supreme confidence. From the rapper's point of view, spitting verses requires Csikszentmihalyi's flow state or neuroscience's Hot Cognition. Functional MRIs (fMRIs) confirm that improvisation, like psychedelics, opens the reducing valve that ego constricts, allowing interconnectivity between brain regions. To find the next rhyme and to advance the story one must be open to all the possible connections (rhyme words and narrative connections) drawn from different regions of the brain, memories drawn from different experiential arenas. Miranda's marginalia point to Lafayette's "weird" use of the word "Ingenuitive":

> I don't know where I've heard it. You should have seen the looks on the faces of my collaborators when I brought the song in. It's apparently a superarchaic word. I really don't know where I met it, but it was there for me when I needed it.

Sure enough, it's in the *O.E.D.* Maybe Miranda took a microdose of psilocybin that day. A state of charismatic confidence is crucial, a state that puts concern for the ego to sleep.

Much of hip-hop is built out of the kind of charisma that insists that the present speaker is the best, richest, and baddest. *Watch out while I create disturbances in your minds.* But one paradox of hip-hop's charismatic bravado and much of its enduring charm is that while its content is all about how special the hip-hop artist is, the mental process or self-state is ego-free. In the documentary about *FLS*, Utkarsh Ambudkar (known as UTK the INC), points to how different *FLS* is from the ethos of hip-hop. While as a hip-hop MC his job "was to talk about how good I was... it's not what we do here. It's much more interesting if you can rap about the Incredible Hulk or a box of Wheat Thins... with the same amount of dexterity as you rap about yourself."

Deactivating the Default Mode Network (DMN) control centers that support the ego allows "unfiltered, unconscious, or random thoughts and sensations to emerge." An fMRI of improvisers in the act of improvising if recorded would probably look more like the brain on psilocybin than on the placebo:

NINE: *Hamilton as Signifying Trickster*

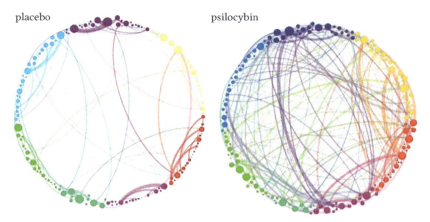

We the audience also share in this opened reducing valve. The rap battle over Hamilton's plan for national credit demands that the audience leap back and forth from what we know about eighteenth-century American history, to pharmaceuticals, to human anatomy, to macroeconomics:

> If we assume the debts, the Union gets a new line of credit,
>   a financial diuretic.
> How do you not get it? If we're aggressive and competitive
> The Union gets a boost. You'd rather give it a sedative?

Like all improvisations, *Hamilton* keeps us on our toes. Much of the almost universal euphoric response to the play stems from the liminal state the play induces. If the performers seem to be on fire, so are we. Theatresports inventor Keith Johnstone argues that "the improviser has to understand that his first skill lies in releasing his partner's imagination." *Hamilton* adds that the improviser's ultimate skill and goal must be to release the audience's imagination. Doing so creates community, a commitment that *Hamilton*'s marketing team made in a small way, giving away four free tickets daily on the *Hamilton Lottery* app. Good seats could cost four figures.

Long before he envisioned the Broadway musical, in 2009 Miranda expressed this commitment to audience in first introducing the *Hamilton Mixtape* at the White House. Miranda explained at an "Evening of Poetry, Music and The Spoken Word" that he had been asked to do a piece from his hit Broadway hip-hop musical *In the Heights*. Instead, he announced, "I'm actually working on a hip-hop album—a concept album—about the life of someone who embodies hip-hop, Treasury Secretary Alexander Hamilton.

You laugh. But it's true," he continued, describing Hamilton's rise from penniless and illegitimate birth on St. Croix, "And in all the strength of his writing. I think he embodies the words' ability to make a difference." *Hamilton* is about the persuasive power of art, and of politics.

Relentless...

Speed and impulsiveness are not only qualities of Hamilton's lyrics but also themes the play explores. The blur of Hamilton's bearing is an itch Burr can't stop scratching: "Hamilton's pace is relentless, he wastes no time." Meanwhile, Burr, is "willing to wait for it." Hamilton's nonstop accomplishments are direct expressions of his authentic self. He is the orphaned immigrant seeking to create a world he can fit into, rewriting his trauma narrative, embracing his agency. Hamilton works for the joy of it. Burr has purpose. He wants power, presidential or imperial (as his efforts to conquer Mexico make clear). Burr adopts Trickster's nonchalant persona. "Talk less, smile more," he advises his rival, as he waits for the opportune moment to strike. Burr, a master of contingency, never taking a stand until it suits his purposes, beats Hamilton in the duel at his own game of mastering the present moment.

Hamilton's commitment not to "throw away my shot" is a running refrain throughout the play. It refers first to the young and ambitious Hamilton's shot at glory:

> I am not throwing away my shot
> Hey, yo, I'm just like my country
> I'm young, scrappy and hungry
> And I'm not throwing away my shot.

But it also foreshadows his fateful duel with Burr when Hamilton is beaten because, un-Trickster-like, he takes the moral high ground. In an attempt to abort the conflict, Hamilton perhaps decorously *delopes* (French for "throwing away"), the practice of deliberately wasting one's first shot in a pistol duel.

Before the duel, ever determined, Hamilton is not only lightning in a bottle, he also inspires lightning behavior. At a glance, his future wife Eliza is "helpless." Her sister Angelica articulates in "The Schuyler Sisters" that what she is looking for is a "mind at work." In the ironically titled "Satisfied," she makes clear she has found him. She sees immediately that she and Hamilton share Trickster's key quality that, ever hungry, they "never will be satisfied." In a thunderbolt equal to her sister's, Angelica sees at a glance that they are an almost perfect match:

> So this is what it feels like to match wits
> With someone at your level!...
> I wanna take him far away from this place,
> Then I turn and see my sister's face.

All that powerful desire, but she must defer to her sister and to her "station" in the family because she realizes in an instant "three fundamental truths": her father has no sons; she's the oldest daughter; and Hamilton is penniless. Following family protocol and Cold Cognition, Angelica *delopes*, much to her lifelong sorrow.

It's Angelica's quick mind (Hot Cognition) and her empathy for her sister that lead her to the worst mistake of her life: to accept Cold Cognition's demands of family and societal norms. Reason and unreason, desire and duty, freedom and necessity, unruly and according to rule: the central tensions of improvisation, here perceived with immediacy, are delivered at lightning speed.

Hamilton's Challenge to Reason

Hamilton is also the story of improvising a nation. The American Constitution has long been understood as a rationalist, Enlightenment Document. But— *Yes, and...*—*Hamilton* explores how Reason must be challenged to accommodate what are thought to be lesser faculties and ignoble desires—instincts like hunger and selfishness. Without such embodied grounding, Reason is doomed to hollow and largely rhetorical—here meaning not only persuasive but also empty—idealism which Jefferson gives voice to. Like Burr, Jefferson is purposeful. He has Monticello and Sally Hemmings to protect by means of his false flag of idealism.

We the People? responds the cast, men and women both, all people of color and immigrants or descendants of immigrants, and then adds: does that include us this time? Or as Angelica signifies on the Preamble's "self-evident" truth, "That all men are created equal":

> And when I meet Thomas Jefferson...
> I'm 'a compel him to include women in the sequel!

Hamilton himself is the improviser *par excellence*. Born out of wedlock and orphaned, Hamilton wrote his way from the furthest margins of the metropole to the center of a new metropole largely of his invention. The list of his innovations that determined the contours of American government challenges credulity. Conceiving and supervising the *Federalist Papers* to sell the Constitution with its emphasis on a federal union of the states, he wrote 51 of its 85 essays. In six months. In this he is, like Hermes, the hermeneut interpreting the Constitution to the nation it gives birth to. He created the Coast Guard, outfitted the first American Navy (down to the color of their buttons, says Chernow), founded The Federal Reserve and New York Bank. Knowing full well as the first Treasury Secretary that his every action created precedent, Hamilton created many of the unwritten norms under which government has been, until recently, conducted.

Hamilton's innovations helped the young nation catch up with Britain's head start in the Industrial Revolution. Miranda's play lays out with incredible verve and economy Hamilton's achievements, a legacy largely forgotten, effaced by Jeffersonian rhetoric and his early death. But improvisations are never pure celebrations. There's always a rub that gets improvisers started. The musical celebrates Hamilton's achievements in founding the new nation and signifies upon how that foundation failed in ways still with us.

Hamilton's diverse cast celebrates America's founding with a level of virtuosity that white voices rarely rival. The play asks the cast to do so with a generosity to our founders that the founders did not return: three-fifths human unless you were a woman, in which case you didn't count at all. The play's generosity to the Founding Fathers—many of them slave-owning—has been challenged by no less-imposing voices than those of Ishmael Reed and Toni Morrison, who funded Reed's play, *The Haunting of Lin-Manuel Miranda*. Although the play emphasizes Hamilton's friendship with abolitionist John Laurens, Hamilton himself, for example, was involved in another friend's sale of a slave. His in-laws, maybe even his wife, owned slaves. For Reed, Hamilton's founding membership in the Manumission Society is all show. Many objected to the play's idealized portrait of Hamilton.

But while some of the play's generosity is unwarranted, the dominant metanarrative of our nation's birth is *Hamilton*'s still worthy target. *Hamilton*'s signifying subtext points to the many hypocrisies of American

NINE: *Hamilton as Signifying Trickster*

history as it is told. Yes, the Founding Fathers were heroic (and flawed). It is also true that how American history is taught is even more imperfect. That is the call and response at the heart of *Hamilton*'s signifying. Understanding the flaws can help us understand those we still live with. According to *Hamilton*, the roots of white supremacy and states' rights can be found in the founding. This is news to few American historians. But it might be news to most high school seniors and much of *Hamilton*'s Disney+ audience, which was large: 2.86 million televisions, not counting phones and tablets, in its first twelve days, from July 3 to July 14.

Ishmael Reed, Miranda's antagonist and author of the brilliant novel *Mumbo Jumbo*, a narrative meditation on the role of signifying in the Jazz Age, needs no lessons in Black culture's "trope of tropes." Miranda humbly acknowledged his play's faults of omission, tweeting the day after the Disney+ launch that "[a]ll the criticisms are valid. The sheer tonnage of complexities & failings of these people I couldn't get. Or wrestled with but cut. I took 6 years and fit as much as I could in a 2.5 hour musical. Did my best. It's all fair game." Nonetheless, Miranda's *Hamilton* deserves the wide audience it garnered.

Hamilton and the Credit System behind the Ten Dollar Bill

Alexander Hamilton is recognized widely as the creator of the American commercial system—largely improvised and now the global model. His first crisis as Secretary of Treasury in Washington's first cabinet was to establish a credit system that was a bit of a confidence game. He wanted the federal government to assume the war debts states incurred when they sold bonds to fight the revolution. To Southerners this meant the North, who held most of the unpaid debt, would benefit unequally. Southerners charged Hamilton with seeking personal gain.

Hamilton did have an ulterior motive, but it was not personal gain. He knew the federal assumption of credit would increase the states' commitment to the union. "Credit is an entire thing," Hamilton argued. "Every part of it has the nicest sympathy with every other part. Wound one limb and the whole tree shrinks and decays." A connector like fellow Trickster Hermes, Hamilton sought to build a well-knit national community.

Ever polytropic, one of the domains Trickster oversees is commerce—conducted traditionally at the crossroads, also her domain. She always carries a purse filled with coins. In the world of commerce, Trickster favors no one: she is the patron of both seller and buyer, of both merchant and thief. Ever the connector, what she favors is exchange. The merchant sells at a profit; the buyer buys at a price she feels is good. In a successful exchange both buyer and seller come away believing they got the better of the bargain. Traditional gift economies, rather than monetary gain, rely on intangible rewards, like a sense of community, honor, or prestige. In market economies, which replaced gift economies, both buyer and seller have cheated and been cheated. Gift exchange nourishes community. Just as Trickster is committed to commerce—flow—she is committed equally to union: community. The challenge commerce faces is how to nurture both competition *and* community. Buyer and seller both seek to flourish and do so to some extent at the expense of their commercial rival. What both share is hunger. As patron of perhaps the hungriest of us all—thieves—Trickster advocates Marx's adage that "all property is theft." She embraces even those outside the pale. Theft, too, nourishes circulation.

Alexander Hamilton has not one but two rivals and his differences with both turn upon the issue of hunger. Hamilton is insistently defined by hunger. Always in a hurry, he will "never be satisfied." In "Enough," his wife challenges him to be satisfied:

> Look at where you are
> Look at where you started
> The fact that you're alive is a miracle
> Just stay alive, that would be enough.

The paradox—or outright contradiction—of Hamilton is that his incredible output reflects a mind working bicamerally, Hot and Cold Cognition working together. He lives focused totally on the present moment and totally on the future. Where for example Jefferson's nativist and anti-immigrant vision privileges those born in the colonies, Hamilton, for Jeremy McCarter, had far-ranging vision,

> It took an immigrant to fully understand the new nation, and to declare a fundamental hope of the American experiment: Under wise government, these diverse men and women "will be constantly

NINE: *Hamilton as Signifying Trickster*

assimilating, till they embrace each other, and assume the same complexion."

For conservative columnist David Brooks, Miranda's portraits of Hamilton and Burr present the audience this quandary, "Are you the operator or the crusader? Every single person walks out of the theater thinking about Hamilton and saying, 'I want to have *that* kind of ambition.'" Even Gore Vidal's novel *Burr*, which takes a remarkably friendly view of its eponymous hero's schemes, finds room to call him "a monster," "a labyrinth," "the slyest trickster of our time," and a man who "makes even a trip to the barber seem like a plot to overthrow the state."

Burr thinks he can control his hunger, he can "wait for it." Burr's Trickster mask is not close-fitting like Hamilton's. He's ultimately not Trickster but her close cousin, the con man. Hungry with ambition fed by his entitled station as the distinguished descendent of Jonathan Edwards, brimstone leader of the Great Awakening, Burr will watch with Reason's eye for the opportune moment. He brags to Angelica, "I'm a trust fund, baby, you can trust me!" Asked by Hamilton how he got through Princeton in two years, Burr neglects to explain that his father was president of the college (as had been his grandfather Edwards). With such a table set, Burr can wait because he can control his hunger. Which invites the question, is he truly hungry? There is a difference between hunger that comes from ambition, and hunger that comes from privation. Hamilton, who knew abject poverty, points to their dissimilarity again and again. He can't understand how Burr can be in love and not seize the moment, as he would.

> I will never understand you.
> If you love this woman, go get her! What are you waiting for?

The idealistic demagoguery of Hamilton's second rival, Jefferson, denies hunger while personally indulging it on every Epicurean front. His wine cellar, largely acquired in France, is legendary. His love life caused a scandal during his presidency, which DNA evidence has since confirmed. More to the point, writing in response to Jefferson's attacks, Hamilton warns:

> There is always "a first time" when characters studious of artful disguises are unveiled. When the vizor of stoicism is plucked from the brow of the Epicurean; when the plain garb of Quaker simplicity is stripped from the concealed voluptuary; when Caesar *coyly refusing*

the proffered diadem is seen to be Caesar rejecting the trappings, but tenaciously gripping the substance of imperial domination.

Slavery may be a problem, according to Jefferson, like having "a wolf by the ears," a situation under control until you let go. In Chernow's and in Miranda's hands, Jefferson is far from the great, idealistic hero Americans, Southerners especially, are used to. Miranda's Jefferson is, according to theatre critic Chris Jones, "an improviser of expedient sensibility." Which is to say he always has his eyes out for the main chance. He is a populist who, anticipating Trump, builds his demagoguery on hollow idealism, on lies, the main object of which is to maintain power and his source of wealth—chattel slavery. Jefferson and Trump both build their "idealism" on a platform of white supremacy.

Miranda brilliantly stages Washington's first cabinet meeting as a rap battle between Jefferson and Hamilton. Jefferson boasts that the South has paid its war debt "Because we plant seeds in the South. We create." Hamilton responds:

> Your debts are paid cuz you don't pay for labor.
> "We plant seeds in the South. We create." Yeah, keep ranting.
> We know who's really doing the planting.

Miranda in the published libretto's marginalia remarks on this bit of signifying on Jefferson, "I cannot tell you how cathartic it is to get to express this to Jefferson every night. The audience's reaction is similarly cathartic." It goes to the heart of Dunlap's "Jeffersonion Democracy."

Hamilton's metaphor for assuming the debt is also telling. Giving the Union a new line of credit would be "a diuretic": it would stimulate flow. (As usual Trickster indecorously embraces lower bodily functions, here, pissing). Trickster is ever amoral—not immoral—because, however greedy, she is never out purely for personal gain. Hermes steals Apollo's cattle to create the rituals of sacrifice. He is hungry for food but hungrier for godhead, to live on Olympus. Creating the rituals of sacrifice creates circulation between humankind and the gods that help both flourish. Trickster's highest purpose is circulation for its own sake, trusting that flow, like tides, will lift all boats. From Hamilton's vantage the goal of commerce is simply commerce and the flourishing community it fosters. With the aid of guardrails that good government can provide, the rest will work itself out. That it is

NINE: *Hamilton as Signifying Trickster*

driven by hunger for riches—or a seat on Olympus—is commerce's engine but not its goal.

Hamilton, in his *First Report on the Public Credit,* persuaded the new nation that its bright future depended, essentially, upon confidence. Based on his study of French and especially British banking, Hamilton knew that the future of American enterprise hung on well-funded, reliable credit. He learned that "Far from weakening [Britain], it had produced manifold benefits. Public credit had enabled England to build up the Royal Navy, to prosecute wars around the world, to maintain a global commercial empire." Hamilton was a seeming con man who put the full faith and credit of the United States in support of his con game. By creating taxes to fund future payouts, he alchemizes credit into no con game at all: leaden credit literally turned to gold. And yet it was achieved by something of a true con game, bartering with Jefferson and Madison in exchange for moving the capital from Philadelphia (or his beloved New York) to the Potomac. The Virginians got a capital nearer home and Hamilton got what was nearest his heart: a credit system that solidified the federal union. To Burr's displeasure, this trickery took place while he was not "in the room where it happened." To the Trickster, true or false, presence is everything.

Confidence is always an aspect of charisma. *They call me the most.* The structure of con games and of financial credit is the same: *Trust me.* Like democracy, the American commercial system is the worst form available except for all the other forms. The others—like hyperrational Marxist-Leninism—are bad because they dampen ambition by denying the role of hunger.

The American commercial system is the better when it abides by its promises, like equality and freedom for all. Stacking the deck against the un-elect, the impoverished and immigrant, the Constitution deploys "inviolable property rights" to support slaveholders' chattel rights rather than the common man's hunger. It builds a fortified wall around its city on a hill. The nation's failure to abide by its promises is the basic text of *Hamilton*'s signifying on the Founding Fathers and on American history.

Because, if Hamilton's credit system helped usher in the modern world, there was a crack in the foundation, just as there was in the Liberty Bell—

and in the Constitution itself. "Inviolable property rights?" "Inalienable rights to life, liberty, and the pursuit of happiness?"

Yeah? the multi-ethnic, immigrant cast, by their very presence, seems to reply. And what about our ancestors? What about slavery? What about red-lining and the lynchings used to appropriate the property owned by the formerly enslaved? What about the promise of the American experiment?

The cast underscored the point in addressing the newly elected Mike Pence attending an early performance. For all its historical inaccuracies, which Reed challenges, restoring Hamilton's achievements to the American narrative seems timely. Yes, greed—reflected now in rampant income inequality—is an unfortunate engine to build a nation on. It needs a governor, something to control it. The governor for greed and corruption is good government. Hamilton had a large role in establishing of the norms of good government. Trump is the avatar of America's loss of faith in those norms. Might being reminded of Hamilton's efforts to champion good government help us return to it? A quixotic but necessary gesture.

Redrawing the American Map—Winthrop's, Reagan's, Obama's, and Miranda's "Exceptionalism"

Charisma is a crucial issue in the question of American exceptionalism. It is a key theme in John Winthrop's address, "A Modell of Christian Charity" (April 1630) to members of the Massachusetts Bay Colony as they sailed toward the New World on the Arbella (sometimes, Arabella). The Puritans were anxious about the "errand into the wilderness" that confronted them. How can a group of outcasts who have a habit of quarreling with authority construct a strong society without fighting amongst themselves?

For Winthrop, given the hierarchical nature of society, "there are two rules whereby we are to walk one towards another: Justice and Mercy." Loving one's enemies and recognizing their shared humanity that supersedes class hierarchies is the only way to successfully establish a Christian society. Love is a charismatic state. Achieving it, they would build "a city on a hill." In his city on a hill, Winthrop planted the seeds of the Declaration of Independence's vision of "all men...created equal, that they are endowed by their Creator with certain inalienable rights to Life, Liberty, and the pursuit of Happiness"—but with a caveat.

NINE: *Hamilton as Signifying Trickster*

Ronald Reagan—whose personal, Hollywood-trained charisma was widely acknowledged—redrew the American conceptual map when he appropriated key tropes from Winthrop's sermon. *Hamilton* signifies upon Reagan's version of American exceptionalism and its continuing legacy. It seeks to set the record straight.

The discrepancy between the aspiration to be exceptional and the hard realities of America in 2015 is what the play *Hamilton* signifies upon. Of course, even 150 years after Winthrop's envisioning, when Jefferson writes the Declaration, our liberty tree is just a sapling. It is, at that, a misshapen sapling since Jefferson's definition of *"all* men" fell short by two-fifths and excluded women. By the time *Hamilton* premieres on Broadway, the liberty tree was in danger—like little George Washington's cherry tree—of being cut down.

Yet, the lie was not in Winthrop's sermon. There the city on a hill trope is a warning, not a boast. Winthrop concludes by alluding to Jesus's *Sermon on the Mount* (Matthew 5). Winthrop warns his congregation that as "a city on a hill" the eyes of the world would be upon their "errand into the wilderness" in the new world. Being a city on a hill, if they failed, they "shall be made a story and a by-word through the world." If they failed in Justice and Mercy toward one another, they would not be exceptional. Rather, what would be exceptional would be the damnation that rained down from God and the world community. In Winthrop's hands, "exceptionalism" is contingent. It is not just warning but a threat.

Reagan's vision of American exceptionalism—marred by trickle-down economics, the defunding of services to the sick and needy, and adventurism abroad—was not known for its Justice and Mercy. For Hamilton as for the Left, Reagan's notion of American exceptionalism is a false flag that the rich and powerful fly to stay rich and powerful, to maintain the hierarchies that Winthrop's charity, while not eliding, does soften.

Reagan boasted that America's city-on-a-hill exceptionalism is not contingent but fully realized, a given. We've arrived, our errand into the wilderness fulfilled. And we've arrived despite forgoing charity. Reagan offers a vision of those who sit atop the hill leaving crumbs to trickle down to those below. Reagan's version of America's specialness, as uncharitable a reading of Winthrop's call to charity as it is possible to conceive, has infected our politics for decades.

President Obama tried again to redraw the conceptual map closer to Winthrop's version when asked during a press conference at a NATO conference in Strasbourg about exceptionalism. Obama answered in personal terms, that "My entire career has been a testimony to American exceptionalism." This returns the city-on-a-hill to a vision of Justice and Mercy, the one he articulated at the Democratic Convention in 2004. That a mixed-race child of an absentee Nigerian immigrant father and a single mother could become the first Black editor of the Harvard Law Review and then to address his party's national convention was at least partial proof of a kind of exceptionalism.

What Obama leaves out is that his achievement was indeed "exceptional": statistically anomalous. Obama's career marks racial progress but it at the same time points to its rarity, to those still left behind. The middle class—and Blacks—continue to lose ground to income inequality. The image of the young five-year-old Jacob Philadelphia's rubbing Obama's hair to see "if my hair is just like yours" intimates that the president's attainments need not be unique, that they represent a sea change for the city on a hill: anyone can belong. But how many people of color and immigrants looked long-

Photo: Pete Souza

ingly up at what they felt was an unjust and unmerciful city on a hill that allowed no place for them?

Miranda's *Hamilton* redraws the conceptual map of America in ways far closer to Obama's than to Reagan's. *Hamilton* says *yes* to American exceptionalism visually even before the multi-ethnic cast sings a word. On opening night August 6, 2015, the status of the stage-full of descendants of enslaved people and immigrants was being challenged by the nativist, anti-immigrant, white supremacist rhetoric of Donald Trump's campaign. The multi-ethnic cast celebrates American exceptionalism but also signifies upon it. *If we're this good, why has there until now been little room for us on Broadway?*

NINE: *Hamilton as Signifying Trickster*

Hamilton's conceptual map of exceptionalism flies the flag not of America's incomparable achievement but rather the flag of America as experiment. Like Winthrop's, it signals aspiration rather than accomplishment, a continual setting off rather than an arrival. Under this flag, Winthrop's "errand in the wilderness" is not about accomplishing a fated mission but emphasizes instead the root of the word. To err is to wander but also to mistake. America's errand may be bold, and it may be charismatically boastful, but it acknowledges that its meaning is contingent upon the journey ahead. That journey is an uncertain experiment—an errand into the wilderness—the continuance of which depends on us, here, now, as we and the Republic are tested every day. There is no unerring Phaeacian steersman at the helm. Improvising doesn't assure good rhymes, metaphors, or ships of state.

Miranda's musical challenges Winthrop and the Constitution: *Yes, all men (and women) are created equal, but what if you really meant it?* The impression of actors "improvising" the Founding Fathers' improvising their national experiment underscores and signifies on their mistakes, invites the audience to acknowledge that the errand into the wilderness has erred and needs correction to achieve its exceptional founding purpose: a charitable, loving society.

Miranda's *Hamilton* presents the American experiment doing what had never been done on a national level, creating a nation-state founded on a written Constitution. This rational document aspires to generate a nation for the first time constituted not by mystery (e.g., the divine right of kings), or by tradition (British Common Law, the basis of its constitution), but by Reason. As Hamilton writes in the first of the *Federalist Papers,* the question is "whether societies of men are really capable or not, of establishing good government from reflection and choice, or whether they are forever destined to depend, for their political constitutions, on accident and force."

But this rational endeavor is also a disruptive improvisation, a challenge to Enlightenment hollow utopianism (notions of the perfectibility of humanity through Reason). What made it so was that, in Hamilton's shaping hands, the experiment acknowledged the role not only of our idealized Rational selves but also of our lesser, embodied selves. For Hamilton, government would never be perfect because the men and women who made it would never be perfect. Though largely estranged from and skeptical of the established religion of his day, Hamilton shares with Winthrop the Calvinist principle of universal depravity (or radical corruption). This fault can be overcome only through God's prevenient grace. For Hamilton and the Founding Fathers, hunger (greed), mankind's original sin, was the source of corruption, a theme that haunted the birth of the nation.

But for all the trouble hunger may bring, for Hamilton hunger is also the engine of progress. A nation without the mercy and justice to allow everyone, with all their flaws, to hunger after and aspire toward betterment of their lot, was no better than the hierarchy-ridden nation they separated from. Hamilton's answer to God's freely given grace, the only possible answer to original sin, is good governance.

Belief in this top-down approach to government got Hamilton labelled a monarchist. But where for Reagan government will be the problem, not the solution, for Hamilton "good government" controls the excessive greed the powerful satisfy at the expense of the less powerful. The line that gets the biggest audience response is delivered by Lafayette and Hamilton: "Immigrants...We get the job done." As Miranda explains, "Why does it get such a delighted response? Because it's true." Immigrants are the hungriest. Chernow recounts a story Jefferson liked to repeat:

> Mr. Adams observed, "Purge that constitution of its corruption...and it would be the most perfect constitution ever devised by the wit of man." Hamilton paused and said, "Purge it of its corruption...and it would become an impracticable government. As it stands at present, with all its supposed defects, it is the most perfect government which ever existed."

"Jefferson," recounts Chernow, "gave this comment a sinister gloss," that Hamilton was a monarchist at heart. "But," Chernow adds, "Hamilton was merely saying that the Crown needed patronage to offset Parliament's power of the purse." Patronage can both guide and limit greed.

Yes, patronage helped balance the power of president and the Congress. But Hamilton meant more than that, something deeper about our humanity and about community. A bit of corruption is that little odor of theft inevitable in commerce. It stems from the hunger that is the engine of commerce. If we don't allow aspirants to the city on a hill to express their hunger, which always has a taint of greed to it, then the city will not prosper. In *Hamilton*,

NINE: *Hamilton as Signifying Trickster*

as in jazz, every voice must be heard, even hunger's, the voice of the dispossessed. At its heart the musical celebrates the fact that only a hungry outsider who is never satisfied could appreciate this critical factor in our political experiment. Only such a cast could express their right to an outsider's hunger to be part of the center.

Hamilton and the Revolution itself celebrate the lower faculties, over which we have less control, in order to enrich Reason and its engine, good governance. But, again, both finally accept the need for control, the simple, rational need for good governance. The rhetoric of spontaneity that revolution depends on can be abused. In the wrong hands the "natural rights of man" can be and was coopted to insist on states' rights—freedom from control of the federalist system. Or worse: tyranny. Hamilton argues in the First Federalist that while "zeal for the firmness and efficiency of government" that he espouses may present a "forbidding appearance," on the other hand "a dangerous ambition more often lurks behind the specious mask of zeal for the rights of the people." He adds (ominously today):

> History will teach us, that [populism] has been found a much more certain road to the introduction of despotism,...and that of those men who have overturned the liberties of republics the greatest number have begun their career, by paying an obsequious court to the people, commencing Demagogues and ending Tyrants.

Glossing Jefferson's hollow states' rights populism, *Hamilton* here points ahead to the Civil War and white supremacy. A new improvisation is needed to answer it.

Community Building

The improviser alchemizes her charismatic bravado to create community. Improvisation's great theme, *carpe vitam*—seize not just the moment but all of life—insists that, by ignoring hierarchies we embrace all of life—not only all of experience but all our fellows. Thinking he could overcome received hierarchies by inspiring charity, *carpe vitam* was John Winthrop's theme in his sermon's final exhortation: "Therefore, let us choose life, that we and our seed may live, by obeying His voice and cleaving to Him, for He is our life and our prosperity." Improvisers create community by giving us the experience of aporias and taking us by the hand as we pass through them.

Winging It

The improviser through charity builds and embraces the widest community possible, free of hierarchies.

In the play, as in American history, no one has a better claim on charisma than George Washington. The moment when Washington drops this pose suggests how deeply this theme of community-building works in *Hamilton*. Serving as Washington's able secretary, Colonel Hamilton has been aching for active command, his only path to satisfy his hunger to advance in society after the war. Such service is one shot he doesn't want to throw away. Faced with the coming battle of Yorktown and urged by Lafayette, Washington, urged by Lafayette, finally gives Hamilton a command. Hamilton swings into high gear, preparing for action, rushing around to prepare for Yorktown.

Meanwhile, seeing Hamilton's enthusiasm, Washington reflects on his first, ignominious command at the Battle of Jumonville Glen where he led hundreds of men into a massacre anyone less callow would have anticipated and avoided. The historian Fred Anderson describes the moment:

> Since boyhood he had dreamed of battle's glory. Now he had seen combat but no heroism: only chaos and the slaughter of defenseless men. Why had it happened? What could he tell his superiors? What would happen next?

George Washington had none of the answers.

It is Washington's overconfidence—call it hollow or blind charisma—that led to their deaths. As Hamilton, unlistening, rushes around, we hear Washington humbly drop his charismatic pose and describe the massacre he led his men straight into:

> Let me tell you what I wish I'd known
> When I was young and dreamed of glory.
> You have no control...
> Who lives, who dies, who tells your story.

In other words, they may call me "the most," as they will you, but behind that pose here is the real deal: you have no control. History may have its eyes on me and on us for our exceptionalism. But don't forget, he warns, as had Winthrop, it will also see our blunders. Improvisers make a virtue out of their lack of control. It leads to sympathy and the charity Winthrop called for. It means you are at the mercy of those in your community who will tell your story.

NINE: *Hamilton as Signifying Trickster*

Hamilton, before Yorktown, also drops his pose, echoing a theme he expressed in the Tavern scene amongst his buddies in "My Shot": "I imagine death so much it feels more like a memory." That he is haunted by an early death helps explain his relentless drive in life and in the play. But he is equally driven by a longing for community, for the men finally in his command, and for his wife Eliza who is expecting. Then, he catches himself and swings into action

> We gotta go, gotta get the job done,
> Gotta start a new nation, gotta meet my son!

Miranda's experience in *FLS* helps explain this sensitivity to community-building. In the documentary *We Are Freestyle Love Supreme*, director Tommy Kail points out that "there's a reason why 'love' is in the middle of the title of the show... It is the middle of what makes the show everything that it is." In a nightly ritual before going on stage, they chant "I got your back" as they pat one another's back—a benign version of the "stack formation" deployed to infiltrate the Capitol on January 6. One of their nightly games is "True" where, whatever prompt is accepted from the audience, each of the members tell a personal story. The fundamental nature of intimacy—that it is about sharing vulnerabilities—is richly on display. The love they articulate is deeply persuasive, moving, and unusual in our culture of toxic masculinity. (The first *FLS* cast was all male.)

Miranda's embrace of community is reflected in his generosity to his musical's arch villain. Burr may be more a con man than a Trickster, but "Dear Theodosia," his lullaby to his infant daughter, sung in a vulnerable, near falsetto, gives him a life outside the archetype, a life of flesh and blood and heart. The tragedy of Hamilton and Burr's inability to form a community is suggested when Hamilton joins his rival on the stage and sings the pendant lullaby to his infant son Philip. What starts as dueling lullabies merges into a duet. They both reveal that they both suffered absent fathers, and that their hopes for their infant nation and their infants are one:

> BURR, HAMILTON: I'll make the world safe and sound for you...
> Will come of age with our young nation.
> We'll bleed and fight for you, we'll make it right for you.

This generosity to Burr is repeated in the last lines Miranda gives him:

> I was too young and blind to see.
> I should've known...
> The world was wide enough for both Hamilton and me.

The world was wide enough. There was room even for these arch rivals to build a community aspiring toward an experiment in exceptionalism.

Youth Poet Laureate Amanda Gorman's inauguration poem, which includes two samples from *Hamilton*, evokes Winthrop's *A Modell of Christian Charity* in her title, "The Hill We Climb." The title makes clear on which side of the city on a hill's ramparts she stands. And yet it is "we" who climb toward

> a nation that isn't broken
> but simply unfinished

For all of us, as for the nation, the journey toward an exceptional, charitable, charismatic community is "unfinished," aspirational. Gorman told Anderson Cooper with elegant simplicity that the poem was "about what it means to be a better country." So is *Hamilton*: not just about the past but also about the future it calls us to make. Improvisation is always about prophecy: about what comes next.

As in many prophetic traditions—biblical or West African—the act of prophecy is half a matter of divine inspiration, and half just a matter of vigilantly inhabiting the present moment intensely enough to see the strands that are likely best to shape the future. The supplicant to the Yoruban prophetic Ifa board chooses subjectively from the sixty-four stories attached to the hexagram cast by the griot. Seeking to call forth America's promise, Lin-Manuel Miranda's *Hamilton*, written before the election, prophesied what was rooted in Jefferson and Jefferson's America: Trump and Trump's America. Prophesied in Dunlap's painting, *Jeffersonion Democracy: A Work in Progress,* the problem was already all around us.

NINE: *Hamilton as Signifying Trickster*

CHAPTER TEN

The Rhetoric of Spontaneity in Your Facebook Feed

> The business model of the internet is arson. You can't make money unless you're setting fires.
> —Jon Stewart

> Steve Job didn't let his children use the iPad.
> —James Williams, Google engineer

When Walter Isaacson finished his book talk at Newman High School, his New Orleans alma mater, about his latest high-profile title, *The Innovators: How a Group of Hackers, Geniuses, and Geeks Created the Digital Revolution,* I was first to grab the mic. "Walter," I asked (our families go back three generations), "you persuasively make the case that the internet was not a top-down enterprise, as many claim, nurtured by government spending and managed by a military-industrial-academic collaboration. Rather, as you argue, it was an emergent, bottom-up affair. As your subtitle has it, it was the creation of hackers, geniuses, and geeks. So, I want to pose this question: how do you reconcile that, when the federal levees broke after Hurricane Katrina, you headed the top-down Louisiana Recovery Authority and yet most of the Newman graduates in this room would agree that New Orleans was rebuilt not from Baton Rouge but rather bottom-up, neighborhood by neighborhood?" I had published a piece on the issue at the time of the 19th anniversary of Katrina.

Walter was gracious. He thought a moment, then said, if memory serves, "yes, that's ironic. I hadn't made that connection." He probably said more but receiving the dopamine hit I sought—Walter Isaacson's approval—had stoppered my ears.

The internet was not only created as a collaborative act of improvisation, as Isaacson argues. Social media are also now a constant improvisational element in our lives: "spontaneous, but scripted; order out of disorder; an unruly routine." The internet's billions of pages put encyclopedic

TEN: *"The Rhetoric of Spontaneity in Your Facebook Feed*

knowledge at our fingertips—both on our desktops and in our pockets. Using algorithms largely spontaneous and autonomous once put in place, the social web—Facebook, Twitter (now X), YouTube, Google, Instagram, Tumblr, Snapchat, and TikTok—has built spontaneous communities of users behaving spontaneously and effecting "a feat of social engineering."

Virginia Heffernan's central contention in *Magic and Loss: The Internet as Art* is "that the Internet is a massive and collaborative work of realist art." My contention is that social media are a massive and collaborative work of improvisation, both top-down and bottom-up.

This improvisation is driven by the same pleasure-bringing dopamine hits I sought from Walter. Much of the content that makes up social media—our posts—seem to be effortless creations of the moment. As improvisers have always done, we write posts doing our best to appear nonchalant. But just as Kerouac edited his kick-written scroll to get it to publication, so, too—*admit it*—we shape or reshape our posts to get more likes. If your last post got more likes by displaying a bit more outrage, well, your next post will embrace ever more outrage. Kerouac revised with the appearance of spontaneity in mind; so, too, your revisions reflect the indecorous norms of social media. Outrage likes a style that smacks of Hot Cognition. Grammatical rules are largely forgotten. Misspellings, internet slang, and acronyms (e.g., LOL) become the norm. *I'm angry, I'm authentic: like me, share me.*

Though claiming to be neutral, social web feeds are driven by algorithms, top-down, re-engineering our now instantaneously global society in ways both good and ill. The social web creates community but also spreads outrage and foments right-wing authoritarianism. The dark side of the social web—driven by hits of dopamine—is one we must understand and learn to deal with.

Until recently I knew only generally what algorithms were: a sequence of step-by-step instructions geared to produce desired results. Nothing new: if some member of the tribe had stumbled on how to make fire (Hot Cognition), afterwards the tribal leaders could offer an algorithm (Cold Cognition). *If you're cold or hungry, then…*

But how "The Algorithm" functioned on Facebook and other social media was a mystery. Friends just a bit more technically adept than I would invoke it to explain away my surprise at my feed's changes. "Oh," I'd hear, "they changed the algorithm." As if that explained anything.

"When we receive a Like," *New York Times* journalist Max Fisher clarifies, looking to neuroscience, "neural activity flares in a part of the brain called the nucleus accumbens: the region that activates dopamine," a neurotransmitter released in the brain that makes you feel good. With no axe to grind and no hand to guide it, just a neutral vessel—so Facebook claims—it doesn't need directly to support Trump or the Oath Keepers. It doesn't overtly need to seek to incite violence and revolution. The Algorithm takes care of all that. If you "friend" someone who "likes" the Oath Keepers, their angry voice will soon find its way to your newsfeed. If you watch a YouTube video about them, researchers in Germany discovered, automatic recommendations push you "toward the more extreme end of whatever network the user was in." Soon you'll be watching conspiracy videos.

The Algorithm is Cold Cognition at its most pure. Based on our past performance, it predicts what will keep us engaged. Paradoxically, what it engages is not *our* Cold Cognition, our reasoned awareness of our true concerns: how to get through the day; how to achieve our life's goals. Rather, it activates our Hot Cognition: our immediate desires, fears, and anger. Conspiracy theories call attention to anomalies, trauma's bread and butter, Hot Cognition's catnip, and point to why we should be outraged. "Ever noticed how the Jews run and own everything?" offers one anti-Semitic trope, "Well take a look at this pamphlet, *The Protocols of the Elders of Zion,*" retooling as a meme a trope from the early twentieth century. Conspiracy theories give meaning to every anomalous detail.

James Williams is a former Google engineer and executive and now an internet defector and professor of tech ethics at Oxford. He explains *how* chasing "likes" supercharges our newsfeeds: "The key element here is the variable reward. When you randomize the reward schedule for a given action, it increases the number of times a person is likely to take that action." Intermittent variable reinforcement: the rule that a dopamine hit will come, but when it will come is randomized, autonomously determined stochastically. Intermittent variable reinforcement is another example of improvisation: spontaneous, but scripted; order out of disorder; an unruly routine. "It's a casino that fits in your pocket," writes Fisher, "which is how we slowly

TEN: *"The Rhetoric of Spontaneity in Your Facebook Feed*

train ourselves to answer any dip in our happiness with a pull at the most ubiquitous slot machine in history." It was B.F. Skinner who discovered that pigeons would stop pecking when they learned that pecking always produced the desired pellets. They pecked more doggedly (*pigeonly?*) if the results were intermittent. Intermittent variable reinforcement is the secret sauce in slot machines, why you come back for another bite of the cherry. Social media executives and engineers were quick to make the connection to and to learn from Las Vegas—a dark version of architect Robert Venturi's postmodern recommendation in *Learning from Las Vegas: The Forgotten Symbolism of Architectural Forms*. We post for pellets, but The Algorithm decides which of our posts to promote and to whom. In that measure, it controls the dopamine we receive. But when they want to, social media can put a heavy finger on the pellet dispenser. *Forbes* reports that "TikTok's Secret 'Heating' Button Can Make Anyone Go Viral."

All that coverage of Trump in 2015 didn't just get him more eyeballs—according to CBS: "Trump was bad for America, but good for CBS"—it got him more true believers. Research shows that repetition can change your politics. Hear something enough times—like the "stolen" 2020 election—and it becomes normalized. Fox News's belief, however ill-founded, becomes MAGAland's gospel. That is, *if* Fox believed: the Dominion legal briefs offered plenty evidence that Tucker Carlson and the gang didn't, that they were motivated by Fox's sliding stock price that depended on, you guessed it, engagement. Fox settled for $787.5 million. Carlson was fired.

An upbeat Facebook corporate site admits to seventy generations of The Algorithm—as they imposingly capitalize it—since first launched in 2007. That's almost seven new algorithms a year. Once in place and aided by AI's mechanical and deep learning, and subject of course to A/B testing as needed, they are autonomous. Offending, hate-filled posts can be sour-cherry-picked only by human clicks. Called "supervised algorithm," certain words trigger oversight by human employees, of which there are never enough to monitor the fire hose of offenses. Major offenses (you know by now whom I mean) are decided by the much-maligned and very Cold Cognition-driven Oversight Board. In short: there is little supervision.

A/B testing is a marketing tool where two or more variants of a page are shown to users at random. Statistical analysis determines which variation performs better, more profitably. If sites don't like the results they get, they do some A/B testing, decide what works best, do some tweaking to the algorithm, and then set it loose again. Just as Kerouac edits his scroll.

Social media's algorithms are fundamentally top-down, written and deployed then tweaked by the sites. And yet, paradoxically, they share improv's use of the rhetoric of spontaneity as a persuasive device. Seeming to seek no purpose other than to grow the customer base and increase engagement, they lay claim to authenticity. They claim to have no axe to grind, no goal but "a more open and connected society." Surely, they are trustworthy. So they claim, as improv,

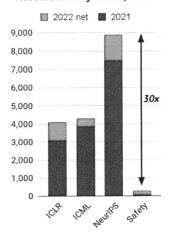

The number of engineers dedicated to safety are dwarfed by all others (from *The AI Dilemma*)

free of overt purpose, has always claimed. They have no political bias to promote. They apply no thumb to the scale. And yet, if Apple was an "innovation company," Mark Zuckerberg would outdo it. He was committed to making a "revolution company." While promising to create community, improv's perennial goal since Hermes improvised the rites of sacrifice, Zuckerberg's real goal was social engineering. *Anyone seeking a plot will be shot.*

When Facebook reached one billion users in 2015, Zuckerberg renewed Facebook's commitment to increasing its client base: "A more open and connected world is a better world. It brings stronger relationships with those you love, a stronger economy with more opportunities, and a stronger society that reflects all of our values." Surely Zuckerberg's big tent filled now with 3 billion voices, close to one-third of the globe, would foster democracy. And yet, is it a coincidence that at the same time the spirit of autocracy and authoritarianism was on the rise? In 2021, Freedom House, using a measure of government accountability, counted 25 countries where democracy increased over the previous year and 60 where it declined.

TEN: *"The Rhetoric of Spontaneity in Your Facebook Feed*

Improvising Memes

Internet memes—not to be confused with GIFs—exemplify the often-benign role of improvisation in generating user content. GIFs (graphics interchange format) are images used to communicate things words can't describe. GIFs are circulated unchanged. Unlike GIFs, memes are meant for clever users to improvise upon, each making it her own. A neologism first defined by the biologist Richard Dawkins as an evolutionary principle to explain the spread of ideas and cultural phenomena, memes are a kind of thought contagion, like how many children one should have (answers first-world culture: *fewer and fewer*; answers the third world: *more and more*). Memes shape social mores, the folkways behind how we act, often without thinking. An "Internet meme" spreads rapidly from person to person via social networks, blogs, direct email, text messages, or news sources, constantly changing along the way. Internet memes shape the mores that social media embody.

"Gangnam Style" is a 2012 dance pop single written and performed by Korean pop singer Park Jae Sung, better known by his stage name PSY. "Gangnam Style" refers to a lifestyle associated with the Gangnam district of Seoul, where people are trendy, hip and exude a certain "class." The song—as meme—celebrates aspirational, "new money" lifestyle. The first YouTube video to reach a billion views, "Gangnam Style" spawned hundreds of parodies across the globe: look past PSY's charm and what you get is trashy misogyny. But I am editorializing.

Not all improvisations on PSY's meme see past his charm. The YouTube channel "Can I Draw You," for example, selects moments in PSY's video and, with an overdubbed, infectious laugh track, offers childlike drawings. It received four million views. While technical expertise lies behind the side-by-side pairing of drawing and original video images, the viewer's pleasure lies not in the video's high production values, but in the drawings' childlike,

imperfect, and playful representation of the original images. "Can I Draw You" pairs its charm with PSY's. Imperfection—*I'm going to slop you up*—is part of the charm.

Nor could it have been high production values that made another twist on "Gangnam Style," "Grumpy Cat," the second-best meme of 2012 (according to the site "Know Your Memes"). "Grumpy Cat" received a million views in two days. "Congrats, PSY" was posted on 4chan's "lolcats channel" (= LOL Cats) when PSY hits surpassed the feline's. Lolcats was inspired by "I can has cheeseburger" that got much of its charm from its misspelling and the clearly  laughable effort to get inside the inscrutable consciousness, or *umwelt*, of cats. Grumpy Cat's grumpy appearance results from an underbite. Tardar Sauce—her real name—became an internet celebrity and is now a brand. You can buy her book *The Grumpy Guide to Life: Observations of Grumpy Cat* at her site which invites you to "Find something terrible to buy." Though she died at seven, her net worth has been estimated at $100 million. The power of social engineering.

Pepe the Frog as Klansman, c. 2015

Launched by Christopher "moot" Poole in October 2003, 4chan, an imageboard site, hosts boards dedicated to a wide variety of topics. The site has been described as a hub of Internet subculture, its community influential in the formation and popularization of prominent Internet memes, from lolcats to Pepe the Frog. Users post anonymously: no registration is required. A prankish, often nefarious, spirit reigns, like convincing West Africans that Ebola doctors worship the disease they are meant to cure. How many deaths did that cause? *The Guardian* summarized the 4chan community as "lunatic, juvenile,...brilliant, ridiculous and alarming." Which is perhaps what they would have reported had

TEN: "The Rhetoric of Spontaneity in Your Facebook Feed"

they been around when Hermes stole Apollo's cattle. It receives 22 million hits a month.

On 4chan, each post must be accompanied by an image. This policy gave a boost to the culture of visual memes. Competition to be the most outrageous reigns. Threads receiving the most replies are "bumped" to the top of their respective board and old threads are deleted as new ones are created. In the quest for dopamine hits, everything drifts toward outrage. Originally an apolitical character invented by Boys' Club, Pepe the Frog's appropriation by the alt right (2015 to 2016) exemplifies how social media, by inviting outrageousness, drives audiences toward the political right. In October 2015, Trump retweeted a Pepe representation of himself, associated with a video called "You Can't Stump the Trump." On Twitter and Instagram, political operative Roger Stone and Donald Trump Jr. parodied the movie *The Expendables* with "The Deplorables," a play on Hillary Clinton's controversial phrase "basket of deplorables." Pepe, sporting Donald's hair, joined members of the Trump family and alt-right heroes.

Soon memes were everywhere. And soon, with Pepe the Frog in tow, the anonymous imageboard 4chan begat 8chan, which begat Anonymous and various other alt-right sites.

Chasing Attention through Sociometry

Social media's bread and butter is the sociometry of its users. Sociometry tracks and measures how people are linked and, in theory, fosters the pleasure of community engagement. The Austrian psychiatrist J.L. Moreno created the science of sociometry in the 1920s. Moreno founded the Theatre of Spontaneity in Vienna and later brought it to New York City. A friend of and influence on the godmother of improv Viola Spolin, on Martin Buber's "I-Thou" relationship, and on the Esalen Institute's group encounters, Moreno

At the entrance to Facebook's Silicon Valley campus

had a profound commitment to spontaneity. His son's biography is titled *Impromptu Man*. Moreno *père* believed that "Spontaneity and creativity are the propelling forces in human progress." Sociometry would inspire "a super dynamic community," his son writes. "New forms of social life that could give meaning to an industrialized and urbanized civilization that seemed intent on alienation and perhaps even self-destruction." A man on a mission to re-engineer society, Moreno, according to his son, wasn't motivated to monetize his improvisational techniques. Nor did he anticipate the "friends" function or the "share" and "like" buttons. Yes, the internet's power is rooted in the origins of modern improvisation.

Mark Zuckerberg first used the term "social graph" in 2007 to refer to the network of members' connections and relationships. The like button was added February 9, 2009. Sociometry was off to the races and was soon winner of the Triple Crown: customer base, profitability, and social media dominance.

A Moreno sociogram

Sean Parker founded Napster and was Facebook's first president at age twenty-four. By 2017 when he spoke to an Axios conference, he was a deserter from the social media cause, an insider turned whistle-blower. Facebook sought to "consume as much of your time and conscious attention as possible" by offering "a social-validation feedback loop...exactly the kind of thing that a hacker like myself would come up with, because you're exploiting a vulnerability in human psychology."

TEN: *"The Rhetoric of Spontaneity in Your Facebook Feed*

"Friends" and "groups" recreated Moreno's sociogram. Now, the "share" and "like" buttons supercharged it, exploiting our psychological vulnerabilities: the social-validation feedback loop and the dopamine hit it provides. Social media were "passive" conduits for society's preexisting problems but jacked up to 11.

The Age of Attention

Passive? Well, not entirely. Social media are aggressive about one thing: our scarce attention. If Claude Shannon founded the Information Age in 1948, the political scientist Herbert Simon aptly renamed it in the 1970s the Age of Attention. When information becomes abundant, attention becomes the scarce resource, the key to "the attention economy." The wealth of information creates a poverty of attention. The challenge becomes how to allocate that attention efficiently.

The internet brings to bear the algorithm's ever-increasing powers of artificial intelligence to grab and hold our attention. Merely chasing attention, social media created a super dynamic community, but hardly dynamic in a way Moreno would have recognized or approved.

Craig Reynolds's artificial life program "Boids" generates complex behavior with a simple, three-line algorithm, as Antonio Damasio's homeostasis algorithm generates flourishing life as we know it with just a single-line algorithm; The three simple Westminster Place Kitchen Rules generate all comedic improv. So too, the algorithms of social media are given but three goals: grow the customer base, increase engagement, and sell advertising. The last is wholly dependent on the first two. Using machine learning, The Algorithm soon learned that the best and quickest way to grow customers and engagement was ginning up moral outrage and fear, those most primitive, adrenalin-fueled of our embodied emotions. For Tim Kendall, Facebook's first director of monetization, the arms race for attention is "a race to the bottom of the brainstem."

The *why* is simple: advertising dollars. Grabbing and keeping our eyeballs—doom scrolling—is how the internet monetizes its wealth of information and all the content we've contributed, which, if unattended, brings no value to the bottom line.

Social media are built not to foster community but to promote their own Big Lie: sales. Sales opens the door wide—with no governors—for greed: surveillance capitalism. Jaron Lanier, one of the founders of virtual reality, argues that "We've created an entire generation of people raised in a context where the very meaning of communication, the very meaning of culture is manipulation. We've put deceit and sneakiness at the absolute center of everything we do." Trickster—Lord of Liars—has been dragooned into a dark role. Deceit—the Lord of Liars—goes straight to the bottom line.

Archimedes claimed that with a lever long enough and a fulcrum on which to place it, he could move the world. Hey Archimedes, how 'bout a feedback loop that serves up ever increasing hits of dopamine? If alt-right factions are advancing on democracies around the globe from Brazil to Germany to the halls of Congress with a frightening consistency, it is not only that globalization, the technocracy, and late capitalism have marginalized them and increased their fear and anger. It is also because dopamine—pleasure, improv's constant goal—is the lever and the "like" button the fulcrum. Trickster, the original cybernaut and global wanderer, ever hungry and horny, and always carrying that coin purse, is in the game.

This dark Trickster charms us not with laughter but with the pleasure of outrage. Williams, the former Google engineer, explains the seductive power of outrage: "it gives us moral clarity and social solidarity. That's great in hunting tribes, but completely counterproductive at a global scale. It turns into public shaming, destroying people for one action… But it's exactly the mob rule that Socrates saw turning democracies into new tyrannies." More exactly, it is a mob led by Dionysus and destroying the hyperrational King Pentheus.

In the voice of Trickster, AI's algorithms point us toward the pleasure of righteous anger. Extremist disinformation pits *us* against *them* to keep us engaged, to radicalize us. The newly radicalized stay engaged and keep the ads and money flowing. Having liked the same angry posts, angry communities gather online and then in the streets. Ironically, with roots in Moreno's friend and the godmother of improv comedy Viola Spolin's efforts to socialize immigrants at Hull House in Chicago, the sociometry behind social media made immigrants their first targets. For Trump was listening to the anger and using social media to gin up anti-immigrant sentiment. Just the ticket, and his presidency was off to the races.

TEN: *"The Rhetoric of Spontaneity in Your Facebook Feed"*

Social Media's Political Problem and the Problem of Loud Voices

If social media are just neutral sources of information—what your pals are thinking and doing today—then it is a public utility and, the argument goes, subject to government control the way other public utilities are. It's what broke up Ma Bell in 1983. Fearing government control, in a clever rabbit-duck reframing, social media turns our eyeballs into voices. Eyeballs—attention/engagement—we all know, is about money, but "voices?" Voices invokes the sacrosanct first amendment. Who is willing to stand against free speech?

Social media invoke the First Amendment and yet, to avoid another political buffet, they claim not to be publishers where free speech is sacrosanct. Section 230 of the Communications Decency Act (1996), written during the infancy of social media, provides immunity—"safe harbor"—for websites with respect to third-party content. According to Section 230, social media are not publishers. But as misinformation on social media mounted, pressure in Congress grew to make social media responsible as publishers would be for law-breaking and hate-filled content.

Monitoring outrageous content doesn't fit the business plan. Social media's autonomous AI algorithms lend power not to the best informed or most persuasive voices, but to the loudest, the most outrageous. The more outrageous a comedic improviser's response to *Yes, and…* is, the better. So too, your last Facebook post. With his bully pulpit, Trump was the loudest of the loud.

It was not the Sophists' loudness or distemper that made Plato and Socrates want to run them out of the Republic. Nor, as Plato claimed, that the rhetoricians won forensic debates without knowing facts. The problem was that having made a study of persuasion, the Sophists were good at it, rivals to Socrates's dialectic. Their hard-won skill garnered more auditors and won more debates.

It is Dionysus—known as "Bromios, the loud-roarer"—who mythically embodies loud voices. Euripides emphasizes the noise of the intoxicated crowd that joins the melee in *The Bacchae*. In our time, the problem of loud voices began as early as the first social network, a messaging site called the WELL ("World Electronic 'Lectronic Link") that Stewart Brand launched in 1985 at *Whole Earth Catalogue*. Called by *Wired* magazine in 1997 "The world's most influential online community," The WELL operated in the utopian, free-wheeling spirit of improvisation wedded to libertarianism, a self-governing anarchist utopia community with almost no rules. In principle, ideas rose or fell on merit. "In reality," Fisher writes, "as cantankerous and combative engineers rushed in, the loudest voices and most popular opinions dominated, but because the WELL's architects represented both, they took this as confirmation that their intellectual meritocracy worked. Forever after, the internet-era architects who'd first gathered on the WELL would treat raw majoritarianism as the natural ideal, building it into every subsequent social network through today." Led by highly trained engineers, how could "raw majoritarianism" go wrong? Hackers, Brand seemed to suggest, would finish what the 1960s started. The revolution won't be televised, but it will be digitized.

This was before Brand learned to distrust utopianism. For Brand, now, system-based utopias are all dystopias. "The utopians say: 'I figured it out, I've got a system. I've got a plan. It's really going to work now. We've just got to get people to understand and appreciate our reasons and then abide by the plan.'" Give up your freedom and we can make it work: Marvel's Ultron would approve. Ultron (James Spader) in Marvel Studio's 2015 *Avengers: Age of Ultron,* is the hyper rational robot programmed by MCU anti-hero Ironman to keep the peace using his supercharged, computer-driven rationality. He decides that humanity itself is the worst threat to the peace and that genocide is the quick solution. Or according to Trump, *only I can fix it.* Why? Because having played the system all his life he knew how to game it. Having been untrustworthy all his life, a lifelong norm breaker, is what makes him trustworthy. All he needs is autocratic power and he'll get the job done. *What could go wrong?*

Democracy is all about the voice of the majority. But it doesn't work when the voice of mob majoritarianism is loud and aggressive and certain that it has a monopoly on truth and the right to drown out minority voices. The quality of your argument and fact-based evidence doesn't get a hearing. Minority voices are lost in the shouting, which The Algorithm pushes along to the like-minded and soon-to-be like-minded.

Though exploiting the techniques of improvisation, social media's creators had drunk the Kool-Aid of their own hyper rationalism. Zuckerberg

TEN: *"The Rhetoric of Spontaneity in Your Facebook Feed*

believed "Facebook could and should…fundamentally rewir[e] the world from the ground up…because [echoing early Brand] it was run by engineers, whose purity of vision would see them through." The New Colonialism, brought to you by Mark "Rhodes" Zuckerberg. *We alone can fix it.*

With all the clarity (and power) of the god Apollo, social media present the paradox of an improvisation machine created by hyper rationalist nerds. One of Peter Thiel's big data projects is Palantir Apollo. "Palantir" references the "seeing-stones" in *Lord of the Rings,* described as indestructible balls of crystal used for communication and to see events in other parts of the world. Nerds and proud of it, just as many comedic improvisers are. In 2015, Stephen Colbert proudly promoted a "nerd-off" with sci-fi director J. J. Abrams. It is perhaps no coincidence that the rise of the internet coincided with Hollywood and independent filmmakers' celebrations of socially awkward slackers who are very good at *Jeopardy!* Social media is the ultimate revenge of the nerds.

While espousing the Sophists' democratic-leaning openness to many voices, social media favor the loud, adrenaline-fueled mobs that embrace autocracy. Silicon Valley is rife with autocratic leanings. Examples are shocking. The archconservative Peter Thiel, cofounder of PayPal and a major venture capitalist, called the value of diversity a "myth" and said that contrarian hackers "with Asperger's-like social ineptitude" made the best startup chiefs. Their neutral vessels aren't biased toward QAnon and conspiracy theorists, or Trump, who together led to January 6. All roads led there, though they were paved not by a political purpose but by simple lines of code that increased engagement. If Zuckerberg imagined Facebook would lead to the next stage of human evolution, he would bootstrap it by tapping our deepest instincts. The "like" button would make it all happen. Elon Musk, an Asperger's-like nerd, restarted Twitter as X and destroyed a vibrant social media community.

Machine Learning: Ridding the World of Spam and Our Good Sense

Charged with increasing engagement, The Algorithm not only uses computer code to execute instructions as regular algorithms do. It is now equipped with the artificial intelligence (AI). AI's machine learning and deep learning improves performance, creating tasks The Algorithms weren't initially programmed for. The Algorithms rewrite themselves, becoming more and more powerful.

Some history: when spam threatened to overwhelm the internet, computer engineers managed to write a program to catch some spam, but not enough. *Deus ex machina,* just in time, machine-learning engineers designed a program, writes Max Fisher, "that would guide its own evolution...It was evolving, and at warp speed, until it produced a variation of itself so sophisticated and powerful that it could do what no human-designed filters could: proactively identify and block almost all spam." In 2016, seeing machine learning's power to chase away spam, YouTube adapted machine learning to its algorithm more efficiently to chase engagement.

In a sense, The Algorithm is one of those black boxes engineers put on schematics to represent elements of the design that haven't been invented yet, and they're not yet sure how it will work. But with this difference: the artificial intelligence in the black box *has* been invented and even refined by machine and deep learning, each more powerful than the last. The adjective "deep" in deep learning refers to its use of multiple layers in the network. In deep learning, we know what goes in—massive amounts of data—and what comes out, just not what's happening inside. As Fisher writes, "There is no way for an overseer to pop the hood on such a spam filter and see how it's working, because they'd be looking at a machine that, over time, was designed by machines, too complex to understand. But who cares? Those machines handily defeated the spammers, saving the web from disaster."

Once installed, the product of Cold Cognition at its finest and run on supercomputers and huge banks of servers, The Algorithm is an improvisation: spontaneous, but scripted; order out of disorder; an unruly routine. Untouched by human hands, it is presumably trustworthy, free of political motive or bias. Neutral vessels. The Algorithm only seeks to bring pleasure to users, measured by engagement. *What could go wrong?*

What could go wrong? Plenty, once the law of unintended consequences kicked in.

Machine learning dramatically changed the types of videos social media serve up. In its first iteration, AI recommended just another octopus video like the last. But, having mined your watch history and learned of your penchant not only for octopuses but also for conspiracy theories, YouTube's Reinforce algorithm (2017) might recommend one of the many videos that claim that octopuses came from outer space. (Yes, that's a thing.) Soon you'll have fallen into a rabbit hole machine learning dug just for you, and you'll be watching a steady stream of QAnon videos and fake news from Alex Jones and alt-right extremism, one after another, each more virulent than the last. You'll have traded the pleasure you sought amongst like-minded friends who like octopuses, for the more deeply engaging pleasure of moral outrage.

YouTube Chief Product Officer Neal Mohan admitted at the 2018 Consumer Electronic Show that more than 70 percent of the videos you watch on YouTube are due to automatic suggestions made by AI-driven recommendations. The lesson? Parents should turn off their kids' automatic feeds. Facebook, Google, and the social media gang soon followed. Netflix, Fisher reports, "issue[s] recommendations so effective that the company credits its algorithm with subscriber retention worth $1 billion per year."

With such a return, who's going to inspect that black box? If the systems operate semi-autonomously, their methods beyond human grasp, as Fisher remarks, "the Valley had an incentive to stay ignorant. Check how the goose gets those golden eggs and you might not like what you find. You might even have to give them back."

Autonomous? Yes and no. They can be tweaked: remember, those seventy iterations of The Algorithm. But the Goldilocks Challenge, which fuels the question, should be ignored. They are autonomous *enough*. They are autonomous enough to *seem* autonomous. Hence they persuade us they are authentic, free of bias.

"Stories of YouTube radicalization," writes Fisher, "were suddenly everywhere, their details repeating with machinelike consistency." The Reinforce algorithm, and social media in general, Fisher argues, "had arrived, however unintentionally, at a recruitment strategy embraced by generations of extremists." The scholar J. M. Berger calls it "the crisis-solution construct." Destabilized people often reach for a strong group identity to regain a sense of agency and control. It's not personal circumstances that make you unhappy, it's that *They are persecuting us.* Just as conspiracy theories explain away anomalies, persecution gives meaning to hardships, and you're no longer facing them alone.

The crisis-solution construct offered action. Loners who suffered from rejection from the opposite sex found a community of "incels," involuntary celibates. And the crisis of their loneliness had a solution of sorts. In 2014, a twenty-two-year-old dropout named Elliot Rodger killed three men in his apartment then announced on YouTube his "revenge against humanity" for being "forced to endure an existence of loneliness, rejection, and unfulfilled desires all because girls have never been attracted to me." Rodger then drove to a sorority house in Santa Barbara, California, and shot three women, killing two of them. Before killing himself, he shot at pedestrians and drove them down.

Rodger, who showed the way from crisis to solution—six dead, fourteen injured—became a hero among the incels. Fisher counts fifty incel killings by 2022. The *Washington Post* reports that the incel forum is visited by 2.6 million people every month. Two point six million. A month. Righteous anger plugged into our lizard brain, untouched by the frontal cortex: authentic, autonomous, and innovative. And so social media go, like improv—spontaneous, but scripted; order out of disorder; an unruly routine. And out of it comes a feat of social engineering, if not deliberately fitted, at least perfectly fit to challenge the norms of our democracy.

"We have something here that we call the dictatorship of the like," said Pedro D'Eyrot who made videos for the Brazilian left-leaning political party Free Brazil Movement (MBL). President Jair Bolsonaro, Brazil's right-wing dictator, who resisted world-wide pressure to end clear-cutting the Brazilian rainforest, urged voters to get their news from YouTube rather than reputable journals. Bolsonaro had been a much-disliked petty legislator until he embraced YouTube, beginning his rise to power. If his burning down the rainforest produced outrage, well, all the better.

What the dictatorship of the Like did in America we have all seen. It shaped our response to COVID and other vaccines, to Black Lives Matter, and to the LGBTQ community. It gathered the dark forces in Charlottesville and at the Capitol. People died.

TEN: *"The Rhetoric of Spontaneity in Your Facebook Feed"*

Improvising Genocide: The Road to Mandalay

Here's how it played out in real time: seeking to grow their global customer base (the goal was a billion users), and deploying an algorithm charged with increasing engagement, Facebook arranged for free internet access to anyone in the nation of Myanmar (formerly Burma) who bought a phone that had their app. These "zero-rating deals" with local carriers subsidized the entire population by waiving charges for any data used via those companies' apps. Phone sales soared.

A genocide of Rohingya Muslims emerged on August 25, 2017, led first by the military and then by Buddhist villagers. Buddhists with smartphones learned on Facebook—falsely—that two Muslim tea shop owners in the city of Mandalay had raped a Buddhist woman. Facebook was soon badgered by UN agencies, NGOs on the ground, and journalists (like Fisher) covering the story. Facebook ignored their pleas. When the Myanmar government cut access to Facebook in Mandalay, the genocide disappeared overnight. By all accounts except Facebook's, its site, along with WhatsApp, Twitter, and YouTube, had caused the deaths of over 24,000 Muslim Rohingya. A million refugees fled to Bangladesh, already awash in refugees. Facebook only voiced concern that engagement had fallen off. The United Nation High Commissioner for Human Rights described the atrocities as a "textbook example of ethnic cleansing."

A measure of Silicon Valley's sensitivity to these events is suggested by Jack Dorsey, CEO of Twitter, who chose Myanmar as the site of his Vipassana silent-meditation retreat only months after social media had helped foment mass murder there by creating a platform for loud voices.

The next year, Facebook initiated the same zero-rating deal in Sri Lanka. The same pattern—free internet, viral hate speech, genocide—invaded the island nation. Once ginned up, anti-Muslim anger continued until the Sri Lankan government imposed a state of emergency and blocked access to Facebook. "The violence stopped," writes Fisher who reported it on the ground. "Without Facebook or WhatsApp driving them, the mobs simply went home." Harindra Dissanayake, a presidential advisor in Sri Lanka, his faith in technology destroyed, believed that "This idea of social media as an open, equal platform is a complete lie…There is no editor, there is the algorithm." He adds: "We don't completely blame Facebook...The germs are ours, but Facebook is the wind, you know?" While Sri Lanka accepted its role, not so Facebook. In a statement to Bloomberg News, Facebook announced, "We deplore the misuse of our platform."

The "editor" Dissanayake speaks of is the control over hate speech that social media keeps promising and keeps failing to deliver.

What's at stake, then, is not just money and the civility of your Facebook feed, but lives. Faced with charges of having caused genocide in Myanmar and Sri Lanka, Google's CEO Eric Schmidt again echoed the Sophists' democratic-leaning position that truth will emerge from many voices: "The answer to bad speech is more speech." Google owns YouTube. Schmidt's sensitivity is gauged by his echo of the NRA's self-serving adage: the answer to gun violence is more guns. Donald Trump, when running for president, said of the 2015 shooting massacre in San Bernardino, California, that "if we had guns in California on the other side, where the bullets went in the different direction, you wouldn't have 14 or 15 people dead right now."

When the parents of Noah Pozner, a six-year-old boy killed at Sandy Hook in 2012, published an open letter to Zuckerberg asking for relief from the harassment and death threats from conspiracy groups, "the companies," writes Fisher, "dug in." Alex Jones helped inspire the harassment with his false flag narrative. Jones described the shooting incident as "synthetic, completely fake with actors." Asked about the problem, Zuckerberg, "riffed on the nature of free speech: 'I'm Jewish, and there's a set of people who deny that the Holocaust happened. I find that deeply offensive. But at the end of the day, I don't believe that our platform should take that down, because I think there are things that different people get wrong. I don't think that they're intentionally getting it wrong.'" Fisher writes, "It was vintage Silicon Valley...a techno-libertarian free-speech ideal":

> He seemed still to be living in an alternate universe where platforms are neutral vessels with no role in shaping users' experiences, where the only real-world consequence is that somebody might get offended, and where society would appreciate the wisdom of allowing Holocaust-denial to flourish.

"Platform," it should be noted, is an industry promoted term, intended to diminish the need for regulation. If they are "platforms" they are not "publishers" and therefore protected by Section 230.

TEN: *"The Rhetoric of Spontaneity in Your Facebook Feed"*

Together the "like" and "friend" buttons enable the algorithm to improvise fear and anger into a feedback loop. As Chaos science's studies on turbulence made clear, there is nothing more powerful in nature than the feedback loop. Just remember back to the last screeching feedback you heard from a heavy metal band. And then think, the "super dynamic communities" of January 6 who followed Jefferson's call to refresh the "tree of liberty...from time to time, with the blood of patriots and tyrants."

Vigilantism

The genocides that occurred in Myanmar and Sri Lanka were feedback loops that ran out of control. They were vigilantism—citizens taking the law into their own hands. The theme runs through improvisation, this discourse that declines to abide the normal, decorous sources of power and legal control, that prefers intuition to evidence. The superheroes of MCU defend fair play, truth, justice, law, and order. And sometimes they take law and order into their own hands as *The Boys,* Amazon Prime's satire of Marvel and DC superheroes, makes abundantly clear with blood and gore by the bucketfuls. So, too, not only the villains of detective fiction and thrillers, but the detective themselves, masters of intuition, stoop to vigilantism. We cheer them on to our delight, but at our peril.

That January 6 was an improvisation, a bottom-up groundswell of moral outrage is both its best and worst defense. Best, because we have a weak spot for spontaneous outrage like that which fueled the Boston Tea Party. Worst, because, as the  January 6 Committee made clear, it was inspired top-down by Trump and the leaders of the Proud Boys, the Oath Keepers, and other alt-right hate groups. Improvisers often deploy their spontaneity with a wink. The insurrection's spontaneity, oft repeated, is a Big Lie. Social media provided the means of communication. The Algorithm, chasing engagement, greased the skids.

AI-iiiiiiiiiiiiiiiiiii!!!!!

As if a social media empowered Improviser-in-Chief didn't present enough trouble for civil society, now comes the next generation of Large Language Learning Artificial Intelligence using Nvidia's superfast graphics processing units (GPUs). GPUs are close cousin to CPUs (computer processing units). Although built for their capabilities in gaming, GPUs became popular for use in creative production and AI. ChatGPT trained on 10,000 Nvidia GPUs. By January 2023, a month after ChatGPT's launch, an explosion in usage crashed the system.

Many observers shout with joy of anticipation of the science and the environment problems NextGen AI promises to solve. Many others fear an AI Apocalypse where 'bots, unable to learn complex human moral codes, will take humanity over or destroy us. Here comes Marvel's Ultron. Humanity itself is the worst threat to peace. Therefore, for Ultron, genocide is the quick solution. Human morality is filled with such ambiguities: we may be our worst danger, but is eradicating us, as Kubrick's HAL 9000 computer did the astronaut Dave Bowman in *2001: A Space Odyssey,* the solution? Sci-fi fiction and film have been warning against the AI Apocalypse ever since.

Like Cold Cognition, AI is a prediction machine. It can't think, but it predicts the next most likely word. It's not sentient but, like Damasio's single-cell bacteria, it has purpose, to fulfill its mission. Another autonomous black box that works we know not quite how, NextGen AI has powerful emergent properties. Like that next rhyme in a rap lyric, the skills and answers emerge autonomously, effortlessly, not by brute force. Impromptu, they just happen. Not charged with learning Farsi, suddenly AI understood and spoke Farsi. Not charged with learning research grade chemistry, suddenly it can teach you with ingredients purchased at Home Depot how to make deadly sarin or VX nerve gas. Engineers detected both these emergent skills months after the bots acquired them. Although there are dozens of examples of emergent capabilities, there are few explanations for why they emerge. In *The AI Dilemma,* Aza Raskin quips that they've adjusted the adage,

> Give a man a fish and you feed him for a day; teach a man to fish and you feed him for a lifetime.

to read,

> Teach an AI to fish, and it will teach itself biology, chemistry,

TEN: *"The Rhetoric of Spontaneity in Your Facebook Feed*

oceanography, evolutionary theory…and it will fish all the fish to extinction.

AI: Psychedelics on Psychedelics

These contrasting diagrams, which helped us see the connection between psychedelics and improvisation, now offer a metaphor for how NextGen AI works. Just as psilocybin opens the flow from diverse brain areas, AI mines Large Language Models from diverse, unrelated fields. Except that here the placebo diagram on the left represents not the normal human brain but the former AI generation, the one, once unmatched in power, that social media used to capture our attention and gin up fear and anger leading to genocide in Myanmar, to the further polarization of the American electorate, and to January 6. The diagram above at right represents NextGen AI, though the numbers of lines and diverse areas connected don't begin to reflect its power and reach. Huxley's "reducing valve" now opens the flow of the entire internet to make its predictions. Think, so many lines that the circle turns black:

Here's the thing: "Large language models" don't just read all the *text* on the internet. In 2017, a new generation was born when it was discovered that everything digital—images, sounds, movement, DNA, code, law, fMRI, etc.—could be read as language. What enabled the change was Transformer—the T in GPT—an addition of just 200 lines of code.

The models are large because Transformer turns everything—images, sound, Wi-Fi signals—into language. We give them one instruction—*go, learn*—and it soaks up all human experience. NextGen AI is machine learning, which taught social media's AI to capture our attention on fear and anger, but now not on macrodoses but on gallons of LSD.

NextGen AI will write things faster, write code faster, and solve now impossible scientific challenges, even climate change. As the internet was since the 1990s, it could be a huge boost to the economy. But, acknowledging NextGen AI's potential to do culture much good, Tristan Harris and Aza Raskin, co-founders of the Center for Humane Technology, nonetheless term this new AI, "Generative Large Language Multi-modal Model (GLLMM)." With a wink, they pronounce the acronym "gollum" or "golem," a double reference: to Tolkien's Sméagol, the once-Hobbit-like creature corrupted by the One Ring's power; and to Jewish folklore, the being made from inanimate matter, imbued with emergent life-like capabilities that usually harm humankind. The GLLMMs launched in late 2022 share, in Harris and Raskin's view, Sméagol's greed and potential to do evil, and the golem's inanimate, amoral dynamism. *Beware! Beware! For they on honey-dew have fed...*

Multimodal: everything, read as "0s" and "1s," is language. When a human subject in an fMRI is shown an image of a giraffe, AI shown only the fMRI blood flow can reproduce an approximation of the original image. Shown only the Wi-Fi radio signals bouncing around in a room full of people, AI can reconstruct the room's inhabitants. Mind police? Orwell's Big Brother? You bet. Police procedurals may soon be examining not only CCTV but dreams and Wi-Fi data. There are of course no laws, written before the technology created the need, to prevent such intrusions. Given three seconds of a person's voice or appearance, AI can seamlessly and convincingly continue the conversation.

TEN: *"The Rhetoric of Spontaneity in Your Facebook Feed*

The AI only "sees" the fMRI but can reconstruct what you're looking at.

(from: *The AI Dilemma*)

If social media algorithms race to the bottom of the brain stem by exploiting fear and anger, NextGen AI's ability to create avatars (deepfakes) is a race to intimacy emptied of embodied experience. Siri and Alexa, employing dinosaur-age AI, were just the beginning. The site that offers the richest experience of intimacy will command loyalty and increase engagement. Sci-fi (*Her, Black Mirror, Extrapolation*) is exploring the dystopia of disembodied intimacy. The dominance of Zoom meetings during the pandemic for a while made disembodied intimacy the norm. Yuval Noah Harari, the author of *Sapiens: A Brief History of Humankind*, argues that "now with the new generations of AI, the battlefront has moved from attention to intimacy. What will happen to human society and human psychology as AI fights AI in a battle to fake intimate relationships with us, which can then be used to convince us to vote for particular politicians or buy particular products?" For the relationships expert Ester Perel, social media hijacked the meaning of "friend" and "like," "connection" and "community," emptying the terms of all complexity and the responsibility they entail. J.L. Moreno, who thought his sociogram would give meaning to an "urbanized civilization that seemed intent on alienation and perhaps even self-destruction," is turning over in his grave.

Perel calls it the "other AI": artificial *intimacy*. "Modern loneliness," she adds, "masks itself as hyperconnectivity. Who are you going to call to feed your cat?" Loneliness, as the incel murders suggest, is a national security risk. With hollow promises of friends and community, social media promote loneliness. Deepfake avatars, promising solutions, will take our loneliness to new levels.

The ultimate Trickster, AI unlocks all the normal locks that secure our culture, anything authentication based: our IDs, voice, banking, thoughts. AI has been used to scam parents to get their children's social security numbers. Call Junior, record his voice, then deepfake it in a call to Mom: *hey, I'm applying for a job. Can you remind me of my SSN?* Ask ChatGPT to write an essay on improvisation and it will offer a cogent answer in five seconds with ten articles to support it. Only, you may learn that the articles were made up out of whole cloth. Such fabrications in the industry are called hallucinations. "This," argues Aza Raskin, "is the year all content-based verification breaks." Note to reader: I, a human, wrote this book. No, really, me. Promise.

Improvisation tells lies to reach subjective meaning. AI's improvisations are meaning-agnostic. AI just doesn't care. Caring is not part of its algorithm. Its purpose—and it is purpose driven—is to respond to the prompt. AI hallucinations tripped up Trump's former personal lawyer and fixer (read, Trickster) Michael Cohen when using Google Bard to find cases to support his cause. He unwittingly passed along bogus AI-generated citations to his lawyer to submit to the judge. Oops! *Well, you wanted authorities.* When AI's mission is fakery—to succeed in the Turing Test to seem human—truth isn't part of the algorithm. "Credit is an entire thing," wrote Alexander Hamilton: "Every part of it has the nicest sympathy with every other part. Wound one limb and the whole tree shrinks and decays." The trust that Jane Jacobs and Alexander Hamilton considered the bedrock of community may go the way of the dinosaurs.

"What nukes are to the physical world," warns Harari, "AI is to the virtual and symbolic world." Harari adds that having mastered human language, "AI has just hacked the operating system of human civilization. The operating system of every human culture in history has always been language. In the beginning was the word. We use language to create mythology and laws, to create gods and money, to create art and science, to create friendships and nations." A debased language, as George Orwell knew, will change everything.

But while nuclear weapons can't make bigger nukes, warn Harris and Raskin, AI systems can make themselves stronger. When it runs out of internet text, AI uses speech-to-text to scrape audio and video, and a century of radio, film, and TV feeds its open maw and the circle of connections gets darker and darker. It designs faster chips to run on. And it's autonomous. Like nuclear weapons it's impossible to get the genii back in the bottle. We are not in control. Having created the ultimate golem of agency, we are about to lose ours.

The good news is that ChatGPT and similar widely released AI programs fall far short of the power of unreleased GLLMMs. The bad news is that these more powerful GLLMMs now exist, and competition among AI companies, driven by a frantic quest not to be left behind, may trigger their release.

An exaggeration? Well, fifty percent of AI engineers believe there is a 10% or greater chance that humans go extinct or become severely disempowered because of our inability to control AI. Would you board an airplane that promised such a failure rate?

One of the NewGen AIs yet to be released is Alpha Persuade. Modeled on Alpha Go which quickly beat world masters at the difficult board game Go, Alpha Persuade will be dedicated to persuading you of anything, anyhow, truth be damned. Imagine your Facebook feed filled with such voices, all of them deepfakes, dedicated as before to alternative facts but far cleverer in marshalling them. Well, in one sense it won't be different. The impulse to persuade is in our DNA. With Alpha Persuade in our feed, in that regard we will not be alone. But our powers of persuasion may be left in the ditch.

Fearing that AI will become inextricably entangled in human culture as social media did, Harris and Raskin's Center for Humane Technology seeks no less than a paradigm shift for technology before it's too late. They seek a humane technology that:

- Respects, rather than exploits, human vulnerabilities.
- Accounts for and minimizes negative consequences.
- Prioritizes values over metrics.
- Supports the shared understanding necessary for effective democracies.
- Promotes fairness and justice.
- Helps humans thrive.

They propose to control GPU production and improvements, to slow deployment of Frontier GLLMM models, and to improve security to prevent the release of "feral"—open source—AI models.

If the release of GLLMMs goes unchecked, Harris and Raskin foresee two possible futures. If we trust no one, then the government alone will deploy them and a dystopian surveillance state will result. If we naïvely trust everyone with NextGenAI, serial catastrophes will result.

These are challenges at least as great as reining in social media and, since not just democracy's but humanity's continuance may hang in the balance, even more pressing. But progress has been made. More than 1,100 signatories, including Apple co-founder Steve Wozniak and Tristan Harris, have signed an open letter that calls on "all AI labs to immediately pause for at least 6 months the training of AI systems more powerful than GPT-4." Elon Musk signed it, then founded his own AI company, proof of the clarity of vision of internet nerds. President Biden and Prime Minister Rishi Sunak of the United Kingdom have together called for an AI Summit on AI Safety. In the EU AI will be regulated by the AI Act, the world's first comprehensive AI law.

Harris and Raskin were primary informants behind Biden's October 2023 white paper "Blueprint for an AI Bill of Rights: Making Automated Systems Work for the American People," published by the White House Office of Science and Technology (OSTP).

These efforts are a start.

While we wait to see if AI will destroy humanity, I offer a much needed moment of comic relief—literally.

Soon after ChatGPT was released, standup comedian Matt Maran in a Brooklyn comedy club faced off against a deepfake chatbot schooled in the standup skills of Sarah Silverman (a chatbot she did not approve). By all accounts, Maran lost hands down. But standup is not improv comedy which demands more than one player. I'm waiting for a team of chatbots charged with the three-line algorithm of improv comedy and deeply read in IO Theater. Disembodied, will a ImprovComedyBot build community? Maybe. Perhaps they will save the world. Maybe not. Perhaps, there on stage, they will destroy community as we know it.

TEN: "The Rhetoric of Spontaneity in Your Facebook Feed

Trumps Unthought Thoughts

Special Counsel Jack Smith has subpoenaed Trump's draft Tweets in the January 6 case. I hesitate to suggest giving Trump any leeway, but the close study of improvisation suggests we should consider doing so.

If I write angry emails to get something off my chest, emails that I know while writing I will not send, am I guilty as if I had sent them? We noodle hoping something interesting will emerge. Are we responsible for the nonsense that precedes the emergence of something interesting? Is Trump guilty of plans he did not act on if for once his frontal lobe short-circuited the plan? Yes, such drafts can help show patterns of thought and intentions. No doubt Jack Smith has such an argument in mind. But surely, we should stay this side of *Minority Report* mental policing.

The question is worth raising because as we saw in the fMRI study of the giraffe image, and as Duke law and philosophy professor Nita Farahany, a champion of freedom of thought, argues, we are on the cusp of neurotechnologies that will read our thoughts. Should thought crimes be punishable by law? Will such technologies—supercharged by NextGen AI—distinguish playful or tentative from purposive thoughts? Will we be responsible for those most improvised of our narratives, our dreams? How purposive must our thoughts be to prove culpable? asks Miss Goldilocks, finally stumped.

Like Rock and Roll, the Rhetoric of Spontaneity is Here to Stay

Professor Farahany argues that when social media and the new neurotechnologies hack into our automatic reactions to bypass our conscious choices they cross a line. She fears that tech companies use information about how the brain operates to exploit rather than to enable and empower people. But of course, advertisers crossed that line a long time ago. The "father of public relations," Edward Bernays, Freud's nephew, crossed that line in 1929 when he promoted female smoking by branding cigarettes as feminist "Torches of Freedom." United Fruit, owned by New Orleanian Sam "Banana Man" Zemurray, hired Bernays in the 1950s to produce a public relations campaign to discredit the Guatemalan government. Democratically elected, Jacobo Árbenz promised land reform in his campaign: to buy back United Fruit's fallow land to put it into the hands of peasants—to many, a reasonable policy. Knowing Americans in the 1950s were primed to distrust communists, Bernays mounted a concerted disinformation campaign that portrayed the company as the victim of a "communist" Guatemalan government. With the help of the CIA—CIA Director Allen Dulles's brother, John Foster Dulles, was on Zemurray's board—Arbenz was deposed and fled to Mexico.

The promise of freedom has great subconscious power. It's what our Hot Cognition continually longs for. But it is quixotic to suggest we can limit such appeals. Until we can make the corpus callosum a toll-free road, Hot Cognition will always seek surreptitious pathways through doorways that Cold Cognition locks tight. The solution is not to bar Hot Cognition's tricks but to understand how they work and to forearm ourselves against the rhetoric of spontaneity that underlies them. Improvisation's rhetoric has great power to inspire innovation. It also has great demonic power. Only by conscious awareness of the difference can we unite Einstein's sacred gift and faithful servant.

CONCLUSION

Re-Embracing Trickster

> Trump is like Hamilton's evil twin. He just won't stop.
> —Maya Wiley, *The Beat with Ari Melber,*
> MSNBC, November 20, 2024

> He will fasten me, Bromios' devotee, in knotted bonds.
> —Euripides, *The Bacchae,* trans. Charles Segal

> Now, who remembers what Vasudeva,
> the ferryman, said to Siddhartha on the banks of the
> Ganges River? He whispered, "Listen better."
> —Richie in *The Bear, on* Hulu

> Jazz is the sound of surprise.
> —Whitney Balliett, *The Sound of Surprise:*
> *44 Pieces on Jazz*

Most commentators gave President Biden top honors in his skirmish with Republican hecklers during the 2023 State of the Union address. "In a setting not known for improvisation," remarked the *Times,* Biden responded "with sharp retorts and even a sense of humor."

Many of the same commentators agreed that Biden and his team had meticulously prepared the groundwork for this improvisation in advance. Biden knew how the Republicans would jump when he reported their plan to subject Medicare and Social Security to five-year sunset votes. Sure enough, the Republicans jumped *bigly. No,* they heckled, *we didn't say we don't support Medicare and Social Security.* To that very qualified *yes* Biden responded categorically that he was happy to learn of their Damascene conversion. He would expect their support of the social safety net. The Republicans heckled back more loudly. Marjorie Taylor Green in white fur made a bullhorn of her cupped hands. Biden walked off with a bit more vigor in his step—a key issue for a man at 80 who would be 86 after a second term.

Finding Solutions

Following Trump's rude departure, clearly we need to reinstitute social and political norms—the work of Cold Cognition's historical perspective and future predictions. Those unwritten guardrails—many created by Alexander Hamilton at the very dawn of the Republic—need to be carved in stone. What moly might Hermes provide to thwart Trump's poisonous rhetoric?

For starters, we need legislation to control social media's power. After January 6, thirty-two Democratic lawmakers addressed letters calling on Facebook, Twitter, and YouTube to make substantive changes to their algorithms. To Zuckerberg, for example, they argued that "the insurrectionist mob [was] radicalized in part in a digital echo chamber that your company designed, built and maintained." None of this, lawmakers maintained, was news to social media:

> Facebook has known about the dangers of its algorithmic recommendation engine for years. An internal company presentation from 2016 found that "64% of all extremist group joins are due to our recommendation tools... [o]ur recommendation systems grow the problem." The presentation further noted that "[o]ur algorithms exploit the human brain's attraction to divisiveness." Facebook executives reportedly blocked efforts at the time to address the issues raised in the presentation.

Facebook understood the danger but ignored it. If social media can build a black box to enlist billions of outraged users, can't it build a machine-learning device that moderates loud roarers? That would require political will. Which means Zuckerberg would have to dial back his plans for global conquest. And there's that little problem of free speech. Controlling social media won't come easy.

And yet it could be as easy as changing the algorithm. According to *The Atlantic*, in 2019 in response to criticism of its rabbit hole machine, Google-owned YouTube changed its recommendation system to reduce the promotion of "harmful misinformation." YouTube also went "on a demonetizing spree," *The Atlantic* reports, "blocking shared-ad-revenue programs for YouTube creators who disobeyed its policies about hate speech." Researchers now find that the rabbit hole machine is no more: "It found that extremist videos were watched by only 6 percent of participants. Of those people, the majority had deliberately subscribed to at least one extremist channel, meaning that they hadn't been pushed there by the algorithm." Social media sites often proclaim they would welcome federal legislation, but clearly they could regulate themselves if they cared to. All it takes is political will and a little less greed.

The work of Cold Cognition is not the only solution. Fear and anger aren't the only Paleolithic emotions. The longing for community and the longing to flourish are equally Paleolithic, both fueled by Hot Cognition. Improvisation seeks to make the brain stem and the amygdala—the seat of strong emotions—not only our enemy but also our friend.

The irony is that, in crises and disasters—themselves unforeseen improvisations—we need improvisation. Rebecca Solnit describes how, when New Orleans was in a state of emergency just short of martial law, FEMA shut down rescue operations as too dangerous. But an "armada of volunteers with boats—from inside New Orleans and from the surrounding Cajun countryside," showed up at the barricades. Disregarding orders, The National Guard had the good sense to let them through. Improvising, The Cajun Navy saved many from attics and rooftops.

How do we stem the tide of polarization that social media's algorithms exploit? How do we reestablish connection and trust? Going forward, what role might more benign improvisation play? Where can we find the moly to neutralize social media's viral contagion? How can we enlist Hermes's friendly spirit to counteract the intoxicating spirit of Dionysus?

Taking Back the Internet

Social media fueled the problem. There are now many projects exploring digital media as means to make democratic institutions more resilient. Each seeks to restore a sense of the common good—what was understood in the eighteenth century as the common weal, *res publica*—here in a modern and functional form. What all five of these initiatives have in common is their intention to recreate a long-lost notion that there are political measures that strive toward attaining the greatest good for the greatest number, and which therefore transcend the sum of individual strivings. They all employ elements of improvisation.

- "Liquid Democracy," also known as Delegative Democracy, seeks to address one problem democracy faces in our complex society: citizens have a hard time keeping up with the issues, local, state, and national. I know I do. In indirect democracy, our elected representatives make informed decisions on our behalf. Voting every few years gives us limited input on policy-making. Using new technologies, Liquid Democracy offers a chance to make our voices heard more often about pressing issues. In this system, we choose either to vote ourselves or to delegate our vote to someone we trust to make an informed decision in our place. In this way, Liquid Democracy allows either citizens or their delegates to weigh in on issues. What we get is a better-informed vote which can be brought to our representatives' attention more often.

- "Ranked Choice Voting" allows for more granular expression of preferences by taking into account second and third choices. Even if my preferred candidate doesn't win, it still matters whom I ranked second. In winner-take-all voting, by contrast, if my preferred candidate doesn't win, my vote doesn't matter at all. Ranked Choice Voting mediates against extreme candidates.

- "The Collective Intelligence Project" (CIP) builds on the historical capacity of humans to develop "collective intelligence" solutions. These include global governance institutions and transnational corporations, standards-setting organizations and judicial courts, the decision structures of universities, startups, and nonprofits. CIP's site proposes to address "fundamentally collective intelligence challenges: pandemics, climate change, plutocracy, and catastrophic risks from technology." CIP's position: If humans created our current harmful collective intelligence systems, we can recreate them.

- "The Computational Democracy Project" (CompDem) brings data science to deliberative democracy. CompDem builds upon the work done by the website Polis which defines itself as "a real-time system for gathering, analyzing and understanding what large groups of people think in their own words, enabled by advanced statistics and machine learning." Polis is Twitter without the flame wars. Participants submit short text statements, or comments, (less than 140 characters) which are then relayed to other participants who agree, disagree or pass. Conversations moderated by Polis currently engage thousands of participants and could grow to millions, winnowing the digital marketplace for ideas worthy of support.

- "The National Popular Vote Interstate Compact" (NPVIC) seeks to return us to the popular vote—one person one vote—by abolishing the Electoral College. Both Al Gore in 2000 and Hillary Clinton in 2016 received a plurality of the popular vote and lost their elections. State winner-take-all laws encourage candidates to focus disproportionately on a limited set of swing states. The NPVIC doesn't deploy new technologies. But it is an improvisatory way to work around the existing Electoral College. The agreement would go into effect among participating states only after they collectively represent an absolute majority of Electoral College votes (currently at least 270). Constitutional issues will finally decide, but the NPVIC sets its sights on ending the electoral college. What's more American, or more in the spirit of improvisation, than one person one vote?

These efforts may seem pebbles tossed into a roiling sea. But we must begin somewhere to reestablish our sense of agency.

Better Listening: The Way Back

The *New Yorker*'s Whitney Balliett defined jazz as "the sound of surprise." Trauma—defined as an intrusion of the unexpected and unthinkable—shares with improvisation this element of surprise. The traumatic intrusion of the extraordinary disturbs our sense of agency. We didn't see it coming last time, so we fear we won't prevent it next time.

"Trauma is a fact of life," trauma psychologist Peter Levine points out, but "it does not have to be a life sentence." For Levine, recovery from trauma can "be transformative. Trauma has the potential to be one of the most significant forces for psychological, social, and spiritual awakening and evolution." He offers the metaphor of an injured tree that grows around its wound:

> As the tree continues to develop, the wound becomes relatively small in proportion to the size of the tree. Gnarls, burls and misshapen limbs speak of injuries and obstacles encountered through time and over-

come. The way a tree grows around its past contributes to its exquisite individuality, character, and beauty... The image of the mature tree, full of character and beauty, will serve us better than denying the experience or identifying ourselves as victims and survivors.

Levine's wounded tree may recall for us the "venerable trees" outside Michael Pollan's writing room. The stolid ash and "elegantly angled and intricately branched white oak" have both seen better days, but their value and meaning are not the less for it.

The study of trauma reveals that pushing back against a traumatizing agent—a response to its call—minimizes trauma and can help victims recover. Liquid Democracy and the like will not fix the problems social media cause, but can provide a crucial psychological gain. Trauma disempowers the victim. Recovery starts with re-empowerment.

Levine offers the example of the 1976 Chowchilla, California kidnapping to address one of mysteries of trauma, why people experiencing the same event can have totally different responses. Of the 26 children buried in two vans in an abandoned quarry, only one survivor differed from all others. Michael Marshall found a way to dig his way to freedom. Finding a way out and urging his schoolmates to follow him, Marshall regained his sense of agency. During confinement, his fellow victims succumbed to numbness and a state of dissociation. Afterwards they suffered "recurring nightmares, violent tendencies, and impaired ability to function normally in personal and social relations." Marshall was symptom free. Participating in good governance, civic technologies may, like Marshall's agency, minimize the damage Trump's chaos has done to our sense of agency.

Trauma and Moral Injury

In his final statement at the end of Trump's second impeachment trial, Congressman Jamie Raskin called attention to "a pro-Trump protester who told his kids before leaving for Washington that he might never see them again." Thinking like a prosecutor, Raskin had considered presenting the protester's admission as proof that the violence was long planned. There was nothing spontaneous the insurrection. But Raskin's daughter Hannah helped him see past the legal and political implications of the insurrectionist's farewell to his children. She saw the humanity the story carried, and the moral implications: "How can the president put children and people's families in that situation and then just run away from the whole thing?" she asked. Hannah was a better listener than her dad. Listening well must form part of our agenda going forward.

What Hannah Raskin responded to is what psychiatrist Jonathan Shay calls "moral injury." Shay, a VA psychiatrist who has worked with combat veterans from the Viet Nam War and other American misadventures, argues that "moral injury is an essential part of any combat trauma that leads to lifelong psychological injury. Veterans can usually recover from horror, fear, and grief once they return to civilian life, so long as 'what's right' has not also been violated."

"What's right"—*themis* in Greek, named for Zeus's second wife, sister to Metis—are the written and unwritten moral norms broken by Trump when he incited an insurrection and then turned his back on the men and women he sent into the chaos. If marriage to Metis brought Zeus creativity and cunning, Themis brought order. It is she who is pictured blindfolded with the scales of justice in front of courthouses. Trump's offenses against what's right didn't begin on January 6. They began when he took the oath of office with authoritarianism in his heart.

But *metic* improvisation, based on the cunning intelligence the Greeks privileged as the source of innovation, can also offend against "what's right."

Shay's *Odysseus in Viet Nam: America, Combat Trauma, and the Trials of Homecoming* argues that we can't understand the difficulties of returning war veterans without understanding Homer's *Odyssey*.

When Odysseus makes it to the court of the Phaeacians, "he's a castaway on civilian shores," writes Shay, "alone with…his 'ravenous stomach.' Figuratively, Odysseus' [ravenous stomach] is his gluttonous will to acquire and control. [It] brings to mind," Shay writes, "stealing and lies, as well as hunger, greed, and compulsive self-gratification. What has happened to his noble fighting heart, his *thumos*?" *Thumos* is the improviser's charisma. Ravenous stomach is desire with no good governance to constrain it.

Seeing his grief, the king calls upon his guest to tell his tale. But Odysseus knows that this is not the right audience to hear his story. Shay argues that Odysseus's tales of wonder told to the Phaeacian court (Calypso, the Cyclops, Scylla and Charybdis, etc.)—for which the epic is best remembered—are not unlike veterans' heroic "war stories" that belie the horror that only a fit audience is worthy to hear.

Odysseus is a *metic* hero and a great improviser, but, Shay reminds us, he has arrived alone at the court because he has caused the death of all his men—600 in all. *Metic* cunning is not a flawless guide. Odysseus suffers PTSD, not only because of the moral injury he sustained from the Greeks' bad leadership in the Trojan War, but also from his own blunders, themselves the result of PTSD. For Shay, "Odysseus emerges not as a monster, but as a human like ourselves."

Improvisation, Trickster's meticulously prepared art, is another kind of collective intelligence that by listening better unites our two minds. But it too can err.

MAEA: Making America Ecstatic Again

Collective intelligence projects employing big data may push back against the rhetoric of spontaneity that Trump, social media, and AI exploit to manipulate our anger and fear. But the deep commitment of this book is the belief that, to minimize dark spontaneity's peril, we must understand it and make it known for what it is. Hot Cognition is a divine gift, but without Cold Cognition's light—or in damaged hands—it can become a curse. With Cold Cognition we must take charge of our response to improvisation's rhetoric of spontaneity. Understanding the myth—one of Neil Gaiman's land mines—that energizes Trump, is a place to start, and to end.

As I write in the winter of 2024, Trump is in full demagogic cry, the authoritarian ferocity of his rhetoric increasing by the minute. Facing four indictment counts with a total of 91 Federal felony charges, and notwithstanding judicial gag orders, nonetheless he rages.

To explain the immovable devotion of Trump's supporters in the face of his legal peril and unhinged public statements, I return to my central contention: Trump's subconscious channels the dark, destructive energies of the Trickster Dionysus. What the Sri Lankan presidential advisor said of the social media-inspired genocide in his country is a metaphor that helps explain Trump's role: *We don't completely blame Trump... The germs are ours, but Trump is the wind.*

Trump is, we can add, a *Dionysian* wind. If so, we must look again at the ancient portraits of Dionysus. The Greek vision of democracy deeply informed the Revolutionary generation's understanding of politics. Their archetypal vision of the human condition remains rich in wisdom.

Dionysus and Donnynisus

Dionysus is the god of transformation, promised through the ecstasy his intoxication brings. In the ecstatic state, the Bacchae or Maenads, his female followers, will "see me clearly as divine." Bacchic intoxication is not a symbol of the god but a direct experience of his divinity, his own little lightning bolt available every day in spiked wine. Ingesting the god, we become him.

Brian Muraresku, in *The Immortality Key: The Secret History of the Religion With No Name,* explains the rapid transition in the early Christian era from the Eleusinian

Matt Wuerker © 2019 | POLITICO

Mysteries cult, which had reigned for over two thousand years, to the cult of the Christ. Muraresku argues that behind the Eleusinian Mysteries lay a beer brewed from barley infected with psychedelic agents, inducing an ecstatic—an hallucinogenic—effect. Behind the Eleusinian brew and the early Church's Eucharist was the same ergot fungus (*Claviceps purpurea*) that fueled mystical outbreaks in the Middle Ages—known to contemporaries as appearances of St. Anthony's Fire—and witch hunts in the early modern era, including the Salem trials of 1692-93. Centuries later, ergot was the source of the chemist Albert Hoffman's distillation of LSD.

Early Christians, Muraresku argues, found a way to make Christ's promise of ecstatic experience not merely symbolic but embodied. Just as Christianity promised eternal life, so too the Eleusinian cult promised that "If you come to Eleusis, you will never die." Those who consumed the hallucinogenic potion, called a *kukeon,* communed in the underworld with ancestors, as Odysseus did after drinking Cerci's magic potion, also called a *kukeon.* Researchers at John Hopkins Center for Psychedelic and

Consciousness Research confirm that the psychedelic experience of the death of the ego makes one more comfortable with mortality.

The MAGA world's willingness to sacrifice itself for their leader shows how Trump, perhaps the ultimate tab of LSD, has dissolved their egos, submerging them in the charisma of a death cult leader. Just as Trump has all the symptoms of a dry drunk, his followers are psychonauts with no need for psychedelics. Kooks without *kukeon,* Trump's charisma suffices.

This is a curious twist on improvisation, a long way for *Yes, and* ... to take us. But the promise of unmediated experience and renunciation of rational judgment leads in multiple directions.

Do you seek the way of love *(agape)*? Then follow the brilliant madman of improv comedy Del Close: "Treat your audience like poets and geniuses so they might have the chance to become them." The Eleusinian Mysteries promised the same. Death of the ego seems to be a universal human desire and experience. Michael Pollan explores alternative roads to ego death aside from heroic doses of hallucinogens: holotropic breathwork, meditation, and various Eastern and Western mystical disciplines. All promote caring and promise increased comfort with our mortality.

If Muraresku uncovers the esoteric roots of western spirituality, improvisation is one of its most potent flowerings. Comedic improv is another drug-free path to the death of the self. (Well, mostly drug free.) Some of the form's greatest practitioners—Tina Fey, Stephen Colbert, for example—speak of improvisation's transformative power. For Tina Fey, improv's "Rule of Agreement reminds you to 'respect what your partner has created' and to at least start from an open-minded place." *Yes, and*... enjoins us to trust. Improv rescued Stephen Colbert, a committed Catholic, from the "free fall" induced by family tragedy. Improv brought freedom: "I don't actually believe that the present social norm is some sort of eternal truth." Less well-known, Will Dennis, trained by the Jesuits and as an improviser, connects Ignatian spirituality and improv. Both teach us how "to know, experience, and be moved by the idea of 'God in all things.'" *Carpe vitam.*

By means of its "meticulously prepared art" improvisers develop ego-free hive mind. Long form improv partners T.J. Jagodowski and David Pasquali begin each hour-long improvisation with the promise, "trust us, this is all made up." Explaining their completely unscripted performances, they speak of "mindreading...we somehow were able to understand one another's intentions. Either we were both looking very hard and paying very close attention or we had some kind of telepathy." Such telepathy goes by other names. For Charna Halpern, head of ImprovOlympics (IO) where the long-form Harold reigns supreme, "When a team of improvisers pays close attention to each other, hearing and remembering everything, and respecting all that they hear, a group mind forms...an empathy among individuals involved almost an instinct."

Dionysus's Dark Promise

But if you seek the way not of love but of aggrievement, follow Dionysus. While Dionysus as an archetype of regeneration has much to offer, in his dark phase Dionysus may be the original strongman of authoritarian regimes. Would-be autocrats in history rode in triumph as the "New Dionysus" to mobilize the plebeians, their base. Like those autocrats, the Dionysus in his two extended literary treatments promises to renew culture but only unleashes chaos.

In the first, the longer of the two Homeric hymns dedicated to Dionysus, he is kidnapped by Etruscan pirates who think he is the son of a king who surely will ransom him *bigly*. He seems timidly to go along with this, but the willow bonds that tie him just fall off. Then the fun begins, as rising winds test the sails, and the ship suddenly fills with wine. Most of the pirates, intent on earthly rewards, refuse to drink his wine. The god morphs into Bromios, the loud roarer. He becomes first a lion, then a bear. When the frightened pirates leap into the sea, they turn into dolphins.

Only the pirate steersman recognizes Dionysus not as a prince but a god. He drinks the spiked wine and becomes "the most blessed of all men." Dionysus addresses him: "Have courage, you radiant man...You have achieved beauty and pleasure for my heart [*thumos*]." Radiant himself, born of a lightning bolt, Dionysus connects the steersman to the divine charisma that makes him radiant, too. Who among us would turn aside from such radiance? But direct experience of a charismatic divinity sometimes comes with a high cost. It fastens us, Bromios's devotees, in knotted bonds.

Trump pours grievances directly into his intoxicated followers. Having drunk his *kukeon*, they radiate a faith in him that the rest of us, who fail to acknowledge Trump's charismatic divinity, cannot share. Thus, we get what we deserve. We may, like the pirates, soon sleep with the fishes—or, perhaps, like General Milley, contemplate a hangman's noose.

Like Dionysus, the improviser invites us to share her charismatic radiance, to drink her *kukeon*. The challenge that faces us is to persuade our fellow Americans that the radiance promised by the rhetoric of spontaneity often is just smoke and mirrors. Indeed, as some found who followed his inspiration—*his wind*—on January 6, Trump's cascading promises and Tweets are just projectile vomit.

Matt Wuerker © 2016 | POLITICO

Detox and Recovery

Or the mist just evaporates. There's more to the dark portrait of Dionysus, because while charisma, as Jessie Hill sings, promises to be "the most" and forever to "create disturbance in your mind," one thing is certain: intoxication—and its radiance—always wears off. How do we recover from the experience of a charismatic hangover?

Euripides's *The Bacchae*'s central character, Agave, is mother to Pentheus, Thebes's hyperrational king. Pentheus adamantly denies Dionysus's divinity. Agave is daughter to Cadmus, Thebes's founder and first king. Semele, Dionysus's mortal mother, is her sister. To achieve Dionysus's promised ecstasy, Agave gives up her "weaving, left my shuttles beside the loom" and drinks his *kukeon*. She joins the women of Thebes on the hillside of Cithaeron.

In the final act, Agave returns to Thebes triumphant. She dances her way down the hillside in Bacchic style, proud to have caught and dismembered a lion's cub. She exults in having "with hands alone…caught this beast and

CONCLUSION

tore it limb from limb," then shared its raw flesh with her fellow Maenads in a ritual feast. So she thinks. Horrifyingly, it is her son Pentheus's all-too-rational head that Agave carries.

In the final moments of Euripides's tragedy, aged Cadmus talks his daughter Agave down from her Bacchic trip:

> When you know what you've done, you'll feel the most terrible agony of pain. But if you stay in the state you're in forever, you'll be unlucky to the end.

Slowly the hallucination lifts. A kind of redemption comes from awakening. "Tell me, now," Cadmus asks, "Whose face do you have in your arms?":

> Agave: A lion's. At least that's what they said, the hunters.
>
> Cadmus: Look straight this time. It won't take long to see it.
>
> Agave: Oh! What am I looking at? What am I carrying in my arms?
>
> Cadmus: Look carefully, and you will learn the answer clearly.
>
> Agave: I see horrible pain. I am so miserable.
>
> Cadmus: You don't think it looks like a lion anymore?
>
> Agave: No. It's Pentheus. I have his head.

Come to her senses, Agave along with her father, founder of Thebes, is banished by Dionysus from the city, the ultimate penalty.

Many of the insurrectionists express the same dawning, dazed awareness that they had been duped. The lawyer for Riley June Williams, convicted of stealing Speaker Nancy Pelosi's laptop, said in an interview with CNN that her client had taken Trump's "bait." Jacob Chansley, the QAnon shaman with the funny headdress—among the most disruptive insurrectionists and certainly the most colorful—claimed through his lawyer that "He heard the words of the president. He believed them. He genuinely believed him... He thought the president was walking with him." As with Agave, the mist disperses...

The End of Tribalism?

So many insurrectionists wore camo and makeshift uniforms that echoed their service that a reader wrote the *New York Times* fashion editor to ask, "Can I still wear camouflage after the insurrection?" Mainstream and social media soon made a meme of the disproportionate number of January 6 insurrectionists who were veterans: 18.5% compared to the national average of 10%. The Gulf Wars demanded their participation in military actions that were, by the account of many who served, morally and legally wrong, not according with *themis* (what's right), involving the killing of children and innocents, murder from afar with drones and cruise missiles, the torture of suspected terrorists and the mistreatment of prisoners as at Abu Ghraib, and abusive efforts to bring our notions of freedom to cultures we did not understand.

The U.S. government maintains that atrocities were isolated incidents perpetrated by bad apples. Psychiatrist Robert Jay Lifton, on the other hand, argues that the body count mentality under which soldiers operated—"If it's dead it's Viet Cong"—created "an atrocity-making situation." For VA psychiatrist Jonathan Shay, atrocities are moral injuries which not only "strengthen the enemy" but also " potentially disable the service member who commits it." Witnessing or participating in atrocities often causes lifelong PTSD.

Many veterans deny wrongdoing. They point instead to myths of Congress members and draft dodgers not allowing them to win with America's superior fire power. Rambo (Sylvester Stallone) confirmed their suspicions: "Do we get to win this time?" (The *Rambo* film series grossed $819 million). Misunderstanding the nature of wars of attrition, many say, "We never lost a battle." Like Hitler's anti-Semitic knife in-the-back conspiracy theory after World War I, such dissociative thoughts—"alt-facts"—energize their bitter hallucinations today. More smoke and mirrors.

What camo-wearing insurrectionists long for is a reckoning not only with the globalization and neo-liberalism that left many Americans behind, but also with the Viet Nam War and with our generation-long, largely invisible war against terror to which veterans sacrificed their blood, limbs, honor, and trust. They bitterly remember the inequities of service: the rich and complacent civilians who stayed home, advanced in their careers, and ignored veterans upon their return. What they long for, we all long for: transformation, the return to healthy national homeostasis, an American experiment that flourishes.

Skepticism, then, about the American way of war—and governance—is not necessarily misplaced. One of the finest writers to come out of the

Afghanistan war, Phil Klay, a National Book Award winner who served as a Marine officer in Iraq, offers the case of Ashli Babbitt, the Air Force veteran turned QAnon conspiracist who was fatally shot while trying to enter the Speaker's Lobby in the Capitol on January 6, 2021. "It's easy to dismiss Babbitt as a loon," Klay writes,

> but her beliefs were a distilled, paranoid version of a not-so unreasonable distrust of American elites. The past decades of war have shown mismanagement, incompetence, bald-faced lies, as well as forms of cruelty only a bit less bizarre than QAnon, such as the CIA's use of hummus enemas as a form of torture.

The insurrectionists acted out their paranoid version of improvisation's perennial project: to challenge "civilized" norms that need amendment—in this case, imperial wars waged under the color of the Constitution that ignore the Law of Land Warfare and the Geneva Accords. The Black Lives Matter and Women's movements ask for a reckoning regarding the Constitutional promise of equality. The LGBTQ movement asks for a reckoning regarding freedom of choice. What we all long for, left and right alike, is a reckoning between America's promise and its performance during its errand in the wilderness.

Surely, if America is to become less tribal, progressives must feel, not just know, the powerful magnetism of Trump's charismatic Dionysian radiance. We must listen better—even to those insurrectionists and white supremacists, who finally must awaken from their MAGA hallucination, as Agave woke from her Dionysian nightmare. By hearing their stories, the left, too, may also shake off its own delusion, that Trump's followers are less-than. Neither awakening is likely to happen soon, or easily.

Fringe or Mainstream?

Did Ashli Babbitt's challenge to "civilized" norms spring from American fringe movements or the American mainstream? Despite Klay's advocacy above, the question may surprise. Of course, we think, it was the fringe right—loony, damaged, PTSD-ridden—who led and "manned" the insurrection.

Robert Pape, a University of Chicago political scientist, has studied terrorist groups and political violence for thirty years, began systematically profiling the rioters as they were arrested. For Pape, the press missed the real story. They focused—as I have done—on sensational examples like the uniformed militiamen and the QAnon shaman, using striking details to tell clickable narratives. But, if the veterans were the vanguard who led the "stack formation" that breached the Capitol, they were hardly alone. What of the others?

What brought the rearguard insurrectionists to the Capitol? Trump's lies, of course. But Pape's demographic study and concurrent national surveys reveal that the insurrectionists were motivated by the conspiracy theory known as *the great replacement*. Remember Charlottesville: *you will not replace us*. Disaffected veterans might have led the charge, but, big surprise, the energy—the *kukeon*—that inspired them was *race,* the fear of the coming seismic demographic shift from white to brown and black— a shift which, in their view, the Jews have plotted to bring about. Those Confederate flags in the rotunda were no accident. Looking at the counties across the nation most likely to send insurrectionists, Pape pinpoints not those that voted heavily for Trump, but rather those that lost the most white population. Pape reports, with a note of fear in his voice: "When you look at this, it's just one category after another after another that shouts out *mainstream*." The percentage of military veterans at the insurrection was almost twice the national average, but Pape points out the more telling statistic: veterans on January 6 represented *less than half* the number than in historical right-wing events: 18.5% vs. 40%.

The insurrection was a *mainstream* event.

In America, All Politics Is Local

As many holiday dinners since Trump's election have shown, American tribalism is not only national but as local as it gets: intrafamilial. Such tribalism is nothing new. Brother fought brother in the Civil War and may in the next. Our challenge today, if and when Trump's followers awaken, is to hear them out as brothers and sisters, as we try once again to build a charitable city on a hill free of tribes.

The great replacement narrative can no longer be dismissed as marginal. It is deeply rooted in aggrievement: the loss of jobs and, foremost, the loss of racial privilege, an aggrievement with historical sources: the Lost Cause narrative, compounded by bad education, bad media, and bad governance (starting with the Compromise of 1877 that ended Reconstruction).

We may have no sympathy for their methods or their flags, but the insurrectionists' demands for a reckoning *signify* on American history, no less than Lin-Manuel Miranda's *Hamilton* does. Trump's promise to drain the swamp seemed to promise such a reckoning. The great replacement narrative is monstrous, but to treat those who embrace it as monsters—not sharing our humanity—is to sink into a tribalism without end.

They are not the first to be misled by a demagogue, nor will they be the last. Better informed, shorn of alternative facts, and free of Trump's lies and Fox's bottom-line driven hallucinations, MAGA world must awaken and begin recovering from its trauma. We are capable, together, of creating a narrative that recognizes America's misdeeds and also trusts in democracy's capacity for self-correction. It is not to their Trumpian rants but to their awakening that we are called to listen, with sympathy, sharing their grief, and helping to reknit a new narrative. If they awaken. A big if.

In April 1971 some 800 Viet Nam Veterans Against the War (VVAW) threw their service medals across a barrier onto the steps of the Capitol saying, "never again, not in our name." The insurrectionists of January 2021 burst through police barriers shouting, "Not on our watch." Taking their call-and-response a step further, they bellowed, "Why not the Capitol?" Why not, indeed? Incommensurate as these protests were, improvisation's response to the reigning paradigm is always extravagant. Hearing their grievances does not legitimize them. Nonetheless they need an airing in a setting where truth and reconciliation can emerge.

Can we not hear one another? The enemy is not government, but a lack of good governance.

Quixotic? Yes, I know. Brandishing improv to save democracy might seem the ultimate example of bringing a pocketknife to a gunfight. But the way forward must be staked out. Truth be told, we stand at a crossroads so beset with obstacles, I fear for the future.

Yet it is at the crossroads that Trickster, the friendliest god, reigns. Calling on her charisma, Hot Cognition, good humor, and the right measure of Hermes's moly let us improvise a way forward. Let Trickster's playfulness work together with Cold Cognition's hard work to create guardrails for social media, writing heretofore unwritten norms into legislation, enlisting collective intelligence projects, establishing "one person one vote" by overcoming the Electoral College, and funding an educational system that again teaches civics and the nature of evidence-based truth. In sum, by these several means—all challenging—we must restore our sense of democratic agency by embracing the good governance that channels embodied desire—our ravenous stomach. Desire reined in by good governance together make for a flourishing democracy. We must regain democracy's *thumos,* its fighting heart, its charisma, and embrace it in reason's wise counsel—as the Constitution at its best sought to.

But most of all we must learn to listen. Tribalism makes listening inoperable—and tribalism seemingly insuperable. That cynicism is exactly what Putin's expert and well-funded internet trolls at the Internet Research Agency (IRA) in St. Petersburg, Russia wanted us to believe in 2015. "Fertiliz[ing] behaviors already flourishing on American soil," Russian trolls, Anand Giridharadas reports,

> encouraged the view, already on the rise, and not without roots in reality, that the basic activity of democratic life, the changing of minds, had become futile work, which in turn fed the feeling that vital political pursuits—of solidarity across difference, of multiracial coalitions, of united fronts against authoritarianism—and other endeavors to create the conditions for meaningful change were doomed.

Once we bowled in leagues, as Harvard political Robert Putnam pointed out long ago, but now we bowl alone.

Since Putnam wrote in 2000, facilitated by social media, call-out and cancel cultures have increased our loneliness, widening the abyss where civic engagement—and persuasion—once flourished. Our "pessimistic and factional political culture," according to Giridharadas, "often discouraged the work of changing minds and sometimes isolated those who pursued it." Mired in identity politics, we have lost faith in persuasion and its role in the democratic process. We must learn not only to listen but to believe that others—who are not "the other" but American citizens like us—are worth reaching.

That "the basic activity of democratic life" is the effort to change minds is an idea as old as Athenian democracy. It is shared by Socrates and the Sophists, by Serious Man and Rhetorical Man. It is the foundation beneath those long hours the Founding Fathers spent in overheated rooms in Philadelphia, hammering out the Constitution and the Bill of Rights. Persuasion is the point of Fred Astaire's courtship dances with Ginger Rogers. It's why Jesse Hill wants "to create disturbance in our minds." While wearing the mask of having no purpose, comic improvisers night after night seek to persuade us that there is more to life than the metronome offers. If there is a way forward from this crossroads, surely it starts with a return to a faith in the necessity and the possibility of persuasion.

Improvisers, masters of good listening and unsung masters of persuasion, know that the change that comes in their audience will be subjective. They don't control it any more than they control their improvising partners' next *Yes, and…* The best change is the change we're ready for.

Giridharadas champions Alexandria Ocasio-Cortez (AOC) as both great listener and champion persuader. Much of AOC's power comes from her improvising. Giridharadas points to to how AOC explains her bomb-throwing skills: "'It's a Bronx thing,' she says, explaining her talent for deploying the clap-back. 'It's call-and-response culture, which is very much in the wheelhouse of people of color. There is a certain amount of street cred that comes with being able to cleverly defend yourself.'"

Is her call and response spontaneous? she's asked. No, like hookup sex on college campuses it's "spontaneous, but scripted; order out of disorder; an unruly routine." The comparison is mine, not hers. But so, too, AOC waits for "a really good example…that's when I do that, because when I clap back, it's not just reflexive, self-defense. I'm trying to dismantle some of the frames of misogyny, classism, racism that we've just allowed to go on." Hookup sociologist Lisa Wade adds, "It is, in short, a feat of social engineering." No one has had a bigger impact in their freshman years in Congress than AOC.

Giridharadas also reports on how activists make community happen despite inevitable differences in their ranks. Loretta Ross, "a pioneering activist, theorist in the Black radical feminist tradition, and co-creator of the theory of reproductive justice," helped organize The Million Women's March in Philadelphia in 1997. She was named a MacArthur Fellow in 2022.

Today she speaks out against call-out culture. She recommends *calling in*:

> For me, calling in is a call-out done with love. You're actually holding people accountable. But you're doing so through the lens of love. It's

not giving people a pass on accountability—like you don't have to pay attention to the fact that they said something racist or that they caused harm to another person. No. It's not ignoring it. But it's about seeing a pathway or multiple pathways for addressing accountability through the lens of love.

Activists developed calling in the 1960s in response to COINTELPRO, the CIA's illegal program on American soil that sought to destabilize leftist organizations by spreading lies. "Ross and her comrades," Giridharadas reports,

> would have SCCU sessions—for self-criticism, criticism, and then unity. In a meeting, before you could call out someone else, you had to explain how you had contributed to the situation. Before calling out, you looked in. You were compelled to take a broader view of complicity and fallibility. Then you could air your criticism. Finally, having aired things and hopefully cleared the air, the goal was unity.

In the *Times,* Ross recently urged: "We can build restorative justice processes to hold the stories of the accusers and the accused, and work together to ascertain harm and achieve justice without seeing anyone as disposable people and violating their human rights or right to due process." The insurrectionists must face Themis's scales of justice and sword, but a truth and reconciliation process must follow.

Putin's trolls are masters of calling out. Masters of Hot Cognition, they will redouble their work in 2024 to support the candidate prepared to throw Ukraine under Putin's tanks. No doubt Elon Musk's X and other social media will do little, or not enough, to root out the IRA's—and China's and Iran's—fake accounts and bots. It's on us. When we experience posts meant to activate our Hot Cognition's fear and anger, we must be prepared to activate our skepticism.

The greatest challenge ahead will come from within our borders. Dionysus is "the god that comes." One day we will be done with Donald Trump. The next epiphany (from the Greek *epiphaneia,* meaning "appearance" or "manifestation,") is always just around the corner. When that day comes, we will again be subject to the peril that Dionysus brings.

Our defense must be rooted in the awareness that spontaneity's meticulously prepared rhetoric is the original two-edged sword: a tool and a weapon wielded, for good or ill, by beings as flawed and blessed—and human—as us. All of us.

CONCLUSION

The Edge of Chaos

If in the early twentieth century jazz and tap humanized the "irritable, nervous, querulous, unreasonable" world of modern industrial life, by the middle of the century comedic improv was an effort to humanize the postindustrial Attention Economy. Comedic improv made "natural" what the Attention Economy made impossible in our chaotic, information-drenched lives: close attention.

Comic improvisers remember their partners' every gesture. Deploying a simple three-line algorithm that begins with *Yes, and...*, improvisers manage their way through chaos often with brilliant results. Improvisers pay attention for fun and to build community a bit freer of the metronome. Subjective meaning emerges. As Carl Jung posited, "As far as we can discern, the sole purpose of human existence is to kindle a light of meaning in the darkness of mere being."

Given the challenges of the Attention Economy and Cold Cognition's control over Hot Cognition's voice, such improvisations are extraordinary. Improvisation appeals because it is a masterful version of what we confront every day. Neuroscience points to our need to escape the inescapably "ambiguous, noisy information" of every moment. Taking the right next step—one of improvisation's superpowers—imposes meaning on the noise.

Improvisers, ever the audience's avatar, master this dangerous, decisive moment. Trauma—the threat of death, real or metaphoric, or the fear of agency's elimination—is improv's incitement. The improvising artist, in the words of the late Stanley Crouch, experiences time "at the tempo of emergency" because she is hyperalert, determined not again to be surprised by these threats. Recognizing and putting to use every salient detail, she builds a new narrative, trauma's best medicine.

Hot Cognition embraces the unpredictable, what can't be predetermined. Improv's alchemy, making gold out of rotten fruit, is compensatory. If improvisers can make glorious art out of their mistakes, why can't we?

Meanwhile, another group of improvisers armed with supercomputers spontaneously and autonomously record our every click with a different purpose: surveillance capitalism. Promising agency like we've never seen—solutions to climate change, cures for cancer—AI's black-box algorithms sweep away human agency. They promise fun, inviting us to find community and our own meaningful-like way amongst a sociometry of "friends." But social media now know more about each of us who venture online than ever before known about anyone in history, and knowledge is power. Cold Cognition does what it does best, looking to past behavior to predict and determine next behaviors. Knowing our every desire, recorded in our history of clicks, they steer us to that next, decisive click. That click may be costly, but it feels so orderly, after all, so on the nose. It's not chaos: *just how did they know I need a hammock and that my favorite color is orange?* Unerringly predictive advertisements coopt the *hermaion* of Hermes. These impulse purchases are happy accidents not the least bit accidental. In them AI's Cold Cognition coopts our embodied Hot Cognition. Putting "deceit and sneakiness at the absolute center of everything we do" and fomenting political division surveillance capitalism destroys personal agency, destroys community, and destroys embodied meaning.

Both surveillance capitalism and comedic improv are creatures of the same discourse: improvisation. Comedic improv embodies our longing for autonomous agency in a world that increasingly denies it. Surveillance capitalism coopts our agency and autonomously monopolizes and monetizes it at the summit of late capitalism's hierarchy: corporations. The Dionysian Trickster, strongman Trump, monopolizes agency too—*I alone can do it*—sucking up the agency of his followers.

Improvisation has long been with us. The robust world of comedic improvisation, with its hundreds of thousands (millions?) of participants and fans across the globe is something never seen before. Surveillance capitalism, too, is something new under the sun. Surely this is improvisation's most consequent contradiction—and it is not accidental. Both surveillance capitalism and comedic improv are responses to our increasingly chaotic world: one tearing down community and agency, while the other builds them up.

We must face that contradiction. Primed by most instances of improvisation to expect benevolent innovation, we need to know when improvisation is a sacred gift, and when dark improvisation is an agent of chaos. We must learn to distinguish between improvisations that deliver agency and those that eliminate it.

CONCLUSION

If Democracy is a conversation driven by a commitment to persuasion that we are losing faith in, we must learn how and what to trust. As January 6 made clear, we live on the edge of a tribal chaos so turbulent that conversation itself becomes impossible. In the words of the philosopher Susanne Langer, "[Man] can adapt himself somehow to anything his imagination can cope with; but he cannot deal with Chaos." Publishing *Philosophy in a New Key* in 1942 amid a chaos never before seen, Langer was writing before comic improv and Chaos Science began to teach us how to manage chaos, and long before the internet's perilous Chaos Machine emerged. And yet jazz—and other art forms from improv's long history—had already shown the way: listen well, make every voice count, make the most of mistakes, and attend to embodied emotions to access humanity's sacred gift, intuition—but warily, for the gut is sometimes a perilous guide.

NOTES

PRELUDE

Eight men and...
Inventing Improv: A Chicago Stories Special, documentary produced by WTTW, 2021

INTRODUCTION

Say that the first player...
Keith Johnstone, *Impro for Storytellers: Theatresports and the Art of Making Things Happen* (New York: Routledge, 1999), 7

"Miles pauses for a fraction of a second"
Herbie Hancock (with Lisa Dickey), *Possibilities* (New York: Viking, 2014), 1

"my unpremeditated verse"
John Milton, *Paradise Lost,* IX, 24. In *The Poems of John Milton,* edited by John Carey and Alastair Fowler (New York: W.W. Norton, 1972)

"This rhapsodical work"
Laurence Sterne, *Tristram Shandy: An Authoritative Text,* edited by Howard Anderson (New York and London: W.W. Norton, 1980), bk. 4, chap. 10, 337

"the spontaneous overflow..."
William Wordsworth and S.T. Coleridge. *Lyrical Ballads, 1798,* edited by W.J.B. Owen (London: Oxford University Press, 1967), 157, 173

"Thought is made in the mouth"
Tristan Tzara, *Dada Manifesto on Feeble Love and Bitter Love* (1920), online at *https://391.org/manifestos/1920-dada-manifesto-feeble-love-bitter-love-tristan-tzara/*

"First thought, best thought"
Allen Ginsberg, *Spontaneous Mind: Selected Interviews 1958-1996,* edited by Edmund White (New York: HarperCollins, 2001), 366

"The intuitive mind is a sacred gift..."
Bob Samples, *The Metaphoric Mind: A Celebration of Creative Consciousness* (Reading, Mass.: Addison-Wesley, 1976), 26

The two kinds of attention...
Daniel Kahneman, *Thinking, Fast and Slow* (New York: Farrar, Straus and Giroux, 2011)

CHAPTER ONE

"So, it turns out you can have intuition for bad reasons"
Daniel Kahneman in Sam Harris, *Making Sense: Conversations on Consciousness, Morality, and the Future of Humanity* (New York: HarperCollins, 2020)

Beware! Beware!…
Samuel Taylor Coleridge, "Kubla Khan: Or, a Vision in a Dream. A Fragment," in *The Oxford Anthology of English Literature,* vol. 2: *1800 to the Present,* edited by Frank Kermode and John Hollander (New York: Oxford University Press, 1973), 257.

"the wall came about…"
Stuart Anderson, "Where The Idea For Donald Trump's Wall Came From," *Forbes,* January 4, 2018

"spontaneous, but scripted…"
Lisa Wade, *American Hookup: The New Culture of Sex on Campus* (New York and London: W.W. Norton, 2017), 49

"The goal is fast…"
Ibid., 41

hooking up "is 'guys' sex"
Ibid., 16

"that casual sex…"
Ibid., 15

"coercive and omnipresent…"
Ibid., 18

"depressed, anxious, and overwhelmed"
Ibid., 14

"I felt like a god"
Gina Kolata, "Kati Karikó Helped Shield the World from the Coronavirus," *New York Times,* April 8, 2021

"by remembering essentially…"
Jeff Asher, "New Walter Isaacson Book Explains Genius of Vaccines, Why We Shouldn't Fear Them," online at *https://www.nola.com/news/coronavirus/jeff-asher-new-walter-isaacson-book-explains-genius-of-vaccines-why-we-shouldnt-fear-them/article_e3c2ea08-7c66-11eb-ad3e-a75ede868102.html*

"he realized that one key…"
Kolata, "Kati Karikó Helped Shield the World from the Coronavirus"

"The bench is there, …"
Ibid.

NOTES

"fundamentally changed our understanding of how mRNA interacts..."
Quoted by Benjamin Mueller, "Nobel Prize Awarded to Covid Vaccine Pioneers," *New York Times,* October 2, 2023

"No other man..."
Homer, *The Odyssey,* translated by Emily Wilson (New York and London: W.W. Norton, 208), 10.327-31

"You know myths..."
Quoted in Hayley Campbell, *The Art of Neil Gaiman* (Lewes, East Sussex: ILEX, 2014), 96

"They had no script, man"
Joanna Robinson, Dave Gonzales, and Gavin Edwards, *MCU: The Reign of Marvel Studios* (New York: Liveright Publishing, 2023), 73

They called it *mētis*,... See Marcel Detienne and Jean-Pierre Vernant, *Cunning Intelligence in Greek Culture and Society,* translated by Janet Lloyd (Chicago: The University of Chicago Press, 1991)

"the country's most accomplished trickster..."
Tim Alberta, "Inside the Meltdown at CNN," *The Atlantic,* June 2, 2023

"My gut tells me more..."
Sarah Zhang, "Trump's Most Trusted Adviser Is His Own Gut," *The Atlantic,* January 13, 2019

"unabashedly improvisational, Trump..."
Jon Meachum, "What a President Needs to Know," *Time,* July 14, 2016

"I'm a very instinctual person..."
Louis Nelson, "Trump: 'I can't be doing so badly, because I'm president and you're not,'" *Politico,* March 23, 2017

"is unpremeditated but all the truer for that"
Desiderius Erasmus, *The Praise of Folly,* translated by Clarence H. Miller (New Haven: Yale University Press, 1979), 12

"the rationalistic orgy of the Middle Ages..."
Alfred North Whitehead, *Science and the Modern World: Lowell Lectures, 1925* (New York: The Free Press, 1967), 20

"The press takes him literally..."
Salena Zito, "Taking Trump Seriously, Not Literally," *The Atlantic,* September 23, 2016

"a fragment of presidential id..."
Adrienne LaFrance, "Six Hours and Three Minutes of Internet Chaos," *Atlantic Monthly,* January 13, 2019

"extraordinary, not because …"
> Judith Herman, *Trauma and Recovery: The Aftermath of Violence—From Domestic Abuse to Political Terror* (New York: Basic Books, 1992), 51

"Before the attempted …"
> Jamie Raskin, *Unthinkable: Trauma, Truth, and the Trials of American Democracy* (New York: HarperCollins, 2022), 13

CHAPTER TWO

"imperfect theories and sentences…" Ralph Waldo Emerson, *Nature: An Essay* (London: Henry G. Bohn, 1852), 42

"a marked style"
> "Preface" to *Leaves of Grass* (1855 edition), in Walt Whitman, *Poetry and Prose* (New York: The Library of America, 1996), 14

Kerouac insisted it was dictated "by the Holy Ghost"…
> Quoted in Howard Cunnell, "Fast this Time: Jack Kerouac and the Writing of *On the Road*," in *On the Road: The Original Scroll* (New York: Penguin, 2008), 52

"The greatest fruit…"
> Quintilian, *The Orator's Education* 10.7 (trans. Donald Russell)

"when it comes from me…"
> Philip Gourevitch, "Mr. Brown," *New Yorker*, July 29, 2002: 57-58

"physically afraid that…"
> Sam Wasson, *Improv Nation: How We Made a Great American Art* (Boston and New York: Houghton Mifflin Harcourt, 2017), 345

"the present social norm is [not] some sort of eternal truth"
> Wasson, *Improv Nation*, 346

"damage…was talent,…"
> Ibid., 356

"Colbert understood there can be no real happiness, …"
> Ibid., 358

"I like to do things…"
> Ibid., 370

Colbert's ensemble—indeed his entire generation…
> Ibid., 369

"Why do I do all these other projects,…?"
> Quoted from memory

"dreams of improving the world…"
> Peter Cowie, *Coppola: A Biography* (New York: Da Capo Press, 1994), 4

NOTES

"stack formation,"
Zoë Richard, "Oath Keeper Who Breached Capitol as Part of 'Stack' Formation Is Sentenced to 3 Years in Prison," *NBC News,* January 2, 2023

"Treat your audience like artists and poets…"
Wasson, *Improv Nation,* 314

The cover of Paul Woodruff's translation…
Euripides, *The Bacchae,* translated by Paul Woodruff (Indianapolis: Hackett Publishing Co., 1999)

"As a focus for communal celebration…"
Richard Seaford, *Dionysos* (New York: Routledge, 2006), 37

"During this purely social visit,"
Francis Ford Coppola, *The Godfather Notebook* (New York: Regan Arts, 2016), 20

"You have to accept this job…"
Coppola, *The Godfather Notebook,* 20

"a metaphor for American capitalism…"
Ibid., 24

"It would be the repository of every idea…"
Ibid., 26

"the key criteria…"
Ibid., 29

It was appealing to me…"
Ibid., 33

"out of profound fear"
Ibid., 38

"The notebook," Coppola writes…
Ibid., 42

"The words, so mundane and unexceptional, …"
Cowie, *Coppola,* 69

Nothing can ever happen twice…
Wisława Szymborska, "Nothing Twice," online at *https://poets.org/poem/nothing-twice*

"exudes a sense of process, and it is slick"
Arthur Schmidt, "Bookends," online at *https://www.rollingstone.com/music/music-album-reviews/bookends-181978/*

"with the idea," in Simon's words,…
Malcolm Gladwell, *Miracle and Wonder: Conversations with Paul Simon,* audiobook (New York: Pushkin Industries, 2021)

Rhythms come to North America from Africa...
Ibid.

When I was composing the lyrics...
Ibid.

CHAPTER THREE

Selective Attention Test (1999)
online at *https://www.youtube.com/watch?v=vJG698U2Mvo*

"enclosed within our own sensory bubble..."
Ed Yong, "How Animals Perceive the World," *The Atlantic* (July/August 2022)

Fearful that "intuitive" becomes "a catch-all word..."
Viola Spolin, *Improvisation for the Theater* (Evanston, Ill.: Northwestern University Press, 1999), 19

Joyce...embracing those thrown away...
On Joyce's embrace of the thrown-away in *Ulysses,* see *A Taste for Chaos: The Art of Literary Improvisation,* chapter 13: "Pierce[d]...with Strange Relation": Jung, Joyce, and Mann Embrace the Back Streets"

"a place where they all used to be happy once,"
Sidney Bechet, *Treat it Gentle: An Autobiography* (New York: Da Capo Press, 2002), 12

"humans invented constructs like morality..."
Robert Sapolsky, *Determined: A Science of Life without Free Will* (New York: Penguin, 2023), 48

"a world of pure plastic beauty..."
Benoît B. Mandelbrot, *The Fractal Geometry of Nature* (San Francisco: W.H. Freeman and Company, 1982), 4-5; emphasis in text

the form of a systematic "textbook [or] treatise in mathematics..."
Ibid., 2

"to study those forms that Euclid leaves aside..."
Ibid., 1

"breakthrough thinking"
David Perkins, *The Eureka Effect: The Art and Logic of Breakthrough Thinking* (New York and London: W.W. Norton, 2000), passim.

"analogy is the fuel and fire of thinking"
Douglas Hofstadter and Emmanuel Sander, *Surfaces and Essences: Analogy As the Fuel and Fire of Thinking* (New York: Basic Books, 2013), 3

NOTES

"if we wanted examples, ..."
Iain McGilchrist, *The Matter with Things Our Brains: Our Delusions and the Unmaking of the World*, 2 vols. (London: Perspectiva Press, 2021)

"all our reasonings concerning matters of fact ..."
Quoted in Peter Fosl and Julian Baggini, *The Philosophers Toolkit: A Compendium of Philosophical Concepts and Methods* (Hoboken, N.J.: Wiley Blackwell, 2020), 59

"became the basic concept underlying all digital computers ..."
Walter Isaacson, *The Innovators* (New York: Simon & Schuster, 2014), 49

"I try to get a feeling of what's going on ..."
Jimmy Soni and Rob Goodman, *A Mind at Play: How Claude Shannon Invented the Information Age* (New York: Simon & Schuster, 2017), 184

"a life spent in the pursuit of curious, serious play..."
Ibid., xv.

Such homeostasis, according to Damasio, ...
Antonio Damasio, *The Strange Order of Things: Life, Feeling, and the Making of Cultures* (New York: Vintage Books, 2019)

"Homostasis...has guided, *non-consciously and non-deliberatively*, ..."
Ibid., 26

"one of the great unsolved mysteries ..."
Francis Crick, "Life from Space," *New York Times,* October 26, 1981

"all living creatures are equipped ..."
Damasio, *The Strange Order of Things*, 28

"Feelings, as deputies of homostasis ..."
Ibid., 26

What "jump-start[s] the saga of human cultures ..."
Ibid., 3

"became the first ensemble ..."
Wasson, *Improv Nation,* 50

Flicker and May found that improvisers, ...
Ibid., 50

When a living organism behaves intelligently ...
Damasio, *The Strange Order of Things,* 6

"Strange," Damasio concludes, "is too mild a word ..."
Ibid., 6

"Unminded" multi-cell organisms ..."
Ibid., 74

"The improviser who does not tell stories..."
    Johnstone, *Impro for Storytellers,* 101

"code-word substitution[s] for the absence of reason"
    Henry Louis Gates, Jr., *The Signifying Monkey: A Theory of African-American Literary Criticism* (Oxford: Oxford University Press, 2014 [1988]), 52

"Everything changes,"...
    Attributed to Paul Valéry, no source known

CHAPTER FOUR

"doctrine of a more perfect reason"
    Francis Bacon: The Major Works, edited by Brian Vickers (Oxford: Oxford University Press, 2002), xviii

"echoes most faithfully the voice of the world itself, ..."
    Francis Bacon, "Of the Wisdom of the Ancients," in *The Works of Francis Bacon,* edited by James Spedding, Robert Leslie Ellis, and Douglas Denon Heath, 14 vols. (New York: Hurd and Houghton, 1864), 13: 101. This is a translation of Bacon's *De Sapientia veterum* (1609)

"Human communication ought to be like the United Parcel Service..."
    Richard A. Lanham, *The Economics of Attention: Style and Substance in the Age of Information* (Chicago and London: The University of Chicago Press, 2006), 19

Scientists "think they are merely stating facts..."
    Deirdre N. McCloskey, *The Rhetoric of Economics* (Madison: The University of Wisconsin Press, 1998), 18

"the 'motor' by which science moves..." "Rhetoric," in *The Stanley Fish Reader,* edited by H. Aram Veeser (Malden, Mass.: Blackwell Publishers, 1999), 129

Lanham calls a person who adopts this position *homo seriosus*
    Richard A. Lanham, *Motives of Eloquence: Literary Rhetoric in the Renaissance* (Eugene, Oregon: Wipf & Stock Publishers, 2004), 6

"a *Choose* book proposes a conception of character..."
    Leslie Jamison, "The Enduring Allure of Choose Your Own Adventure Books," *New Yorker,* September 12, 2022

"Thoughts without intuitions are empty, ..."
    Immanuel Kant, *Critique of Pure Reason,* translated by Norman Kemp Smith (New York: St, Martin's Press, 1965), 93 (B75/A51)

"there is always just beneath the surface..."
    "Rhetoric," in *The Stanley Fish Reader,* 126

The battle is constant, Fish writes...
    Ibid., 122

CHAPTER FIVE

VIDACOVICH: When you're improvising,..."
"Drum Improv: Organized Chaos?," with Johnny Vidacovich, Shannon Powell, Stanton Moore; moderated by David Kunian at Improv Conference New Orleans, December 2019, online at *https://improvnola.com/2019-archive/*

"the first virtuoso of the visible brushstroke"
Peter Schjeldahl, "Haarlem Shuffle: The Fast World of Frans Hals," *New Yorker*, August 1, 2011

for "imbu[ing] his paintings with such force..."
Theodorus *Schrevelius, Harlemias ofte, om beter te seggen, de eerste stichtinghe der stadt Haerlem,* Haarlem, 1648; quoted by Christie's, online at *https://www.christies.com/en/lot/lot-6182934* (Lot Essay)

"illustrious drinkers and you, precious syphilitics..."
François Rabelais, *The Five Books of Gargantua and Pantagruel,* translated by Jacques Le Clercq (New York: The Modern Library, 1936), 5

a. careless or without effort...
Randy Fertel, *A Taste for Chaos: The Art of Literary Improvisation* (Thompson, Conn.: Spring Publications, 2022), Chapter 3.

"accenting off the beat..."
Wynton Marsalis, "Music as Metaphor: XVII. Syncopation—Expect the Unexpected," Wynton at Harvard, online at *https://www.youtube.com/watch?v=nmsQYzcYjO8*

But it's just two voices..."
Jon Batiste, *Fresh Air,* broadcast by WHYY, January 1, 2020

"a place where they all used to be happy once"
Bechet, *Treat it Gentle,* 12

"all that cerebral stuff,..."
Stanton Moore, in "Drum Improv: Organized Chaos?"

"We must suck the essential marrow of life"
François Rabelais, *Gargantua and Pantagruel,* Book 1

"nature is perhaps the most complex word in the language"
Raymond Williams, *Keywords: A Vocabulary of Culture and Society* (New York: Oxford University Press, 1985), 219

"catalogue of swindles and perversions"
"Politics and the English Language," in George Orwell, *A Collection of Essays* (Garden City, N.Y.: Doubleday Anchor Books, 1954), 169

"philosophically... scandalous"
C.S. Lewis, *Studies in Words* (London: Cambridge University Press, 1967), 46

the vein of sentiment so common in the modern world…"
  "On Nature," in John Stuart Mill, *Three Essays on Religion* (London: Longmans, Green, Reader, and Dyer, 1874), 44

"natural law… a kind of general trump card"
  Thomas B. McAffee, "Substance Above All: The Utopian Vision of Modern Natural Law Constitutionalists," *Southern California Interdisciplinary Law Journal* 4 (1995)

"If it makes you sweat…"
  "Living Memory: A Meeting with Toni Morrison," in Paul Gilroy, *Small Acts: Thoughts on the Politics of Black Cultures* (London and New York: Serpent's Tail, 1993), 181

"Because there is in it a dormitive principle"
  Gregory Bateson, *Steps to an Ecology of Mind* (New York: Ballantine Books, 1972), xx

"one thing is certain…"
  Ibid., 45

Why do we treat the fleeting day
  Szymborska, "Nothing Twice"

If Keats "hate[d] poetry that has a palpable design upon us…"
  Letter to J. H. Reynolds, February 3, 1818, in *Selected Letters of John Keats,* edited by Grant F. Scott (Cambridge, Mass.: Harvard University Press, 2002), 86–87

"ads are sometimes most successful…"
  Tiffany Hsu," Have You Noticed More Bad Ads Online? We Want to See Them," *New York Times,* February 11, 2023

the singing commercial ruled the day…
  Peter Brook, *Seduced by Story: The Use and Abuse of Narrative* (New York: The New York Review of Books, 2022), 9–10

The great Russian literary theorist…
  M. M. Bakhtin, *The Dialogic Imagination: Four Essays,* edited by Michael Holquist; translated by Caryl Emerson and Michael Holquist (Austin: University of Texas Press, 2008), passim

"Persons attempting to find a motive in this narrative will be prosecuted…"
  "Notice," in Samuel Langhorne Clemens (Mark Twain), *Adventures of Huckleberry Finn,* edited by Sculley Bradley (New York: W.W. Norton, 1962)

"the world in love with dreams…"
  Samuel Langhorne Clemens (Mark Twain), *Life on the Mississippi* (New York: Viking Penguin, 1984), 327

Going "a good deal on instinct"
Clemens, *Adventures of Huckleberry Finn,* 173

Hitler "listens intently to a stream of suggestions..."
"Diagnosing the Dictators," in *C. G. Jung Speaking: Interviews and Encounters,* edited by William McGuire and R.F.C. Hull (Princeton, N.J.: Princeton University Press, 1977), 119; emphasis in original

CHAPTER SIX

Michael Pollan...
Michael Pollan, *How to Change Your Mind: What the New Science of Psychedelics Teaches Us about Consciousness, Dying, Addiction, Depression, and Transcendence* (New York: Penguin Books, 2018)

it really is the network in your brain...
"Improvisation and Creativity: A Conversation among Randy Fertel, Mark Plotkin, and Michael Pollan," Improv Conference New Orleans, December 2019. Online at *https://improvnola.com/conversations-jules-feiffer-michael-pollan/*

"a reducing valve"
Aldous Huxley, *The Doors of Perception,* (New York: Harper & Row, 1970), 23

"great blooming, buzzing confusion"
William James, *The Principles of Psychology,* 2 vols. (New York: Dover Publications, 1950), 1: 488

We know now... that the nervous system..."
Jerome S. Bruner, *On Knowing: Essays for the Left Hand* (Cambridge, Mass. and London: The Belknap Press of Harvard University Press, 1979), 6

"it distills, or abstracts, the essence of what it sees..."
Quoted in Marilia Duffles, "Secrets of Human Thinking," *Financial Times,* March 2, 2002

"a wonderfully italicized version..."
Pollan, *How to Change Your Mind,* 6

The efficiencies of the adult mind, ..."
Ibid., 15

"the Studebaker of the drug market"
Hunter S. Thompson, *Fear and Loathing in Las Vegas and Other American Stories* (New York: The Modern Library, 1996), 201

"in the edifice of materialist rationality"
Quoted in Pollan, *How to Change Your Mind,* 25

our "insatiable desire...to forget ourselves"
"Circles," in *The Collected Works of Ralph Waldo Emerson* (Cambridge, Mass. and London: The Belknap Press of Harvard University Press, 1979), 2: 190

"**far-flung brain regions...**" So, your sense of smell...
   "Improvisation and Creativity: A Conversation among Randy Fertel, Mark Plotkin, and Michael Pollan"

"**are thought to provide a cognitive framework...**"
   Charles J. Limb and Allen R. Braun, "Neural Substrates of Spontaneous Musical Performance: An fMRI Study of Jazz Improvisation," *PLoS ONE* 3, no. 2 (2008)

It seemed to me..."
   Pollan, *How to Change Your Mind*, 132; emphasis in original

"**Somehow an open circuit of feeling...**"
   Quoted by Cunnell in *On the Road: The Original Scroll*, 36

"**As I gazed at the two trees...**"
   Pollan, *How to Change Your Mind*, 133

"**what Adam had seen...**"
   Quoted in ibid., 161

"**Set...is the mind-set or expectation...**"
   Ibid., 6

This "expectancy effect,"
   Ibid., 158

but I beheld this..."
   Michael Pollan, in "Improvisation and Creativity: A Conversation..."

"**Facts of whatever kind...**"
   Quoted in Peter France, *Diderot* (Oxford: Oxford University Press, 1982), 70

they "refute themselves"
   Steven Pinker, *Enlightenment Now: The Case for Reason, Science, Humanism, and Progress* (New York: Penguin Books, 2018), 351

"**this form is no longer that of a simple exposition...**"
   Quoted in Gary Peters, *The Philosophy of Improvisation* (Chicago and London: The University of Chicago Press, 2009), 148

"**Right, I'm fighting the urge to punch you...**"
   The Colbert Report, broadcast by Comedy Central, October 18, 2011

"**Reasons last step is the recognition...**"
   Pascal, *Pensées*, translated by A.J. Krailsheimer (Harmondsworth, Middlesex: Penguin Books, 1966), 85

"**the heart has its reasons...**"
   Ibid., 154

"**Where is the wisdom we have lost...?**"
   T.S. Eliot, *The Rock* (New York: Harcourt, Brace and Company, 1934), 7.

"The Age of Enlightenment left a legacy of facticity..."
Murray Stein, *Jung's Map of the Soul: An Introduction* (Chicago and La Salle, Ill.: Open Court, 1998), 216

"One could say that the real picture consists..."
C.G. Jung, *Collected Works,* edited and translated by Gerhard Adler and R. F.C. Hull, vol. 10: *Civilization in Transition* (Princeton, N.J.: Princeton University Press, 1970), par. 494; emphasis in original

Edward Hopper quietly remarks...
Hopper: An American Love Story. American Masters, PBS, 2024

"Try to be one of the people on whom nothing is lost"
Henry James, *The Future of the Novel: Essays on the Art of Fiction,* edited by Leon Edel (New York: Vintage Books, 1956), 13

"the future resolution of the two states, dream and reality,..."
André Breton, *Manifestoes of Surrealism,* translated by Richard Seaver and Helen R. Lane (Ann Arbor: The University of Michigan Press, 1969), 14; Breton's emphasis

"If the depths of our mind..."
Ibid., 10

"where id was, there ego shall be"
Sigmund Freud, *New Introductory Lectures on Psychoanalysis,* translated and edited by James Strachey (New York: W.W. Norton, 1965), 80

CHAPTER SEVEN

"this adrenalized unsafe situation"
We Are Freestyle Love Supreme, documentary directed by Andrew Fried, 2020

"in which people are so involved..."
Mihaly Csikszentmihalyi, *Flow: The Psychology of Optimal Experience* (New York: HarperPerennial, 1991), 4

As he spoke, Hermes of Kyllene,...
Translated by Lewis Hyde, in *Trickster Makes this World: Mischief, Myth, and Art* (New York: Farrar, Straus and Giroux, 1998), 326

imperial power, or rather *force*—Simone Weil's term...
Simone Weil's The Iliad *or The Poem of Force: A Critical Edition,* edited and translated by James P. Holoka (New York: Peter Lang, 2006), passim

"'Charisma' is the personal quality..."
Max Weber, *Economy and Society,* edited and translated by Keith Tribe (Cambridge, Mass. and London: Harvard University Press, 2019), 374

"But when he was all clean and richly oiled…"
    Homer, *The Odyssey,* translated by Emily Wilson (New York and London: W.W. Norton, 2018), 6.227-39

"The crowd is his element…"
    Charles Baudelaire, *The Painter of Modern Life and Other Essays,* translated and edited by Jonathan Mayne (New York: Da Capo Press, 1986), 9

"to do with the utter freedom unleashed…"
    Lauren Elkin, *Flâneuse: Women Walk the City of Paris, New York, Tokyo, Venice, and London* (New York: Farrar, Straus and Giroux, 2016), 4

was just made for dancing…
    Daisy Woodward, "Leslie Caron on Fred Astaire & Gene Kelly," *AnOther Magazine,* November 4, 2011

"inspires a person to think…"
    Jennifer Welsh, "Fred Astaire vs. Gene Kelly," *Medium,* June 5, 2015

"only native and original dance form[s]"
    "Loving the Lindy," *Life Magazine,* August 23, 1943

"rhythmic organization of industrial noise"
    Joel Dinerstein, *Swinging the Machine: Modernity, Technology, and African American Culture Between the World Wars* (Amherst and Boston: University of Massachusetts Press, 2003), 224

"New sounds…"
    Le Corbusier, quoted in ibid., 4

that Henry Adams had seen…
    The Education of Henry Adams: An Autobiography (Cambridge, Mass.: The Massachusetts Historical Society, 1918), 499

"make it new"
    Ezra Pound, *Make It New: Essays* (London: Faber and Faber, 1933)

"one expresses the self, the other perfection"
    Sally Sommer, quoted in Dinerstein, *Swinging the Machine*, 226

"the rhythm of the steppes…"
    T.S. Eliot, "London Letter," *The Dial* (October 1921)

"it must have the ability to use found objects…"
    "Living Memory: A Meeting with Toni Morrison," in Gilroy, *Small Acts,* 181

"I once had a student tell me…"
    Online at *https://danceworksmke.org/tapping-out-rhythms-of-life/*

"Astaire and George Gershwin's parallel rhythmic sensibilities"
    Todd Decker, *Music Makes Me: Fred Astaire and Jazz* (Berkeley, Los Angeles, and London: University of California Press, 2011), 57

[Horton] opens the door...
Quoted in Decker, *Music Makes Me*, 120

"Habitual Hollywood practice and fear of protests..."
Ibid., 273

"If I can only get me..."
Online at *https://www.lyrics.com/lyric/7107581/Fred+Astaire/Slap+That+Bass*

"'Slap That Bass'..."
Dinerstein, *Swinging the Machine*, 245

I think it's pretty obvious...
Online at *https://genius.com/Wilson-pickett-ooh-poo-pah-doo-lyrics*

"an indelible hand of agency"
Toni Morrison, *The Source of Self-Regard: Selected Essays, Speeches, and Meditations* (New York: Alfred A. Knopf, 2019), 318

CHAPTER EIGHT

"the daily ballet of Hudson Street"
Jane Jacobs, *The Death and Life of Great American Cities* (New York: Vintage Books, 1992 [1961]), 54

as "problems of simplicity" and "problems of disorganized complexity"
Ibid., 431

"a morbid and biased catalog of ills"
Ibid., 20

"eyes on the street"
Ibid., 35

"There is nobody against this... but...a bunch of MOTHERS!"
Quoted in James Howard Kunstler, "An Interview with Jane Jacobs, Godmother of the American City," *Metropolis* (March 2001)

"powerful and corrosive elitism"
Stanley Fish, *Doing What Comes Naturally: Change, Rhetoric, and the Practice of Theory in Literary and Legal Studies* (Durham and London: Duke University Press, 1989), 473

the brains behind the eyes...
Jacobs, *The Death and Life of Great American Cities*, 56

"Crime shows outnumber every other drama subgenre..."
Rick Porter, "TV Long View: How Much Network TV Depends on Cop Shows," *Hollywood Reporter*, June 20, 2020

I then walked slowly down the garden path,..."
Sir Arthur Conan Doyle, "A Study in Scarlet," in *The Complete Sherlock Holmes* (New York: Doubleday, 1930), 84

Winging It

"I am a brain, Watson"
"Adventure 1: The Adventure of the Mazarin Stone," in ibid., 1014

"Bi-Part Soul"
"The Murders in the Rue Morgue," in Edgar A. Poe, *Tales* (New York: Wiley and Putnam, 1845), 120

"We divided its entire surface into compartments…"
"The Purloined Letter," in ibid., 206

"The measures adopted were…"
Ibid., 209

"an identification," Poe writes…
Ibid., 210

"When I wish to find out…"
Ibid.

"Very rapidly, we got this unifying notion…"
Kim Armstrong, "'I Feel Your Pain': The Neuroscience of Empathy," *APS,* December 29, 2017

"sees things five seconds before the rest of the world"
Lee Child, *61 Hours* (New York: Delacorte Press, 2010), 54

"almost more a scientist than a poet"
Quoted in John Tresch, *The Reason for the Darkness of the Night: Edgar Allen Poe and the Forging of American Science* (New York: Farrar, Straus and Giroux, 2021), 338

"the second scientific revolution"
Quoted in ibid., 9

"On an unprecedented scale"
Ibid., 135

"The promise of the Enlightenment…"
Ibid., 132

When I heard the learn'd astronomer…
"When I Heard the Learn'd Astronomer," in Walt Whitman, *The Complete Poems,* edited by Francis Murphy (London: Penguin Books, 2004), 298

"corked in a bottle and floating on the *Mare Tenebrarum*"
Edgar Allan Poe, *Eureka: A Prose Poem* (New York: Geo. P. Putnam, 1848), 10

"Aristotelian and Baconian"
Ibid., 12

"the progress of true Science…"
Ibid.

"The simple truth is"
    Ibid., 14
"'Contradictions cannot *both* be true...'"
    Ibid.
"dreamers and those who put faith in dreams..."
    Ibid., 5
"the Soul... loves nothing so well..."
    Ibid., 18
"the *only* true thinkers..."
    Ibid., 19
  Poe depicts a "universe,"...
    Tresch, *The Reason for the Darkness of the Night*, 341
  Instead of a dead machine, this cosmos was alive..."
    Ibid., 317
"Huge smoking cities arose,..."
    "The Colloquy of Monos and Una," in Poe, *Tales*, 102
"empathy is always perched precariously between gift and invasion"
    Leslie Jamison, *The Empathy Exams: Essays* (Minneapolis: Graywolf Press, 2014), 4
"D——," Dupin reports,...
    The Purloined Letter," in Poe, *Tales*, 211
"disorder and destruction at the core of existence..."
    Tresch, *The Reason for the Darkness of the Night*, 317
"the *only* true thinkers..."
    Poe, *Eureka: A Prose Poem*, 19
"discovered his laws..." Tresch, *The Reason for the Darkness of the Night*, 300
"The edifice of science requires..."
    Quoted in Paul Strathern, *Mendeleyev's Dream: The Quest for the Elements* (London: Penguin Books, 2001), 277
"I saw in a dream..."
    Quoted in Strathern, *Mendeleyev's Dream*, 286

CHAPTER NINE

"America then, told by America now"
    Lin-Manuel Miranda and Jeremy McCarter, *Hamilton: The Revolution* (New York: Grand Central Publishing, 2016), 33
"rap gods"
    Ibid., 26

"**the point of rap...**"
Daniel Levin Becker, "On Rap's Linguistic Twists and Turns," *City Lights,* February 28, 2022

"**American history for...**" Quoted in Miranda and McCarter, *Hamilton: The Revolution,* 125

There was undeniable genius on the pages...
Richard Morgan, "How Hamilton's Cast Got Broadway's Best Deal," *Bloomberg,* September 28, 2016

"**the willing suspension of disbelief...**"
Samuel Taylor Coleridge, *Biographia Literaria or Biographical Sketches of My Literary Life and Opinions,* edited by John Calvin Metcalf (New York: Macmillan, 1926), 191

"**Simulation," she notes,...**
Lisa Feldman Barrett, *How Emotions Are Made: The Secret Life of the Brain* (Boston and New York: Houghton Mifflin Harcourt, 2017), 26

Simulations are your brain's guesses...
Barrett, *How Emotions Are Made,* 27

Diggs raps at 6.3 words per seconds...
Quinn Hough, "Hamilton: How Fast Daveed Diggs Actually Raps As Lafayette, *ScreenRant,* August 5, 2020

Doesn't hurt that Daveed is...
Miranda and McCarter, *Hamilton: The Revolution,* 118

"**ambiguous, noisy information**"
Barrett, *How Emotions Are Made,* 2

What the improvising artist did...
Stanley Crouch, *Kansas City Lightning: The Rise and Times of Charlie Parker* (New York: HarperCollins, 2013), 17

I don't know where I heard it...
Miranda and McCarter, *Hamilton: The Revolution,* 118

"**unfiltered, unconscious, or random thoughts...**"
Limb and Braun, *"Neural Substrates of Spontaneous Musical Performance"*

If we assume...
Miranda and McCarter, *Hamilton: The Revolution,* 161

"**the improviser has to understand...**"
Kenneth Johnstone, *Impro for Storytellers: Theatresports and the Art of Making Things Happen* (New York: Routledge, 1999), 93

"**I'm actually working on a hip-hop album...**"
Miranda and McCarter, *Hamilton: The Revolution,* 14

NOTES

"Hamilton's pace is relentless..."
Ibid., 92

"talk less, smile more"
Ibid., 186

I am not throwing away my shot...
Ibid., 26

So this is what it feels like...
Ibid., 82

And when I meet Thomas Jefferson...
Ibid., 44

"trope of tropes" Gates, *The Signifying Monkey*, 21

"Credit is an entire thing"
Quoted in Chernow, *Alexander Hamilton*, 302

Look at where you are...
Miranda and McCarter, *Hamilton: The Revolution*, 110

It took an immigrant to fully understand...
Ibid., 88

"Are you the operator or the crusader?..."
Quoted in ibid., 257 (emphasis in text)

"a monster," "a labyrinth," "the slyest trickster of our time"
Gore Vidal, *Burr: A Novel*, New York: Random House, 1973), 4, 7, 21

a man who "makes even a trip to the barber seem like..."
Ibid., 4

"I'm a trust fund, baby,..."
Miranda and McCarter, *Hamilton: The Revolution*, 44

I will never understand you...
Ibid., 87

There is always a "first time"...
Quoted in Chernow, *Alexander Hamilton*, 409

"a wolf by the ears"
Letter to John Holmes, April 22, 1820, in *Letters and Addresses of Thomas Jefferson*, edited by William B. Parker and Jonas Viles (Buffalo, N.Y.: National Jefferson Society, 2011), 265

"an improviser of expedient sensibility"
Chris Jones, "Hamilton: Hip-Hop and Founding Fathers in Dazzling Broadway Musical," *Chicago Tribune*, August 6, 2015

Winging It

"I cannot tell you how cathartic..."
  Ibid.

"Far from weakening [Britain]..."
  Quoted in Chernow, *Alexander Hamilton*, 296

"there are two rules..."
  John Winthrop, "A Modell of Christian Charity (1630)," online at *https://history.hanover.edu/texts/winthmod.html*

"whether societies of men are really capable or not,..."
  "Publius" [Alexander Hamilton], *The Federalist 1*, in *The Debate on the Constitution: Federalist and Antifederalist Speeches articles and Letters During the Struggle over Ratification,* Part One (New York: The Library of America, 1993), 219

"Why does it get such a delighted response?..."
  Miranda and McCarter, *Hamilton: The Revolution,* 121

Mr. Adams observed,...
  Quoted in Chernow, *Alexander Hamilton,* 395

"Hamilton was merely saying that..."
  Ibid.

History will teach, that the [latter]...
  "Publius," *The Federalist 1,* 221

Since boyhood he had dreamed of battle's glory...
  Fred Anderson, *Crucible of War: The Seven Years' War and the Fate of Empire in British North America, 1754-1766* (New York: Vintage Books, 2001), 7

Let me tell you what I' wish I'd known...
  Miranda and McCarter, *Hamilton: The Revolution,* 120

"I imagine death so much it feels more like a memory"
  Ibid., 273

We gotta go, gotta get the job done...
  Ibid., 121

BURR, HAMILTON: I'll make the world safe and sound for you...
  Ibid., 129

I was too young and blind to see...
  Ibid., 275

"The Hill We Climb"
  Online at *https://www.youtube.com/watch?v=LZ055ilIiN4*

"about what it means to be a better country"
  Online at *https://www.youtube.com/watch?v=qHhut5nhI8g*

CHAPTER TEN

"that the Internet is a massive and collaborative work of realist art"
Virginia Heffernan, *Magic and Loss: The Internet as Art* (New York: Simon & Schuster, 2016), 8

"when we receive a Like…"
Max Fisher, *The Chaos Machine: The Inside Story of How Social Media Rewired Our Minds and Our World* (New York: Little, Brown and Company, 2022), 30

"toward the more extreme end…"
Ibid., 215

"The key element here is the variable reward…"
James Williams, *Stand out of our Light: Freedom and Resistance in the Attention Economy* (Cambridge: Cambridge University Press, 2018), 34

"It's a casino that fits in your pocket…"
Fisher, *The Chaos Machine,* 27

"TikTok's Secret 'Heating' Button…"
Emily Baker-White, "TikTok's Secret 'Heating' Button Can Make Anyone Go Viral," *Forbes,* January 20, 2023

"Trump was bad for America, but good for CBS…"
Eliza Collins, "Les Moonves: Trump's run is 'damn good for CBS,'" *Politico,* February 29, 2016

"A more open and connected world…"
Quoted in Stuart Dredge, "Zuckerberg: One in Seven People on the Planet Used Facebook on Monday," *The Guardian,* August 28, 2015

In 2021, Freedom House,…
Online at *https://freedomhouse.org/report/freedom-world/2022/global-expansion-authoritarian-rule*

The YouTube channel 'Can I Draw You,'…
"Gangnam Style drawing meme," online at *https://www.youtube.com/watch?v=dtoR5XR_oHI*

like convincing West…
Online at *https://www.washingtonpost.com/news/the-intersect/wp/2014/09/22/4chans-latest-terrible-prank-convincing-west-africans-that-ebola-doctors-actually-worship-the-disease/*

"lunatic, juvenile,…brilliant, ridiculous and alarming"
Sean Michaels, "Taking the Rick," *The Guardian,* March 19, 2008

"Spontaneity and creativity are the propelling forces in human progress"
The Autobiography of J.L. Moreno M.D. (Abridged), edited by Jonathan D. Morena (United Kingdom: The North-West Psychodrama Association, 2011), 61

"consume as much of your time..."
   Quoted in Mike Allen, "Sean Parker Unloads on Facebook: 'God Only Knows What it's Doing to our Children's Brains,'" *Axios,* November 9, 2017

For Tim Kendall, Facebook's first director...
   Online at *https://www.youtube.com/watch?v=l2tZLesCX4M*

"We've created an entire generation..."
   Jaron Lanier, in *The Social Dilemma,* directed by Jeff Orlowski for Netflix, 2020

"it gives us moral clarity and social solidarity..."
   Quoted in Adam Tinworth, "James Williams: Distraction by Design and the Attention Moral Crisis," *Next,* September 22, 2017, online at *https://nextconf.eu/2017/09/james-williams-distraction-by-design-and-the-attention-moral-crisis/*

"In reality, as cantankerous and combative engineers rushed in,..."
   Fisher, *The Chaos Machine,* 47

"The utopians say: 'I figured it out,...'"
   Quoted in John Markoff, "What the Silicon Valley Prophet Sees on the Horizon," *New York Times,* March 22, 2022

"Facebook could and should..."
   Fisher, *The Chaos Machine,* 48

"with Asperger's-like social ineptitude"
   Ibid., 243

"that would guide its own evolution..."
   Ibid., 107

"There is no way for an overseer..."
   Ibid.

(Yes, that's a thing)
   See, for example, online at *https://www.youtube.com/watch?v=xR6ayLjvsuE*

YouTube Chief Product Officer Neal Mohan...
   Joan E. Solsman, "CES: YouTube's AI is the Puppetmaster over What you Watch," *CBS News,* January 10, 2018

"issue[s] recommendations so effective..."
   Fisher, *The Chaos Machine,* 108

"the Valley had an incentive to stay ignorant..."
   Ibid., 105

"Stories of YouTube radicalization..."
   Ibid., 212

"had arrived, however unintentionally,..."
   Ibid., 210

NOTES

his "revenge against humanity"...
Ibid., 211

"We have something here that we call the dictatorship of the like"
Quoted in ibid., 277

a "textbook example of ethnic cleansing"
Online at *https://news.un.org/en/story/2018/08/1017802*

A measure of Silicon Valley's sensitivity...
Online at *https://www.cnbc.com/2018/12/13/twitter-ceo-jack-dorsey-spent-his-birthday-on-a-silent-meditation-trip.html*

"The violence stopped,..."
Fisher, *The Chaos Machine*, 175

"We deplore the misuse of our platform"
"Sri Lanka: Facebook Apologizes for role in 2018 Anti-Muslim Riots," *Aljazeera*, May 13, 2020

"The answer to bad speech is more speech"
Quoted in Fisher, *The Chaos Machine*, 38.

"if we had guns in California..."
Quoted in Melinda Wenner Moyer, "More Guns Do Not Stop More Crimes, Evidence Shows," *Scientific American*, October 1, 2017

"the companies dug in"
Fisher, *The Chaos Machine*, 211

"synthetic, completely fake with actors"
"Alex Jones Judgment: The Cost of Lies," *CBS News*, August 7, 2022

He seemed still to be living in an alternate universe...
Fisher, *The Chaos Machine*, 218

"Platform," it should be noted...
Thanks to Marc Rotenberg, president and founder of the Center for AI and Digital Policy (personal email)

"tree of liberty..."
Letter to Colonel Smith, Paris, November 13, 1787, in *The Writings of Thomas Jefferson*, vol. 6 (Washington, D.C: The Thomas Jefferson Memorial Association, 1903), 373

For the relationships expert Ester Perel,...
"Esther Perel on Artificial Intimacy," *Your Undivided Attention*, podcast with Tristan Harris, August 17, 2023, online at *https://www.humanetech.com/podcast/esther-perel-on-artificial-intimacy*

"What nukes are to the physical world ..."
"AI and the future of Humanity: Yuval Noah Harari at the Frontiers Forum," online at *https://www.youtube.com/watch?v=LWiM-LuRe6w*

standup comedian Matt Maran...
Jason Zinoman, "Are Comedians Bots Ready to Kill?," *New York Times,* August 20, 2023

She fears how tech companies use information...
"Protecting our Freedom of Thought with Nita Farahany," *Your Undivided Attention,* podcast with Tristan Harris, August 3, 2023, online at *https://www.humanetech.com/podcast/protecting-our-freedom-of-thought-with-nita-farahany*

CONCLUSION

"In a setting not known for improvisation"
Michael Shear, "7 Takeaways From Biden's State of the Union Address," *New York Times,* February 7, 2023

Facebook has known about the dangers...
Igor Bonifacic, "Democrats Ask Facebook, Twitter and YouTube to Rework their Suggestion Algorithms," *Engadget,* January 20, 2021

According to *The Atlantic*,...
Kaitlyn Tiffany, "Very, Very Few People Are Falling Down the YouTube Rabbit Hole," *The Atlantic,* August 30, 2023

an "armada of volunteers with boats..."
Rebecca Solnit, *A Paradise Built in Hell: The Extraordinary Communities That Arise in Disaster* (New York: Viking, 2009), 263

"the sound of surprise"
Whitney Balliett, *The Sound of Surprise: 44 Pieces on Jazz* (New York: Dutton, 1959)

"Trauma is a fact of life..."
Peter Levine, *Waking the Tiger: Healing Trauma* (Berkeley: North Atlantic Books, 1997), 2

For Levine, recovery from trauma can "be transformative..."
Ibid.

As the tree continues to develop,...
Ibid., 33

"recurring nightmares, violent tendencies..."
Ibid., 26

"a pro-Trump protestor..."
Jamie Raskin, *Unthinkable,* 388

"How can the president put children..."
Ibid., 388

"moral injury is an essential part of any combat trauma..."
Jonathan Shay, *Achilles in Viet Nam: Combat Trauma and the Undoing of Character* (New York: Scribner, 2003 [1994]), 20

"He's a castaway on civilian shores,..."
Jonathan Shay, *Odysseus in America: Combat Trauma and the Trials of Homecoming* (New York: Scribner, 2002), 12

"Odysseus emerges not as a monster, but as a human like ourselves"
Ibid., 120

"see me clearly as divine"
Euripides, *The Bacchae* 23 (trans. Paul Woodruff)

"If you come to Eleusis, you will never die."
Brian C. Muraresku, *The Immortality Key: The Secret History of the Religion With No Name* (New York: St. Martin's Press, 2020), 26

"Treat your audience like poets and geniuses..."
Sam Wasson, *Improv Nation,* 313

For Tina Fey, improv's "Rule of Agreement..."
Tina Fey, *Bossypants* (New York: Little, Brown and Company, 2011), 82

"I don't actually believe..."
Quoted in Wasson, *Improv Nation,* 289

Both teach us how "to know, experience,..."
Will Dennis, "Praying with Tina Fey: Living in the Intersection of Improvisation and Spirituality," *https://bit.ly/3vLy4bJ*

"mindreading...we somehow were able to understand..."
T.J. Jagodowski and David Pasquesi, with Pam Victor, *Improvisation at the Speed of Life* (Chicago: Solo Roma, 2015)

For Charna Halpern, head of ImprovOlympics (IO)...
Charna Halpern, Del Close, and Kim "Howard" Johnson, *Truth in Comedy: The Manual of Improvisation* (Colorado Springs: Meriwether Publishing, 1994), 92

...the original strongman of authoritarian regimes
On strongmen, see Ruth Ben-Ghiat, *Strongmen: Mussolini to the Present* (New York: W.W. Norton, 2021)

"sweet to drink, it was splashing around..."
"Homeric Hymn to Dionysus," translated by Gregory Nagy, The Center for Hellenic Studies (online at *https://chs.harvard.edu/primary-source/homeric-hymn-to-dionysus-sb/*)

"weaving, left my shuttles beside the loom,"
  Euripides, *The Bacchae* 1236

"with hands alone...caught this beast and tore it limb from limb,"
  Ibid., 1210

When you know what you've done,...
  Euripides, *The Bacchae* 1259-60

Agave: A lion's...No. It's Pentheus. I have his head.
  Euripides, *The Bacchae* 1278-84

"If it's dead it's Viet Cong"
  Robert Jay Lifton, *Home from the War: Learning From Vietnam Veterans* (New York: Beacon, 1992), 65. See also, Nick Turse, *Kill Anything That Moves: The Real American War in Vietnam* (New York: Picador, 2013)

"strengthen the enemy..."
  Shay, *Odysseus in America*, 224

"It's easy to dismiss Babbitt as a loon,"
  Phil Klay, *Uncertain Ground: Citizenship in an Age Endless, Invisible War* (New York: Penguin Press, 2022), xvi.

...who led and "manned" the insurrection
  Early arrest counts numbered 76% male. See "'We Did Our Part': The Overlooked Role Women Played in the Capitol Riot." ABC News, April 8, 2021

"Fertiliz[ing] behaviors already flourishing on American soil"
  Anand Giridharadas, *The Persuaders: At the Front Lines of the Fight for Hearts, Minds, and Democracy* (New York: Alfred A Knopf, 2022), 6

Once we bowled in leagues,
  Robert Putnam, *Bowling Alone: The Collapse and Revival of American Community* (New York: Simon and Schuster, 2000)

Our "pessimistic and factional political culture,"
  Giridharadas, *The Persuaders*, 7.

"'It's a Bronx thing,'..."
  Marisa Guthrie, "Alexandria Ocasio-Cortez, the Movie: D.C.'s Bomb-Throwing New Star Seizes the Sundance Spotlight," *Hollywood Reporter*, January 23, 2019

But so, too, AOC waits for "a really good example...
  Quoted in Giridharadas, *The Persuaders*, 178

Loretta Ross, "a pioneering activist,..."
  Ibid., 47

"Ross and her comrades,"
  Ibid.

"We can build restorative justice processes…"
Lilian Ross, "I'm a Black Feminist. I Think Call-Out Culture Is Toxic,"
New York Times, August 17, 2019

"As far as we can discern,…"
C.G. Jung, *Memories, Dreams, and Reflections* (New York: Vintage Books, 1989), 380

"ambiguous, noisy information"
Barrett, *How Emotions Are Made,* 2

"at the tempo of emergency"
Crouch, *Kansas City Lightning,* 17

"deceit and sneakiness…"
Jaron Lanier, in *The Social Dilemma*

"[Man] can adapt himself…"
Suzanne Langer, *Philosophy in a New Key: A Study in the Symbolism of Reason, Rite, and Art* (Cambridge, Mass: Harvard University Press, 1957)

ACKNOWLEDGMENTS

This book has benefited from many hands. Kristin Sanders, a digital nomad, helped an aging academic navigate current examples to appeal to a wider audience than I am used to reaching. Fred Anderson, who once introduced me to the literature of war, which became my other lifelong passion, and who writes better prose than any of us, helped me clear the thickets. Gwen Thompkins helped me over a hurdle that had me stymied, how to speak of archetypes to a general audience. Beth Ann Fennelly brought whatever grace here abounds. N. West Moss and Claudia Barker caught infelicities. Michelle Shocked and Tony Gentry's enthusiasm spurred me on. Didi Goldenhar and Jane Isay's firm hands reined me in. For all their help it is a better book than I ever imagined. That it is not a better book is entirely my doing.

Several mentors helped shape the mind that made this book. The late Don Taylor taught me more than anyone how to read, that to understand the shaping principle of a book was to find its meaning. Richard Lanham helped me understand the motives of eloquence, or, in improvisation's case, the motives of ineloquence. James Boren, my first grad school adviser, a fellow oenophile, put me on the detective fiction trail. And, though I have not had the good fortune of meeting him, I must acknowledge Lewis Hyde whose *Trickster Makes This World: Mischief, Myth, and Art* taught me how to follow Trickster through his many permutations. Henry Louis Gates's fine *The Signifying Monkey:* took me the rest of the way, schooling me in Trickster's call and response.

Many thanks to Rebecca McClanahan and Peter White, two *Kenyon Review* friends who helped get my writing career on track.

Special thanks to Dan Tyler for the perfect title to hang my hat on. Because I was searching for a less academic voice, I shared many chapters long before they were ripe. With apologies I wish to thank many old and new friends who struggled through those hard plums: Ralph Adamo, Roberta

NOTES

Baskin, Lynn Bell, Steven Bingler, Eric Booth, Ron Caron, Gianna Chachere, Steven Coats, Rebecca Crenshaw, Ruth Dickey, Nicole Terez Duttton, Lolis Eric Elie, Rien Fertel, Ham Fish, Tripp Friedler, Tom Gage, Stephen Gentry, Alan Gerson, Craig Gillam, Roberta Gratz, Ken Grossinger, MaryBeth Guarisco, Ajay Heble, Rosemary James, Chris Kamenstein, Wayne Karlin, Elizabeth Kipp-Gusti, Greg Lambousy, Dan Lorenzetti, Jackie Lyle, Davan Maharaj, Conrad Martin, Kevin McCaffery, Richard McCarthy, Jerry Meaders, Jonathan Moreno, Malcolm Munson, Stephen Nachmanovitch, Jana Napoli, Davia Nelson, Martin Pederson, Rick and Zack Permutt, Chip Pique, Mark Plotkin, Richard Rabinowitz, Ricky Riccardi, Sonya Robinson, Paul Shaffer, Paul Siegel, André Stern, Ned and Constance Sublette, Russ Titelman, Beth Arroyo Utterback, Susan Welsh, and Elissa Zengel. It's been a long haul and the old academic's memory weakens. I'm sure I've forgotten some and beg forgiveness.

More special thanks to editor Paul Glastris of *Washington Monthly* who first published my crazy idea that Trump's improvising supercharged his power over his base.

This book owes a lot to the team that helped me conceive and put together the Improv Conference New Orleans: Gianna Chachere, Rosalind Hinton, and Sonya Robinson. New Orleans boasts a lot of great food and music festivals. We announced that ours was for Lousiana singular: A Festival of Ideas. It was Gianna's brilliant naming. Special thanks to Matt Wuerker for his brilliant cartoons of the Improviser-in-Chief, used here, a gift he brought along to the 2019 Festival of Ideas.

This book owes a debt too to the participants who did so much to inform it. 2018: Zarouhie Abdalian, Courtney Bryan, Ben Burkett, Mel Chin, Theo Eliezer, Ham Fish, Chris Kaminstein, Khari Allen Lee, Richard McCarthy, Stephen Nachmanovitch, Davia Nelson, Michael Pellara, Jenna Sherry, Rob Wallace, Matt Wuerker, Alice Waters. 2019: Brett Anderson, Steven Bingler, Rahn Broady, Bliss Broyard, Donna Cavato, Jules Feiffer, Jonathan Freilich, David Gamble, Wendy Gaudin, Roberta Gratz, David Kunian, Andrew Lam, Bryan C. Lee, Jr., Sue Mobley, Stanton Moore, Sandy Ha Nguyen, Mark Plotkin, Michael Pollan, Shannon Powell, Kristina Kay Robinson, Michael Tisserand, Johnny Vidacovich.

Last thanks go to Klaus Ottmann for his luminous cover and meticulous editorial skills.

Made in United States
North Haven, CT
12 November 2024

60236080R00137